# Where Liberty Dwells
## *True Texas Tales*

## BY JIM MCLAUGHLIN

*Cover Photo: The San Jacinto Monument*

*On April 21, 1836, Sam Houston slept late for the first time in months. It is said that when he awoke, he saw an eagle, his Cherokee talisman, circling overhead. A good omen.*

*That afternoon, Houston led 918 men, mostly farmers without military experience, into battle with 1200 crack Mexican troops. The battle lasted eighteen minutes by Houston's pocket watch. It was a stunning and unexpected victory for the Texians.*

*Houston's victory at San Jacinto resulted in the independence of Texas. Texans, with their usual understated modesty, claim the battle changed the world. It led to the creation of an America that stretched from the Atlantic to the Pacific and added all of California, Nevada, Arizona, New Mexico, Colorado, and Utah to the United States, along with parts of Wyoming, Kansas, and Oklahoma.*

*Construction of the San Jacinto Monument was started on April 21, 1936, and completed three years later, on April 21, 1939. The monument was designed by a Texan, Alfred C. Finn, and engineered by Robert J. Cummings. It is the world's tallest masonry column - typical of Texans. The monument was built to commemorate the Battle of San Jacinto and celebrate the Centennial of Texas Independence.*

Where Liberty Dwells

True Texas Tales

Jim McLaughlin

ISBN (Print Edition): 978-1-54398-765-2

ISBN (eBook Edition): 978-1-54398-766-9

# TABLE OF CONTENTS

# Introduction

I'm serious about Texas history, but I think it needs to be fun. If it's not fun, no one will read it except historians, and everybody knows they're no fun. I want to get the facts straight, but I don't want to skip a good story just because it's funny.

The Apache Indians had a sense of humor. In 1758, the Apaches convinced Spanish priests to build a mission in the heart of Comanche territory near San Saba, then hid and giggled while they watched to see what the Comanche would do.

Chief Flacco, a Lipan-Apache scout used often by the Texas Rangers, commented on the unusual bravery of Captain Jack Hays. "Flacco and Red Bird much brave. We go to Hell together. Capt'n Yack more brave. He go to Hell by himself."

John Adair, Charles Goodnight's financial partner, shot his own horse in the back of the head while trying to shoot an elk from the saddle. He twisted his ankle when the dead horse collapsed.

It is hard to forget the El Paso madam who shot a rival madam in the "Public Arch."

Clay Alison's tombstone announces, "He never killed a man who didn't need killing."

Most history books are all about men. Men fought the wars, blazed the trails, shot the deer, and played the poker. Most all of these men had a woman at home, taking care of the kids, raising a garden, chopping firewood, washing clothes, sewing, and cooking all day, every day. One of these women was supposed to have said," Texas is paradise for men and dogs, but hell on women and horses."

When I looked up that quote, to see who said it, I discovered it was said many times, about many places. Ohio, Louisiana, Indiana, etc. That's the trouble with history. If you look long enough, you'll find someone who disagrees with everything you've ever known.

History is a collection of stories cobbled together by someone with a motive. I want to tell true stories and have fun doing it. I want to talk about the women who worked shoulder to shoulder with the men to civilize this primitive land and the people in it. I want everyone to know and love Texas as I do.

*Jim McLaughlin*

# CHAPTER ONE
# Very Early Texas History

Texas History starts whenever the historian wants it to start. Some have placed the beginnings of Texas at the time man first crossed the land bridge at the Bering Strait and began to filter down between the glaciers into North America and naturally settle in the garden spot of this continent, around present-day Lubbock, Texas.

Newer evidence suggests that this migration happened but may not have populated Texas. The first humans on Texas soil may have come from Europe or Africa, by sailing across a narrow part of the Atlantic, landing in South America and working their way north. Then again, they may have floated over from Polynesia and landed in Chile. Perhaps all of the above contributed to the settlement of early Texas. Because of advances in the study of DNA, all these theories have some merit and are being investigated.

No matter how they got here, there is solid evidence that humans lived near Lubbock over 12,000 years ago. At the Lubbock Lakes Archeological Site, one excavated cliff wall shows proof of continual habitation from before that time. This site is the only place in North America showing such evidence. Indications are that early Texans hunted Wooly Mammoths and Giant Bison in this area, butchered their kill here, and dried and preserved the meat. A variety of artifacts, flint spear points, arrowheads, and cutting tools show that these Indians were nomads. Some lived near here and others came from afar or perhaps traded with distant people.

Instead of getting into an argument about who came first from where, fast forward 12,000 years to 1211 A.D. The Moors from North Africa conquered most of the south half of the Iberian Peninsula and the Pope in Rome was worried they would take the rest of Spain, and then Europe, which would put him out of a job. He was so worried that he ordered the Christian Kings of the area to quit squabbling among themselves and join together in a Crusade against the Muslims. Most everyone joined. It is not a big surprise that the French didn't like the rules and took their 30,000 soldiers and went home.

Pope Innocent III ordered this Crusade. Thinking this might be the first example of an oxymoron in modern history, I read everything I could about him. He was not the first oxymoron—at least two examples preceded him—Innocent I and II.

Pope Innocent III

King Alphonso VIII of Castile; Jimenez De Rado, the Archbishop of Toledo; Sancho VII of Navarre, and Pedro II of Aragon followed Innocent III's orders, pooled their armies, and set out with some 50,000 soldiers to fight the Saracens. The Muslim horde, estimated to be over 125,000 men, was camped in a secure valley near Las Navas, protected on all sides by impassable mountains. They rested peacefully, knowing they controlled the high ground at the only known pass into the valley.

A local shepherd, Martin Alhaja, (or Halaja) told the soldiers of a secret pass into the valley which he had marked with a cow's skull. The troops found the pass, staged a forced march through the night, and surrounded the surprised Muslims on the morning of July 16, 1212. The ensuing Battle of Los Navas de Tolosa was a slaughter.

The caliph in charge of the Muslims, Muhammad al-Nasir, camped in a splendid tent on a rise near the center of his army. His tent consisted of "three-ply crimson velvet flecked with gold; strings of pearls descending from its purple fringes." Rows of chain radiated from the center of his camp and tied in place 3,000 camels. Inside the ring of camels, 10,000 black slaves were chained together in a circle, their steel tipped lances facing outward at an angle, with the bases buried in the ground. According to reports by the Christians, the caliph stood inside this protection, "wearing the green dress and turban of his ancestral line," holding a scimitar in one hand and a Koran in the other. He read passages from the Koran which promised all the delights of paradise to any young man who perished in religious battle and the torments of hell to any coward who should desert his ranks.

The Spanish attacked eagerly. Sancho VII drove his war horses through the lines of camels and made short work of the chained, immobile slave guards. Muhammad al-Nasir was evidently not interested in the "delights of paradise" because he fled on a mare and "did not rest until he had reached Jaen," where he spent long hours writing elaborate excuses as to why he lost the battle. The Spanish soldiers roamed the mountains for the next few days, slaughtering Muslim stragglers. Causality estimates are perhaps exaggerated, but approximately 100,000 Muslims are claimed to have perished, while the Spanish only lost some 2,000 men.

Written accounts of the battle are available from both sides and are interesting in their contradictions. Moorish reports tend to stress the unavoidable series of unfortunate circumstances which befell the competent commanders, while most of the Spanish reports come from various letters to the Pope and uniformly cite the hand of God and the influence of the Pope in the victory. Self-serving statements praising the authors are scattered through all the documents, no matter which side they represent.

The caliph's elaborate tent was sent to Innocent III as a gift from Alphonse VIII, in case the Pope needed a folding three-bedroom, two-bath place to sleep. Perhaps in deference to the Pope, no mention was made of the dispensation of the harem contained in the back bedroom. The poor shepherd, Martin Alhaja, was appointed a nobleman, and given appropriate lands and a coat of arms. He was bestowed the title Cabeza de Vaca—the head of the cow.

The heirs of Cabeza de Vaca prospered, and almost three hundred years later, in 1490, Francisco de Vara and Teresa Cabeza de Vaca had a son named Alvar Nunez Cabeza de Vaca. Two years later, in 1492, King Ferdinand and Queen Isabella's armies finally drove the Moors out of Granada and across the Mediterranean into North Africa. That same year, Isabella backed an unknown Italian, Christopher Columbus, on a quest to find a short cut to India. Spain was on a roll.

In 1492, when Alvar Nunez Cabeza de Vaca was just two years old, Columbus left Portugal, crossed the Atlantic Ocean and sailed, more or less aimlessly, around the Caribbean Sea trying to figure out where he was. He realized the world was round, but it was about twice as big as he imagined. He was convinced that everything would be fine if he could just find India. Or maybe China. Instead, he kept finding islands.

Posthumous portrait of Christopher Columbus by Sebastiano del Piombo, 1519

The islands he found were inhabited by friendly indigenous people called Tainos. After his first encounter with the Tainos, in the Bahamas, Columbus wrote King Ferdinand and described them as tall, well formed, handsome people. He went on to say "They traded with us and gave us everything they had, with good will...they took great delight in pleasing us. They are very gentle and without knowledge what is evil; nor do they murder or steal....Your Highness may believe that in all the world there can be no better people....They love their neighbors as themselves, and they have the sweetest talk in the world, and are gentle and always laughing."

Regardless of Columbus' feeling that there were "no better people" on earth, the Spaniards were more than ready to give these "gentle and ...laughing" people knowledge of "what is evil." Because they believed India was near, they called the natives "Indians." Columbus believed the "Indians" would make great slaves, and on his second voyage in 1493 and 1494, set about to conquer and enslave them. He decided the subdued natives would pay a tribute which he would split with the king. Every three months, every native over fourteen years of age was required to deliver a hawk's bell full of gold to Columbus. If there was no gold, Columbus would accept twenty-five pounds of seeded and spun cotton. If the Tainos did not pay, Spanish soldiers cut off their hands and left them to bleed to death.

The Indians rebelled against these harsh methods without much success. Many died in battle, and many, forced into slavery and not allowed to work their fields, starved to death. The biggest killer of all was disease—the natives had no immunity to smallpox, measles, influenza, typhoid, or other European maladies and hundreds of thousands were infected and died. In 1492, the apex of Taino society and not coincidentally, the arrival of Columbus, historians estimate one and a half million natives lived on the island of Hispaniola alone, with at least that many more scattered among other islands.Some estimates put the entire Caribbean population at over eight million, and "long counters" estimate over thirty million. In any case, only fifty years later, in 1540, the Taino population of the islands stood at forty thousand and falling. The Spaniards were forced to import slaves from Africa to do the work.

It is believed that the Tainos moved into the islands from the South American continent about 400 BC, and thrived there almost 2000 years, until the Spanish came. Taino language gave us the words *canoe, hammock, barbeque, tobacco,* and *hurricane.* Tainos named Cuba and Haiti. The Karankawa Indians who lived along the Texas coast are believed to have migrated from the Caribbean. They were large, handsome people and may have been distant relatives of the Tainos.

Columbus discovered Cuba but was not sure if it was an island or a continent. Perhaps it was China. In 1494, he sailed along the south side of the island and finally, in 1508, Sebastian de Ocampo proved Cuba was not a continent by sailing around it. Columbus never saw the mainland of either continent that blocked his way to China, but he kept searching.

Also in the year 1492, Spain drove the Moors out of their last European stronghold, Granada. Suddenly, a number of young Spanish soldiers were left without a war to wage. Many of them volunteered to help explore the "New World," and hurried west to make their fortunes. Spain conquered and enslaved the native population of Cuba and built the city of Havana on the South Coast in 1514. The city was moved to its current location on the north side of the island in 1519 because of the superb natural harbor there.

·HERNANDO·CORTES·

In 1519, Hernan Cortes, a cousin of Pizarro, ignored orders to return to Cuba and proceeded to conquer the Aztecs in Mexico. He enslaved the indigenous people, put them to work in the gold and silver mines, and began systematically looting the country. For forty percent of the bounty, the Spanish king forgave his transgressions and appointed him ruler of Mexico in 1523. Ruthless and universally disliked by his contemporaries, Cortes became one of the richest and most powerful men in the New World. Cuba soon became the hub of commerce and culture in the Carribean. Ships arriving from Spain unloaded their cargo into Havana's warehouses. Treasure ships returning to Spain stopped in Havana to take on fresh food, water and supplies for the voyage back to Europe. Conquistadors and explorers planned their trips and outfitted their ships among the wharves in Havana. About this time, a twenty-one-year old Cabaza de Vaca joined the army in Spain and began making a name for himself on the battlefield.

The Spanish conquistadores were young, ambitious and utterly ruthless. They shared a complete disregard for the welfare of the natives in whatever area they conquered, enslaved them, killed them in battle, and wiped out whole populations with European diseases. The Spanish king had no knowledge of the treatment of the natives and didn't really care. So long as he got 40% off the top he was satisfied. When the native populations died off, the Spaniards imported slaves from Africa to do the work.

Most of these conquerors knew each other, or at least knew of each other. Ponce de Leon arrived in the New World with Columbus, on his second voyage in 1493, as one of 200 "gentlemen volunteers." DeSoto fought alongside Pizarro and Balboa and became rich in the conquest of Peru. Ponce De Leon became the first governor of Puerto Rico before he decided, in 1512, to lead an expedition to search for gold, explore, and colonize lands to the north. He discovered and named La Florida, which he thought was another big island. A popular legend was born fifty years after his death, when a writer wondered if De Leon had been searching for the "Fountain of Youth."

17th Century Engraving of Ponce De Leon

In 1519, at the direction of Francisco de Garay, governor of Jamaica, Alonso Alvarez de Pineda set out to map the coast of the gulf from the "island" of Florida to the Panuco River, just north of Veracruz. He hoped to find an ocean route to China. Pineda was the first to see and map the Gulf Coast of Florida, Alabama, Mississippi, Louisiana, and Texas, land which he called "Amichel." His explorations verified the fact that Florida was a peninsula, and he was the first European to see the Mississippi River. His notes describe the river and the Indian settlements on its banks. He sailed eighteen miles upriver from the coast before he returned to the Gulf. Historians are always ready to dispute the findings of each other. Some suggest he missed the Mississippi River altogether and, instead, sailed eighteen miles into Mobile Bay.

On June 24, 1519, Pineda sailed into a lovely, deep water bay on the Texas coast which he named "Corpus Christi" because it was the day of the Roman Catholic Feast of Corpus Christi. Later, he sailed up the Panuco River in Mexico and spent forty days repairing and refurbishing his ships. During this time, he was killed in a battle with local Indians, but his map was saved and delivered to Francisco de Garay, who financed the expedition.

Pineda's map, done in 1519, was the first document in Texas history. By today's standards, it is a rather crude rendition, with an oversized Cuba dominating the center of the Gulf, a misshapen Yucatan Peninsula to the left, the coast curving past Texas, Louisiana, Mississippi, Alabama, and finally terminating at a rather boxy-shaped Florida on the far right. Pineda proved La Florida was not an island, proved there was no outlet to China from the Gulf, and proved the Gulf was much larger than previously believed. Cortes disputed his findings, probably in an attempt to keep from sharing any of the discovered lands with one of his many rivals, the Governor of Jamaica, Francisco de Garay.

A Cleaned Up Version of Pineda's Map

Pineda's discoveries were taken to Seville and entered into the Patron Real, a master map of the Caribbean set up for the king to keep track of all discoveries, claims, and counter claims in the area. These maps were shared with any Spanish ship's captains, explorers, or conquistadores bound for the New World. One of the first explorers to use Pineda's information was Panfilo de Narvaez, who, in 1527, mounted an expedition to explore, colonize, and settle La Florida. A thirty-five-year old soldier with the unlikely name of "Head of a Cow," Alvar Nunez Cabeza de Vaca, was the king's accountant and second in military command of this expedition.

To encourage colonization, the Spanish established an encomienda system, whereby Spanish noblemen were awarded tracts of land or islands and assigned Taino slaves. The landowners made huge fortunes and part of the profit (usually 40 %) from these colonies was paid directly to the king as tribute. Spanish soldiers-of-fortune flooded the islands, seeking riches. Encomienda grants were doled out on a first come, first-served basis, and the competition was fierce.

Panfilo de Narvaez, a tall, blond native of Castile, came to the Caribbean as a soldier determined to make his fortune. Even though he was of noble birth and had friends in high places, Panfilo exhibited a natural tendency toward stupidity. According to contemporary reports, he had an authoritarian personality and was unusually cruel to the Taino natives. Considering some of his decisions, he was less than bright. Indications are that de Narvaez was an arrogant, cruel and stupid soldier, dependent on relatives for his position and oblivious to the needs of his subordinates.

Panfilo de Narvaez

In 1511, Panfilo's uncle, Diego Velázquez de Cuéllar, the first governor of Cuba, put him in charge of the army with orders to conquer the unarmed Tainos and subject the island to Spanish rule. Father Bartolome de Las Casas watched as de Narvaez's troops murdered 2500 peaceful natives whose only crime was bringing food offerings to the soldiers. Watching the massacre, which de Narvaez called the "conquest of Cuba," Las Casas sympathized with the helpless Tainos. He began a fight against the encomienda system, slavery, and mistreatment of native people that lasted for the rest of his life.

When Cuba was secure, Governor de Cuellar sent Hernando Cortes to conquer Mexico for him. After launching the expedition, the governor had second thoughts. He realized the ambitious Cortes might take over Mexico and keep it for himself. He ordered Cortes back to Cuba. Cortes ignored the order. In 1520, de Cuellar appointed his nephew, de Narvaez, governor of Mexico and sent him with 1400 men to arrest Cortes, put him in irons, and bring him back to Cuba.

Cortes, with 250 troops, proved his military worth by whipping de Narvaez and his army. De Narvaez not only demonstrated military ineptitude but lost an eye in the battle. Cortes threw him into prison in Veracruz for two years. Narvaez's Cuban soldiers, promised gold and recognizing competent leadership, deserted Narvaez and joined Cortes. With his new army, Cortes decided to keep Mexico for himself, demonstrating that de Cuellar was a shrewd judge of character.

When Cortes released him from prison in Veracruz, de Narvaez made his way back to Spain. Working through contacts in the government, he convinced King Charles V to back him in a mission to explore and colonize the land along the Gulf coast, from Florida to Mexico. The king provided ships, soldiers, and colonists, and de Narvaez was to provide leadership. In June of 1527, with five ships and 600 men, de Narvaez sailed back to the New World, planning to conquer and colonize all the land north of the Gulf of Mexico, and expecting to find untold wealth.

King Charles, wishing to protect his interests, sent a bright young man along to keep records and to act as second in command. Alvar Nunez Cabeza de Vaca joined the expedition for his first trip to the new world. Most of what we know of the de Narvaez expedition is because of de Vaca's journals.

There were problems from the beginning. Coming from Spain, the expedition first landed on the island of Hispaniola, where about one-fourth of the crew deserted. The soldiers had no confidence in their one-eyed commander, and desertion was a constant problem. Two ships and more men were lost in a hurricane off the Cuban coast. De Narvaez planned to start at the mouth of Rio Panuco, north of Vera Cruz, and work his way east, but became lost and confused. Very confused. He managed to land some three hundred men on the east coast of Florida, near present Tampa Bay. Because of the confusion and his reluctance to admit a mistake, de Narvaez decided to work west to the Panuco, which he thought to be about fifty miles. The expedition most likely used the crude map drawn by de Pineda eight years before, which Narvaez did not trust. The map showed Florida to be a peninsula and not an island.

De Narvaez, in a decision openly opposed by Cabeza de Vaca, sent the ships back to Havana and decided to march his troops overland to explore and occupy the country. Local Indians, having learned from de Leon that Europeans could not to be trusted, were less than happy to see de Narvaez's expedition. Unable to fight the well-equipped Spaniards in the open, they hid in the jungle and picked off the Spaniards one or two at a time with arrows or lances. Rather than allow the soldiers to occupy their villages, the Indians burned them. There was no gold or silver and very little food. The Spanish were soon reduced to eating their horses.

Six months of struggling through the swamp, fighting Indians and starving, convinced de Narvaez to abandon his ambitions and return to civilization. There was, however, a problem—no ships. Cabeza de Vaca felt the expedition should go to Mexico across country, but de Narvaez overruled that notion. The soldiers built a forge and melted down every bit of metal they could find—horseshoes, stirrups, bits, fasteners, buttons, armor, anything metal—and made tools and nails to build rafts. They built five rafts, each designed to hold forty men with oars. The soldiers used their clothing to make sails.

De Vaca protested separation of the rafts, thinking it best that they work together. Instead, Narvaez picked the forty strongest men to row his craft and made it clear that each barge and every man was on his own. As they sailed and rowed close to shore, the heavy current of a river, probably the Mississippi, swept de Narvaez's raft and two others out to sea, leaving Cabeza de Vaca to make his way along the coast with the two remaining rafts.

Cabeza de Vaca, with two rafts and eighty-six men, kept close to shore and made his way west, planning to follow the coast to civilization in Mexico. A hurricane washed them ashore and destroyed the rafts on a barrier island off the coast of Texas. It may have been Galveston Island, but most historians believe it was a few miles down the coast at Follets Island. De Vaca named the island "The Isle of Misfortune."

# CHAPTER TWO
# Cabeza de Vaca

When Cabeza de Vaca and his crew washed ashore on Follet's Island, a few hundred yards west of Galveston Island, they managed to start a fire in a ravine and found pools of fresh water from a recent rain. Local Indians were curious and friendly, and brought their wives and children to see these strange men. The Spaniards gave the women and children trinkets they had saved for trading, and the Indians brought edible roots and fish.

Cabeza de Vaca

After a good night's sleep near a warm fire, the Spaniards dug their raft out of the sand. They were eager to get back to sea and make it to the settlement at the mouth of the Panuco River, which they felt must be near. The helpful Indians provided them with dried fish and other provisions, and they put everything on the raft. The men stripped down to nothing and used their remaining clothing to chink the cracks in the vessel. They pushed the craft through the surf and climbed aboard, stark naked. Three hundred yards from shore a wave washed over the raft, ripping loose the steering oar. The crew lost control of the vessel. A second wave hit them broadside and capsized the whole affair, dumping everything on board into the sea. Three men drowned. The rest washed ashore, naked and shivering, with every-thing—tools, clothing, food, provisions—lost, and a blue norther blowing in.

The amused Indians provided the Spaniards with food and a warm hut for the night, and the next morning led them to another raft that had washed ashore four miles away, on Galveston Island. This was the craft of de Vaca's friends, Captains Andres Dorantes and Alonzo del Castillo. All their men were safe. From the two rafts, eighty-six survivors remained.

The shipwrecked Spaniards took stock of their situation and decided to repair Captain Dorantes raft and sail it on to the Panuco, which they estimated to be about fifty miles. Some would have to remain, but the others would send help as soon as they reached the village in Mexico. Forty men were selected to go and the hastily repaired barge was launched, only to break into pieces when it hit the surf. With both rafts destroyed, all eighty-six men were forced to winter on the Isle of Misfortune.

The Panuco River was over six hundred miles away, near present day Tampico. The survivors were convinced that it was not far and a rescue party would be sent as soon as word reached there. De Vaca chose four men—Feandez, Mendez, Figueroa, and Astudillo—all healthy and good swimmers, to travel overland and send help as soon as they reached civilization. Five men actually left the camp to make the trip. An Indian from Cuba, the faithful servant of one of the men chosen, went with his master. According to the custom of the time, slaves were sub-human, so he was not counted.

De Vaca and the eighty men left on the island prepared for the winter. As time passed, the Indians, no longer amused and curious, grew tired of the Spanish, became less friendly and ceased to share their food. De Vaca went to the mainland and stayed for a time with the chief of a neighboring tribe. A disease passed through the area and killed many Indians and some Spaniards. De Vaca was stricken and almost died. He was nursed back to health in the hut of the chief that befriended him.

The Karankawa's attitude toward the Spaniards evolved. Their initial curiosity was replaced by mistrust. They blamed the visitors for bringing strange diseases to their villages. Life was hard for the natives, and they didn't want the additional burden of feeding the white men. They decided to leave alive only those useful as slaves.

The winter was long and cold, and many Spaniards died of exposure and starvation. The Indians killed some in battle and some for sport. In the springtime, April of 1529, Andres Dorantes and Alonzo del Castillo, both men of action, decided to walk to the Panuco, which they believed was only fifty miles. Only fifteen of the original eighty-six men remained alive, and their acknowledged leader, Cabeza de Vaca, was on the mainland not expected to live. Two men chose to remain as slaves on the island. The others escaped to shore and started the trek to the Panuco, with Dorantes leading. They went first to the friendly village to see Cabeza de Vaca, but the Indians there said he was dead, or would be shortly, so they continued without his blessing.

In a few months, Cabeza de Vaca recovered, went back to the island and found Lope de Oviedo and Hieronimo Alaniz living there alone. Everyone else from the expedition had died, except the dozen who walked away with Dorantes. Alaniz died later that year and the timid non-swimmer, Oviedo, refused to leave the island. Cabeza de Vaca gathered seashells to trade with the mainland Indians.

The Indians on the island were belligerent, and Cabeza de Vaca moved to the mainland, where he established a trading network that took him inland to the north and east of Galveston Island. He may have roamed as far north as Oklahoma. The red clay he traded came from a riverbed near present day Nacogdoches. He brought seashells, conch shells and other objects from the sea coast to the interior and carried animal hides, bows and arrows, and colored clay back to the coastal Indians. The Indians allowed him to travel anywhere he pleased, even among their enemies, because he remained neutral, learned their languages, and traded things they wanted.

He visited the Island of Misfortune annually and urged Oviedo to go with him in search of the Panuco, but the nervous non-swimmer, afraid he would drown crossing the rivers, always put him off until the next year,

The Indians forced Cabeza de Vaca into faith healing. He came into a village where there were three sick people and the Indians asked him to heal them. He declined, saying he had no talent for that sort of thing. The Indians became angry and refused to feed him if he did not heal their sick.

Cabeza de Vaca was well educated for the time, but he knew little about medicine. He placed his hands on the sick Indians, made the sign of the cross and prayed aloud for God's healing power. The Indians immediately said they felt better and were well by morning. Cabeza de Vaca felt that God had guided his hands and heard his prayers. The Indians believed the Spaniard was a "Child of the Sun" and gave him food and other items of value. De Vaca believed God had intervened. He became a very religious man.

The castaways lived in this manner for six years. Cabeza de Vaca traded and travelled and Oviedo remained a slave on the Island of Misfortune. Finally, Oviedo gave in to Cabeza de Vaca's pleadings, and the two escaped. Cabeza de Vaca carried Oviedo on his back across to the mainland and over several rivers. Some Indian women with canoes helped them across Matagorda Bay. The Indians told them of three other "men like you" living with a tribe near the River of Nuts, as the Guadalupe River was known. Had

Cabeza de Vaca traveled this direction while trading, he would have discovered the other survivors years earlier.

Unconcerned that he owed a measure of loyalty to Cabeza de Vaca, and fearful of the unknown, Lope de Oviedo decided to stay with the Indian women who helped him cross the bay. Cabeza de Vaca could not convince him to continue, so Oviedo dropped from history and stayed in South Texas with two agreeable squaws.

Cabeza de Vaca went into the pecan groves along the Guadalupe River, where he had a joyous reunion with his old friends, Andrés Dorantes and Alonso del Castillo. The third survivor was Dorantes' Moorish slave, Estevan. These men had thought Cabeza de Vaca dead for six years. All were overjoyed to find each other alive. The men realized they were the only survivors of Perfilo de Narvaez's expedition, and vowed to escape and make it back to Mexico to tell their story. Or die in the attempt.

During their happy reunion, Dorantes and Castillo brought Cabeza de Vaca up to date on the other members of the original expedition. They let him know the four swimmers he sent, and the faithful Cuban servant, were dead. They told the fate of the other three rafts. One of them, commanded by Alonzo Enriquez and Fray Juan Suarez, had been washed ashore and destroyed near the mouth of the San Bernardo River, some sixty miles west of Galveston Island. All the priests and the religious contingent of the expedition were aboard this craft and made it safely to shore. Narvaez and his crew saw the wreckage and landed nearby. His crewmen were tired of the sea and wanted to walk to the Panuco with the priests.

Narvaez, suffering the late stages of leprosy, was weak and sick. He and two men caring for him chose to stay on his raft. During the night a north wind blew the craft out to sea and Narvaez and his two companions were never seen again. It is not unlikely that Narvaez sailed away on purpose, abandoning his men and planning to make it to the Panuco on his own. Either way, it was a fitting end to the most inept conquistador who ever lived.

Of the one hundred or so priests and soldiers remaining in the vicinity of the San Bernardo River, many starved to death, many died of disease, some killed each other, and Indians killed others. Some of those who died were eaten by the starving survivors. A few tried to walk to Mexico and starved to death in the desert.

The final raft, commanded by captains Tellez and Penaloso made it to the vicinity of present-day Corpus Christi, and probably landed on Mustang Island near Aransas Pass. The Camones, a bloodthirsty tribe that lived in the area, killed them. According to de Vaca's writings, the Indians said the Spaniards were so weak they offered no resistance while being killed. The Camones killed all of them and showed de Vaca their clothing and weapons as proof.

De Vaca and his friends became slaves of coastal Indians. They would be killed if they attempted escape, but even so, in late September of 1534, they left the coastal tribe and headed inland. Unfortunately, they were caught and enslaved by another tribe, some miles away from the coast. The captives were separated and lived in different villages, but they managed to communicate while spending another year in captivity. They planned their escape for the next "tuna season," when their captors went inland to gather prickly pear tunas, a staple of their diet.

On September 8, 1535, the four escaped for good and travelled inland until discovered by a tribe that knew of their reputation as healers. They were taken to a village where one man appeared to be dead and four others were very ill. Even though Cabeza de Vaca could detect no pulse, and the man's eyes were "rolled back," he uncovered the man, massaged his body, breathed on him, made the sign of the cross, and prayed loudly for God's mercy. He treated the other sick in a like manner.

In the morning, the man who appeared dead woke up, asked for food, and walked around the village praising Cabeza de Vaca. The others also recovered and the Indians in the village begged the Spanish to stay and showered them with gifts. The Indians believed the white men had the power of life and death, and no one could die while they were present.

When the Spaniards decided it was time to leave, the Indians escorted the little group to another friendly tribe. The natives believed the white men and the Moor were "children of the sun" and were full of magic. They carefully kept them away from their enemies, fearing the enemies might be blessed if they even looked at the Spaniards. An entourage of Indians began to accompany the Spaniards from village to village, to sing their praises, feed and protect them, and carry their possessions.

Each new tribe brought out their children to be blessed by the white men. Without fail, all the sick in every village claimed to be healed, and the tribes provided gifts of food and anything of value they had. When the Europeans decided to move on, the Indians would protest loudly, weep and wail, and escort them to another village where the natives were happily awaiting the arrival of the healers. Dorantes and Castillo also became "healers," and appeared to be as talented and effective as Cabeza de Vaca. Castillo was reluctant at first because he had thoroughly enjoyed a life of sin. He feared that would make him ineffective as a healer. God evidently forgave him.

Some of the villages Cabeza de Vaca visited consisted of permanent structures, but most were temporary huts, made with sticks and woven mats. One place with permanent buildings was in a valley, near a river just south and east of the first mountains de Vaca saw in this land. Historians who have researched his route feel this permanent village was located where San Antonio now stands. If that could be proved, San Antonio would officially be the oldest continuously occupied city in North America.

That distinction now goes to Acoma, the Zuni Pueblo that Coronado's guides mistook for a city of gold. Acoma had been occupied at least three hundred years when Coronado found it. No one knows how long the Indians might have lived at San Antonio.

The vagabonds and their entourage left San Antonio and worked their way northwest. They crossed the Concho River near what would become San Angelo and spent some time at the "Big Spring," (located just south of the present city by that name). Following the waterholes and rivers, current research indicates they crossed the Pecos River near what is now Carlsbad, New Mexico, and followed the Rio Penasco into the Sacramento Mountains.

After a seventeen-league crossing over a mountain pass near Cloudcroft, New Mexico, the group was welcomed by a village on the western slope near the Rio Tularosa. The usual blessing of the children and bestowing of gifts took place, and the village elders brought the Spaniards a young man who had been wounded in the back by a spear. The shaft had been removed, leaving the flint spear point embedded. The wound had healed. The projectile had worked its way to the vicinity of his heart and was causing constant pain and recurring sickness for the teenager.

Cabeza de Vaca was reluctant to attempt a cure, but the elders left him no choice. In their view, it was a simple matter. If these men were deities, as they claimed, it would be a simple matter to heal this boy. If they were not deities, it would be a simple matter to kill them.

Cabeza de Vaca gathered supplies and equipment, made the sign of the cross, prayed aloud, and prepared for the first heart operation in North America. Four strong men held the boy down for the procedure. Using the flint knife he always carried, Cabeza de Vaca cut into the boy's chest from the front and probed for the arrowhead. He discovered it very near the heart, lodged crossways to his incision. Probing with the point of his knife, he loosened the flint, and burying his knife to the hilt, managed to pull the projectile free and remove it. It was huge.

The boy gushed blood. Cabeza de Vaca tied two stitches of deer tendons to close the incision and used a piece of hair-on buffalo hide to bind the wound and stop the bleeding. Later, when he removed the two stitches, Cabeza de Vaca was proud of his work. He said after the wound healed, it resembled a "crease in a man's palm." The young man felt no more pain, not even tenderness in the vicinity of the incision.

The villagers cleaned the piece of flint and passed it around for all to see. They sent it by runner to surrounding villages so others could know of this wonderful thing. To the Indians, these white men were surely gods and nothing was too good for them.

*In 1915, the Texas Surgical Society was formed and chose Cabeza de Vaca as their Patron Saint. The operation performed by Cabeza de Vaca was named a Sagittectomy, Latin for" the removal of an arrow from the heart." It is rarely performed these days. The operation was written up in an article in the prestigious New England Medical Journal. In 1965, Tom Lea, the famous El Paso artist, did an etching of Cabeza de Vaca performing the surgery. The original was purchased by Dr. Sam Dunn, a Lubbock surgeon, who donated it to the University of Texas Medical School at Galveston. Since that time, much research has been done on de Vaca's route. The operation credited as the "first heart surgery in Texas" almost certainly took place near the Rio Grande River, downhill from Cloudcroft, New Mexico. (This area was part of Texas until 1850, when Texas sold it to the United States, along with a third of Colorado and parts of Wyoming, Oklahoma, and Kansas)*

The size of the entourage increased and the attitude of the Indians towards the Spaniards changed. The Indians were afraid to make eye contact with the white men. To the natives, these men held the power of life and death and must never be displeased. When they entered a village, everything in the village was given to them, even the houses. The Indians looked at the ground and spoke in whispers. To capitalize on this attitude and enhance their importance, Cabeza de Vaca and his friends ceased to speak directly with the Indians. The Moor did all the communication with the natives and relayed all information and questions to the Spaniards. Estevan enjoyed the attention and soon learned to take advantage of his position. He enjoyed the best of food and drink available, and required the most desirable young women in each village be sent to his bed.

Hundreds of Indians now escorted the Spaniards on their journey. They crossed the Rio Grande near present-day Rincon, New Mexico, about seventy miles north of El Paso, and made their way almost due west to Arizona, then across the southeastern corner of that state and into Mexico, moving southwest. When they came near the Gulf of California, which they knew as the South Sea, they turned south to follow that body of water toward civilization.

For the first time in all their travels, food was plentiful. The Indians in this area grew corn, squash and beans, and the climate was such that they got three crops a year. The Spaniards ate only once a day, at dusk, and, by the Indian's standards, they ate very little. Their bodies were tight and lean. Walking had toughened them so they didn't tire as ordinary men. The Indians could see this and it strengthened their belief that these Spaniards were gods.

Natives in this area had been exposed to Christians and were aware of some of the concepts of Christianity. Anything they couldn't explain or understand was "from Heaven." They believed Cabeza de Vaca and his friends were "from Heaven." Cabeza de Vaca realized they could be easily converted to Christianity and said that if he could speak and understand their language better, he would have left them all Christians. Cabeza de Vaca developed an admiration and sympathy for the native people of the Americas that would cause trouble for him the rest of his life. Sympathy toward native peoples was not a popular attitude in Colonial Spain.

At the village of Onovas, Castillo noticed an Indian with a small metal buckle and a horseshoe nail on a thong around his neck. The Indian said it was "from Heaven." When asked who brought it from Heaven, the Indian said some bearded Christian soldiers had passed through and lanced two villagers. One of the Spaniards had dropped the buckle and the Indian retrieved it and the nail.

The excited Spaniards hurried south to find the Christians. As they did so, they found abandoned fields, vacant villages and starving Indians. The Indians were in the woods, hiding from the soldiers who were riding through the country capturing slaves. The natives preferred death to enslavement in the silver mines. They went into hiding, ceased to work their fields, and did not plant their crops.

When de Vaca realized the Spanish soldiers were near, he took the Moor and eleven Indians and hurried ahead of the group to find them. All through the countryside, fields were neglected. Nothing had been planted and the people were gone. The Spanish had burned the empty villages.

On the afternoon of the second day, about thirty leagues from the city of Culiacan, (the northernmost Spanish city in Mexico at the time), Cabeza de Vaca hailed four Spanish soldiers, resting their horses in the middle of a vacant field. It was mid-March of 1536.

The horsemen were dumbfounded. A bearded, emaciated, Spanish-speaking man, afoot in the uncharted wilderness, dressed in rags, accompanied by a negro and surrounded by Indians, did not fit their worldview. They stared. De Vaca may have said, "Take me to your leader."

Cabeza de Vaca was taken to Diego de Alcaraz, a Spaniard in charge of procuring slaves to work the silver mines. He explained to de Vaca that the ignorant natives refused to voluntarily become slaves, and, rather than surrender to the Christians, they hid in the woods, allowed their fields to sit idle, and starved. De Vaca, furious at this treatment of the Indians, was less than tactful in his comments to the bureaucrat. Alcaraz did not need a ragged, half-naked Spaniard giving him orders, and he arrested de Vaca and his friends, put them in irons, and sent them under guard to Mexico City. He ordered the capture of the Indians in de Vaca's entourage and put them to work in the silver mines.

When the government in Mexico City realized that these four vagabonds were the survivors of the Narvaez expedition, de Vaca and his companions were warmly welcomed. The Mexican Government and the Spanish Crown were hungry for any news of the mysterious land north of the Rio Bravo. A commission was established to debrief each survivor, thereby getting four versions of each incident. With this information, a comprehensive report of the whole episode was created. These findings, called the "Joint Report," were assembled and shared by government officials.

Based largely on the Joint Report, a friend of the Viceroy, Francisco Vazquez de Coronado, used his wife's fortune to outfit an expedition and went north to explore and look for gold in 1540. The Joint Report was lost but a summation of it written by a historian, Gonzalo Fernando Oviedo y Valdez, was published in 1547.

De Vaca's friends, Dorantes and Castillo, both married rich widows and settled quietly into Mexico City society. Dorantes' Moorish slave, Estevan, was given or traded to the Viceroy, who sent him to lead a priest, Friar Marcos de Niza, to the golden city of Cibola in preparation for Coronado's expedition.

Cabeza de Vaca went back to Spain and wrote a detailed narrative (La Relacion) of his eight years among the Indians, covering the events, the geography, the plants, the people, their food, and their languages. His broad education and keen observation skill made such a study possible. When his memoir was finished, he returned to the King's service and was appointed Governor of Paraguay. While there, De Vaca loudly protested the treatment of the native people by the Spaniards. His attitude was so unpopular he was eventually arrested and sent back to Seville in chains.

De Vaca was tried and found guilty, exiled to North Africa, and forbidden to visit any colony of Spain with native inhabitants. His wife spent her fortune appealing the verdict, and eventually was successful. King Carlos V released de Vaca, paid him a monetary settlement, and appointed him Chief Justice of the Tribunal of Seville in 1556. He lived less than a year after and died in 1557, broke and unknown. He is buried somewhere in Spain, but his gravesite is lost.

## CHAPTER THREE
# White Men Come to Texas

Starting about 400BC, the Karankawa Indians lived along the Texas coast from Galveston Island to present-day Corpus Christi. They were handsome people, tall and well built, and probably descended from the Tainos, the friendly natives that lived on the Caribbean Islands when the first white men arrived in the "New World." The Karankawa were not friendly—they were constantly at war with neighboring tribes and trusted no one.

The Karankawa

These Indians ate fish and lived along the coast much of the time but moved inland each year to eat pecans and prickly pear tunas during their seasons. They used longbows as tall as a man, with three-foot arrows to hunt deer and buffalo on the mainland.

The Karankawa's first exposure to European men happened in the summer of 1519, when Alonso Alvarez de Pineda led an expedition with three ships and 270 men to map the northern coast of the Gulf of Mexico. In late June of 1519 the expedition anchored in a large bay that Pineda named Corpus Christi, after the Roman Catholic feast day on June 24th.

Although there is no record of contact, Pineda's men must have come ashore in Texas for food and water. The shy Karankawa may have watched from the woods and marveled at the large canoes which moved without oars and the deadly crossbows and fire sticks the Spaniards used for hunting. Within a short time, all the coastal Indians were aware of the strangers.

The first recorded contact happened nine years later, in late 1528, when Cabeza de Vaca and some eighty companions from the ill-fated Narvaez expedition washed ashore and gave the curious Indians a closer look at white men. It soon became apparent that these men were weak and not well equipped to survive in the wilderness. Many died of exposure and disease. The Karankawa grew tired of feeding them and killed some for sport. Those who didn't eat too much were kept as slaves.

The Indians of that day communicated with each other through traders that moved from village to village. Because there was little to talk about, any news of interest moved quickly and was discussed at length. After Cabeza de Vaca and his three companions escaped, the Karankawa heard that they survived and found Spanish soldiers in a land far to the south. They knew that several hundred Indians had accompanied de Vaca, to sing his praises, carry his belongings, and assist him with his healing endeavors.

The Karankawa also knew that many of these camp followers had been captured by Spanish soldiers and taken to be slaves in the mines. It was not important to them that de Vaca opposed this enslavement and worked to free the people. They understood the important lesson—white men were treacherous.

Hernando de Soto

The Karankawa did not know, or care, that the King of Spain had given permission for Hernando de Soto to mount an expedition to explore and colonize La Florida and the southeastern section of the North American Continent.

In May of 1539, De Soto landed 620 men, 220 horses, 200 pigs and other livestock on the west coast of Florida, near present day Tampa. De Soto and his men spent three years meandering through the swamps and woods of present day Florida, Georgia, the Carolinas, Tennessee, Alabama and Mississippi. De Soto's troops fought many skirmishes with the natives and killed hundreds of Indians and lost dozens of soldiers in a great bloody battle near Mobile Bay. He led the first white men to cross the Mississippi River, probably near present day Memphis. They found no gold or other valuables. De Soto is believed to have traveled as far west as Caddo Gap, Arkansas, where he fought yet another battle with the local Indians.

About the same time De Soto set out, Fray Marcos De Niza followed Estevan, the Moor that travelled with De Vaca, into the land of the Zuni.

Viceroy Mendoza, with a substantial personal investment in his friend Coronado's expedition, wanted some assurance that riches were available in the lands to the north. He sent Marcos de Niza, with the Moor as a guide, to determine the location and amount of the riches. The Viceroy and Francisco Coronado hoped for and expected another land as rich in gold and silver as Peru.

The Moor, always looking for advantage, had no idea of the location of Cibola, but was aware that no one else did either. He slipped back into his old habits, lording it over the natives and arrogantly demanding lovely maidens be sent to his bed. Fray de Niza, at the Moor's insistence, followed two days behind and was unaware of Estevan's activities. With the help of local Indians, they reached the Zuni stronghold, and the Moor made his usual demands. The Zuni did not understand how important he was, so they killed him.

When de Niza learned that the Indians had killed Estevan, he decided not to enter their city, but to observe it from the safety of a nearby mountain. He reported a city of size equal to Mexico City, which was true. Past that truth, his imagination filled in the blanks a bit too vividly. Fray de Niza reported what the Viceroy wanted to hear, but he did not specifically say that he had seen gold or precious jewels. He was convinced wealth was there, even though he had not seen it. Nothing in his report discouraged the Viceroy or Coronado.

On April 22, 1540, even though he had not heard de Niza's final report, Coronado moved north from Cullican with 400 soldiers, about 1500 camp followers, a few priests and some slaves, 500 horses, 700 pigs, and some cattle and other livestock. The expedition was well organized, and, at the suggestion of Melchor Diaz, was broken into several stages, with slightly different routes and different starting dates, to allow water sources and grass for grazing to replenish between visits. Two shiploads of supplies were sent ahead, with Hernando de Alarcon in charge. The ships sailed up the Sea of Cortez and into the Colorado river where they were to meet Coronado's soldiers. The

Spaniards had no idea of the distances involved, and after waiting a considerable time at the intersection of the Colorado River and the Gila River, Alarcon had the supplies buried. He and the sailors returned to Mexico.

Francisco Vázquez de Coronado

The Zuni People did not welcome Coronado's soldiers. They had no food to share with outsiders, and the Spanish demanded they give up what little they had. When they resisted, Coronado led an attack and subdued the natives, but he was wounded in the skirmish. Afterwards, the soldiers raided the villages, took food and anything else of value, and, as was their custom, raped the wives and daughters of the natives.

As he recuperated from his wounds, Coronado sent expeditions in all directions, looking for gold or other valuables. Melchor Diaz, one of Coronado's most trusted and competent captains, was assigned to return Fray de Niza to Mexico. The Father's descriptions of Cibola were so distorted and untrue that his life was in danger from some of Coronado's soldiers.

Diaz was an intelligent officer, respected by his men. His troops were well trained, disciplined soldiers. He treated the local Indians as equals and dealt with them with kindness and respect. He shared much-prized coffee and sugar with them and successfully gained their confidence and cooperation. Unlike other Spaniards, they considered him a friend.

Captain Pedro de Tovar was sent by Coronado to the Hopi villages northwest of Cibola to search for riches and information about the area. After trying friendly persuasion with little success, Tovar attacked and subdued the Hopis. They told him of a large river to the west. (The Colorado)

Coronado's second in command, Garcia Lopez de Cardenas, was dispatched to the northwest to find the large river and locate the supply ships. Cardenas and his soldiers were the first to see the Grand Canyon. They could see the Colorado River in the canyon, two thousand feet below, but were unable to descend the sheer walls to get at the water. They reported that it would be impossible to unload the supplies on that river.

When Melchor Diaz returned from Mexico after delivering the disgraced de Niza, Coronado sent him west, to find the ships and supplies de Alarcon was to deliver. The local Indians, happy to please their friend, led Diaz to the intersection of the Colorado River and the Gila River to show him where the supplies were buried. He became the first European to cross the Colorado River and the first to see eastern California. (Viceroy Mendoza had another expedition on board ships exploring the west coast of California at the time.) Diaz's troops unearthed the supplies and loaded them for return to Cibola.

A few days into their return, Melchor Diaz grew tired of a stray dog that had attached itself to their unit early in the expedition. The dog was pestering the pigs the soldiers herded along for food. When Diaz started toward the dog, it trotted away. Diaz spurred his horse to a gallop. The dog ran across the desert with Diaz in hot pursuit, much to the amusement of the soldiers nearby. With his quarry directly ahead, Diaz threw his lance. The dog swerved and the lance missed and buried itself into the ground at an angle. The horse was moving too fast to avoid collision, and Diaz impaled himself on the butt end of his own lance. The lance penetrated his groin area and Diaz suffered for twenty days before he died of his wounds. The last opportunity for a peaceful relationship with the local Indians died with him.

Hernando de Alvarado, another of Coronado's captains, took a troop east and discovered the Rio Grande River and several Indian pueblos nearby. Coronado recovered sufficiently to move and relocated his headquarters to a pueblo which he commandeered near present day Bernalillo. During the winter the Spaniards demanded food and supplies from the Tigua Indians who lived nearby.

The Tiguas resisted, and Coronado had his troops burn their pueblo. (After his injury, Coronado no longer engaged in battle.) As a lesson to all the Indians, Coronado had every man, woman, and child who lived in the Tigua pueblo killed. Coronado dealt with the natives as the Spanish had always dealt with them, but a set of statutes called "The New Laws" were being drafted in Madrid. The priest who witnessed Narvarez' cruelty, Fray Bartolome de Las Casas, after a lifetime of resistance to the encomienda system, finally gained the king's ear and laws against mistreatment of Native People were being enacted. When Coronado returned to Mexico, in addition to being a dismal failure married to a woman with no money, he and Cardenas, his second in command, faced charges for their treatment of the Indians. Activities that were routine when they left Mexico City were now against the King's Law.

At the Pecos Pueblo, Coronado picked up an Indian guide, which the Spaniards called El Turco—The Turk, because of his dark skin.

Coronado Sets Out to the North, by Fredrick Remington

El Turco offered to take the Spaniards to a rich and prosperous land, Quivira, far across the Llano Estacado. The Llano Estacado was as yet unnamed—Coronado may have been the first to use the term to describe the area. Coronado left most of his expedition in New Mexico and took about forty soldiers with him to follow the Turk. El Turco led the Spaniards east, some sources insist through the Lubbock area, and then into Blanco Canyon. El Turco's motives are unknown, but he was nowhere near Quivira. He may have planned to lose the Spaniards in the wilderness and then slip away. Other natives told Coronado that Quivira was to the north and led him through Oklahoma and Kansas to a pitiful little village of mud huts and naked people near the Arkansas River in Kansas. Here is Quivira! Coronado had El Turco throttled and headed back to Mexico City. El Turco is celebrated as an Indian hero because he led the Spaniards away from the Pecos Pueblos and, for a time, gave the natives some relief from the invaders.

Coronado returned to Mexico City in the spring if 1542. He was tried for war crimes but was acquitted by his friends in Mexico City. Cardenas was tried in Spain on virtually the same charges and found guilty. Coronado spent most of his wife's fortune on the unsuccessful quest, and lost his cushy government job, but he and his family lived in relative comfort until he died of an illness in 1554. The family's comfort should come as no surprise. Coronado was a boyhood friend of Viceroy Mendoza, and his wife was, after all, a blood relative of the king.

In 1554, all was excitement in Vera Cruz. Four treasure ships prepared to sail to Havana, then on to Spain. They carried gold, silver and cochineal as cargo, with a 2016 value of about forty-five million dollars. (Cochineal is a highly-prized natural red dye, made from tiny insects that live as parasites on Prickly Pear Cactus. It was a major export from the new world.) Each ship carried a hundred or so passengers, mostly noblemen and their families. Half a dozen priests were on board, returning to Spain, along with active and retired soldiers moving to new duty stations or going home on leave.

In an attempt to get ahead of hurricane season, the four ships left Vera Cruz on April 9, 1554, to head for Cuba, then on to Spain. As they neared Havana on April 29, they encountered a fierce storm that blew three ships back to the Texas coast. The *San Andres* made it to Havana but was so badly damaged that her cargo was off-loaded and she was scuttled.

The *San Esteban, the Santa Maria de Yciar*, and the *Espiritu Santo* were wrecked and sunk a few hundred yards from shore on Padre Island, about fifty miles north of the mouth of the Rio Grande River. About half of the three hundred passengers survived and made it to shore.

One of the ship captains, Francisco del Huerto, gathered healthy sailors for a trip back to Vera Cruz to arrange a salvage operation. The masts of his ship, the *San Esteban*, were plainly visible in the surf, about three hundred yards offshore. The ship rested upright in 15 feet of water. Survivors off-loaded barrels of water and other supplies and stored them among the dunes on the island.

Captain del Huerto and thirty sailors left in a salvaged long boat for the trip back to Vera Cruz. The Indians, with sign language, invited the remaining survivors to a feast. The hungry survivors happily joined the Indians. They looked forward to the meal, their first real food in days.

During the meal, as soon as the Indians were certain the Spaniards had no "fire sticks", they attacked with flint knives, war clubs and longbows. The survivors, confused and frightened, ran away in panic with only the clothing on their backs. The Indians herded them south, down the island and away from their supplies.

One sailor, Francisco Vazquez, hid in the weeds and made his way back to the beach where the salvaged provisions were stored. Everyone else walked south along the shore, thinking they were near enough to walk to the Panuco River settlement in Mexico.

The survivors fled through the night and waded across the lagoon to the mainland. The natives followed, keeping the crowd moving by picking off stragglers with their arrows. The Karankawa intended to kill every man, woman, and child in the group, but first, they wanted to make them suffer.

The Indians captured two sailors, which they treated well. They had the captive sailors strip, then fed and released them, indicating that all they wanted was their clothing. The Spanish hurried to obey. The women and children, because of modesty, stripped and went ahead of the group, and the men followed. Four men that refused to strip were soon riddled with arrows. Everyone else stripped and left their clothing on the beach. The Indians continued to follow and sent a group ahead to prepare an ambush.

When the Spaniards made it to the mouth of the Rio Grande, the Karankawa patiently waited and watched as they constructed crude rafts of driftwood to cross the river. The survivors lost what few crossbows they had when the rafts capsized, but most of the people made it across. Pestered by mosquitoes, naked, painfully sunburned, thirsty, hungry and miserable, those who were still able walked into the waiting ambush a few miles down the beach.

One of the priests, Fray Marcos de Mena, was shot many times with flint-tipped arrows. His fellow priests, thinking death was near, administered last rights and buried de Mena under a shrub in the warm sand, leaving his head exposed under the bush so he could breathe and be relatively comfortable until he died.

Marcos de Mena awoke late that night, refreshed with renewed energy. He dug himself out of the warm sand and started to remove the seven arrowheads lodged in his body. The pain caused him to pass out, but he revived and managed to get out most of the flint fragments. He found some water and food among the bodies left on the beach. Everyone was dead. The Karankawa were gone.

Some weeks later, two peasants working in a cornfield outside the mission at Panuco discovered a starving, naked man at the edge of their field. De Mena had walked over 500 miles to civilization. Plagued by painful arrowhead fragments for the rest of his life, he lived thirty more years and died in Peru in 1584. Some of the facts are disputed, but much of what we know about the shipwreck comes from his memoirs, published by a fellow priest after his death.

Captain del Huerto and his longboat made it back to Vera Cruz and a salvage fleet was quickly organized and dispatched to the site of the ship-wrecks. When the salvage ship anchored near the wreck of the *San Esteban*, the crew saw an excited sailor, waving from the beach. Francisco Vazquez had survived, hiding in the sand dunes near the salvaged water barrels.

The Spanish salvage operation located all three ships along the beach, less than six miles apart. They worked long hours and recovered about 40% of the gold and silver lost in the wrecks. The wrecks may have been plundered later by treasure-seekers, because the location was no secret. It was shown on Spanish maps of the area for the next two hundred years.

The wreck of the *Santa Maria de Yciar* was evidently directly in the path of the dredges when the Mansfield Cut was widened and deepened in the 1950s. From that ship, only the anchor was found intact, and a few coins were recovered from the debris piles left by the dredges. The *San Esteban* and the *Espiritu Santo* were located in the mid-1960s and are still being explored and salvaged. After many lawsuits, the courts ruled that all shipwrecks and artifacts (and oil wells) located within nine nautical miles of the coast belong to the state of Texas. Much of the salvage from these wrecks is on display at the Corpus Christi Museum of Science and History. Something over 51,000 pounds of gold and silver is still missing.

Most of the Karankawa living at the time never saw another white man. It was over fifty years before another expedition visited that part of Texas. The Indians continued to live as they had for centuries, annually moving from the coast to the mainland in search of food. They resisted all efforts to become "civilized" and refused to give up their lands or live in peace with white men.

One of Stephen F. Austin's stated purposes in the formation of his "ranging company" (the original Texas Rangers) was the annihilation of the Karankawa. Austin and others, including Mirabeau Lamar, were successful. The last Indian of that tribe died before the American Civil War. The Karankawa are no more.

While Coronado's men were camping in West Texas and searching for Quivira, remnants of Hernando De Soto's expedition to explore the southeast came into Texas from Arkansas. De Soto never made it into Texas. He died on May 21, 1542 and was buried by his troops, most likely in the Mississippi River. The soldiers' plan was to cross Texas and make their way to Mexico City overland. While still in East Texas, they realized Texas was too dry and undeveloped to feed their army, and the native villages had no extra stores of food they could plunder, so they returned to the Mississippi River valley, where food was more plentiful, but the Indians were unfriendly.

The arrogant Spaniards made no friends with the native people during their early expeditions. They demanded food and took everything they wanted by force. Many of the natives were taken as slaves and made to carry the Spanish soldiers' supplies and equipment. The women were raped. Native Americans distrusted white men for centuries after the visits of Coronado and De Soto.

De Soto's soldiers wintered in Arkansas and Louisiana, near the Mississippi River. After the rainy season, they built longboats called "pinnacles" to sail down the Mississippi and along the Gulf Coast to civilization in Mexico. Indians pursued them in canoes, picking off unlucky individuals with arrows. Almost seven hundred men started the expedition, but only 311 managed to make it to safety at the Panuco River in the fall of 1542. Of the many that tried, these men and Father Marcos de Mena in 1554 are the only recorded survivors who reached the Panuco.

De Soto's exploration of southeast America, and Coronado's visit to the southwest were both considered failures. They returned to Mexico within months of each other and because there was no easy wealth, the Spanish lost interest in the land to the north. For almost a hundred years, the Spanish ignored the North American continent, except for a few scattered attempts to establish missions in Florida and Texas.

In 1629 a Spanish priest, Father Salas, with the help of Indian guides, left Santa Fe and made his way past the Pecos Pueblo in New Mexico, then followed the Pecos River until it intersected the Portales Draw. He followed that draw east, and it became the Black Water Draw which eventually intersected with the Yellow House Canyon in what is now Mackenzie State Park in Lubbock. There is some evidence that Coronado followed this same route from the Pecos Pueblo in 1541.

For many years, Spanish artifacts have been discovered at various sites in the panhandle area of Texas. In one case, about 1927, Dr. H. Bailey Carroll, who later became a history professor at the University of Texas, went duck hunting on George Wolffarth's farm, west of Ropesville, near Lubbock. As he crawled along in the mud (men do strange things when trying to outsmart a duck), he discovered the edge of a copper pot, just showing in the undisturbed soil. He forgot about the ducks and dug up the pot. It was a great specimen of hammered copper and brass. Alexander Whitmore, an authority at the Smithsonian Institute, identified the pot as being the age and peculiar manufacture of those in use at the time of Coronado's expedition.

From Lubbock, Father Salas followed a fork of the Brazos River into what is now Garza County, then picked up a tributary of the Colorado River and followed it to its intersection with the Concho. Almost 250 years later, Ranald Mackenzie followed that same route, in reverse, during the Red River Wars.

Father Salas built a crude mission (the first in Texas) near the Concho River among the Jumano Indians. He stayed several months, then returned to Santa Fe. In 1632, he returned by the same route to minister to the Indians at his makeshift mission. This time he returned to Santa Fe with a few dozen freshwater pearls he gathered in the sandy bed of the Concho River.

The water of the South Concho is crystal clear but contains minerals in which freshwater mussels thrive. These mussels produce beautiful pearls, in pastel colors, ranging from pink to peach to light purple. When the mussels die, the shells separate and the pearls are deposited in the sand and gravel of the riverbed.

When the Viceroy in Mexico City heard of the pearls, he sent word for an expedition to go back and gather what they could find. In 1650, Captains Martin and Castillo followed the same route through Lubbock County to the San Angelo area. The soldiers, with the help of the Jumanos, picked up gallons of pearls, enough to make a necklace for "every fine lady in Spain." Four years later, the Viceroy sent word for another expedition to return and gather more pearls.

In 1654, Captain Diego de Guadalajara and thirty soldiers followed the same route through Lubbock County to the Concho River. Martin and Castillo had done a thorough job and fewer pearls were available, so the harvest was unsatisfactory. Guadalajara and his troops stayed several months gathering pearls and during that time helped the Jumanos fight their local enemies.

Having cemented their relationship with the Jumanos, the Spaniards returned to the area often. Over the next hundred or so years, unknown to the Texians near the Gulf Coast, scores of expeditions crossed from Santa Fe into the Concho River country. Legend has it that San Angelo Pearls are included in the Crown Jewels of Spain. Pearls became too scarce to justify an expedition, but dozens of hunting trips and trading parties crisscrossed the South Plains, and the Spanish soldiers in Santa Fe became familiar with the high plains.

In 1952, a Spanish dagger was dug up in the alley behind the Coca-Cola bottling plant on Texas Avenue in Lubbock. Texas Tech officials sent it to an authority on Spanish Arms at the Metropolitan Museum of Art in New York. The dagger was identified as being made in Spain between 1629 and 1683. The knife was not available during Coronado's time, but could have been lost in either of the expeditions searching for pearls, or any ot the many later visits to or from the Concho River area.

Spanish activity in the area ceased about 1800, as the domination of the plains by the Comanche took hold. Maps were lost, and old-timers who knew the routes died off. The Llano Estacado became the mysterious, uncharted, dangerous land of the Comanche.

René-Robert Cavelier, Sieur de La Salle

In early 1682, a Frenchman, Sieur Robert de La Salle, left the Great Lakes area and canoed down the Mississippi River to the Gulf of Mexico. On April 9, he buried a plaque and a cross near what is now Venice, Louisiana, claiming the whole Mississippi watershed for France. He named it La Louisiana, after King Louis XIV of France.

La Salle returned to France and, with the king's blessing and assistance, assembled three hundred colonists and loaded four ships to establish a French

Colony at the mouth of the Mississippi. When the expedition reached the Caribbean Sea, pirates attacked and took one of his ships. The three remaining ships, lost in the Gulf of Mexico, could not find the Mississippi. One ran aground and another sank in Matagorda Bay on the Texas coast. La Salle may have mistaken the Brazos River for the Mississippi, but the Spanish didn't buy that story. They thought France was trying to steal Texas.

La Salle knew that he had picked the wrong river. He knew he was in Spanish territory and the local Karankawa Indians were none too friendly. He decided to establish a colony despite the difficulties. Fort St. Louis was established near present-day Victoria, flying a French flag deep inside territory claimed by Spain

The soldiers who remained with La Salle were none too happy. They began to question his competence. The original 300 colonists were now reduced to about fifty, two ships rested at the bottom of Matagorda Bay, and La Salle could not find the Mississippi, one of the largest rivers in the world.

On March 19, 1687, during their third overland trip searching for the Mississippi, the soldiers mutinied and killed La Salle. Historians, of course, disagree about where this happened. Most think it was near the site of present-day Navasota, but others think it was farther east, on the banks of the Trinity River. All agree that it was nowhere near the Mississippi River.

Fort St. Louis lasted less than a year. Karankawa Indians killed the colonists, except for six children that were taken as slaves. Five of the children were from the same family, the Lavons, and were rescued a few years later by Spanish troops.

The ruins of the colony were discovered within a year by the Spanish. It was identified as a French settlement, and the nervous viceroy in Mexico City immediately took steps to prevent French incursion in New Spain. A fort, La Bahia, was built in the vicinity of the French Fort St. Louis. Missions were to be established, each with a presidio to house troops for protection from the Indians and enemies of Spain.

One of the first missions, called Tejas, was set up in 1690 for the Caddo Indians in the piney woods near present-day Wenches in East Texas, just across the Sabine River from the French in La Louisiana. The attempt failed within three years and the priests buried the mission bells and burned the chapel before fleeing the angry Caddos. The Indians became hostile toward the priests because European diseases they brought caused the death of hundreds of natives.

In 1713, Louis St. Denis, a French trader and soldier of fortune, established a settlement at Natchitoches, in Louisiana on the Red River. He planned to establish trade with Spanish Texas, even though it was against Spanish law. Smuggling was a profitable way of life in most of the world, and St. Denis intended to introduce it to Texas. To get his business started, he loaded a wagon train with trade goods and travelled across Texas to the Rio Grande River. At San Juan Bautista, he was apprehended by the Spanish army and charged with smuggling. St Denis was held in relative comfort under house arrest at the home of the commandant of the presidio.

The smuggling law had never been used or questioned before, the goods St. Denis brought were desirable and reasonably priced, and the politicians had no idea what to do with him. While he suffered a somewhat "friendly" house arrest, St. Denis wooed and won the hand of the commandant's teenage granddaughter. He talked himself out of trouble and married his child bride. St. Denis worked at San Juan Bautista, assisting his wife's grandfather in setting up Spanish Missions.

St. Denis and his wife returned to Natchitoches in 1721, where they lived under French rule for the rest of their lives. St. Denis attempted to retire, but the French had no one to replace him. He died in 1744, still serving the King of France as head of the military detachment at Natchitoches.

In 1747, the Spanish moved La Bahia inland to the San Antonio River, and spent the next twenty-five years constructing a stone fort, chapel and presidio on the site. This became the only fort for protection of the Spanish holdings between the Rio Grande and the Mississippi River. The town of Goliad grew up next to the presidio.

The Chapel at La Bahia

In the early 1750's, Apache Indians asked Spanish Priests in San Antonio to construct a mission for them far out in unsettled territory, near present day San Saba. The Apaches promised to live on the mission grounds and convert to Christianity. The priests were excited. Their prayers had been answered. They ignored the military leaders, who said the mission site was not in Apache territory. Even with opposition from the military, by early 1757, the mission was complete. No one could say why, but the Apache did not settle in to mission life as they had promised..

The Spanish knew that a mission so far from civilization would need protection, so they insisted that a presidio with a contingent of soldiers be built adjacent to the mission. The priests, knowing that soldiers were not the best example for their converts, insisted the fort and the soldiers be located a proper distance from the mission. The resulting compromise placed the presidio across the river and three miles upstream from the mission.

Destruction of the Mission of San Saba in 1757 by Jose de Paez, 1765

On the morning of March 16, 1758, the priests looked up and 2,000 Indians, mostly Comanche, surrounded their mission. The Apache had convinced the priests to build a mission in the heart of Comancheria, and then simply waited to see what the Comanche would do.

The Comanche attacked. They killed and mutilated every priest they could find. They burned the entire complex. By the time the soldiers arrived from the presidio, the priests were dead, all the livestock was dead, the mission was on fire, and the Comanches were gone. The San Saba Mission was the only mission ever destroyed by native forces on Texas soil. The Spanish sent troops into Comancheria to extract revenge, but they were not successful.

Texas remained relatively quiet for the next half century, as the Spanish attempted to pacify the native tribes, establish missions, and introduce settlers. Starting with Philip Nolan in 1800, General James Wilkinson introduced a string of American filibusters into the territory. "Filibuster" at that time did not mean a talkative senator—it was a name given to land pirates.

# CHAPTER FOUR
# General James Wilkinson

When President Thomas Jefferson bought Louisiana from France in 1803, no one could say exactly where Louisiana stopped and Texas started. The east bank of the Mississippi was sparsely settled and, if you were not an Indian, it was downright lonesome on the west side of the river. Everyone knew that Spanish-owned Texas was out there somewhere, but no one was sure where. Before 1800, the location of the border made no difference because Spain owned most everything west of the Mississippi and south of Canada. After Louisiana changed hands, Spain wanted the Texas border as far east as possible, and the United States, of course, wanted it moved westward. Many Americans, especially southerners, wistfully thought the Louisiana Purchase included Texas.

Spanish and English-speaking people mistrusted each other long before the Middle Ages. The Spanish word for Anglo-Saxon, *anglosajon*, has negative connotations, ranging from petty thief to outright pirate, depending upon the user. The Spanish did not understand the energy and ambition of the Anglos, and the Anglos considered the Spanish a lazy race of bean-eaters who took naps during the workday.

Seeing an opportunity in this situation, General James Wilkinson, Commander of the United States Army, stepped forward to aid the Spanish. The general, an absolute scoundrel, had no particular loyalties, other than his own interests. His accommodating personality inspired trust and put people at ease. He was polite and gracious and had no trouble convincing people of his sincerity and integrity. Virtually unheard-of today, General James Wilkinson was the most outlandish traitor in American history.

General James Wilkinson

General Wilkinson, in a secret document, swore allegiance to the King of Spain in 1787, and began to actively work on Spain's behalf. Esteban Rodriguez Miro, Spain's Governor of Louisiana, paid Wilkinson with gold coin, land, and commercial favors. The general, in keeping with his long-standing practice of self-promotion and self-preservation, neglected to reveal his Spanish citizenship and went about his duties serving both countries in whatever manner most benefited his personal needs. The extent of his treason was not fully known until seventy-five years after his death, when documents discovered in Cuba after the Spanish-American War were made public.

Wilkinson was well prepared for his role. As a young man, he had been commissioned a captain in the Revolutionary Army, and served as an aide to General Benedict Arnold, and later General Horatio Gates. Wilkinson was forced to resign in 1778 when it was suspected that he conspired in the "Conway Cabal," a plot to replace George Washington with General Gates. In 1779, he re-entered the military and a forgiving George Washington appointed him Clothier-General to the Army. In 1781, he resigned that position amid charges of corruption and bribery. His stated reason for the resignation was a "lack of aptitude for the job."

Philip Nolan, a seventeen-year-old Irishman, came to work as clerk, bookkeeper, and aide for James Wilkinson in 1788. At the time, the general was living in Kentucky, on Spain's payroll and temporarily out of favor with the U.S. Army. The ambitious young Nolan learned quickly and soon started smuggling trade goods into and out of Spanish Texas. He left Wilkinson's employ in 1791, but continued to receive advice, moral and financial support from the general for the next ten years as he "mustanged" in Texas. Nolan illegally caught wild horses in Texas, broke them, and drove them to Louisiana where he sold them. It was a lucrative business. A typical raid would take less than six months and net a thousand horses worth $25.00 each.

During this time, Nolan lived two years with the Indians in Texas and became familiar with the territory. Using the general's connections, he obtained a Spanish passport and travelled extensively in Texas, settling for a time in San Antonio, then called Bexar. He married a local Spanish girl, Maria Gertrudis Quinones, and fathered a daughter. The Spanish authorities, paranoid of Anglos, became suspicious of his motives, revoked his passport, and banned him from the territory. Nolan abandoned his wife and daughter and went back to Mississippi.

Once there, Nolan renewed his relationship with General Wilkinson, and, displaying a flexible set of morals, courted and married Frances Lintot, daughter of a prominent Natchez businessman. Again, using the general's connections, Nolan corresponded with Thomas Jefferson and was invited to Monticello to discuss the wild horses of Texas, a subject of interest to the multifaceted Jefferson. There is no evidence Nolan ever made the trip.

Likely at the urging of General Wilkinson, Nolan decided to invade and conquer Texas. He promised those who would join him free land and vast wealth. Early in 1801, he led twenty-seven heavily armed men into the territory. To avoid Spanish troops at Nacogdoches, the group entered through a little used northern route. They brought wagon loads of trade goods and set up camp deep inside Texas, between present-day Cleburne and Hillsboro. At the campsite, they built corrals to gather horses.

Nolan's motivation for this campaign is unclear. Members of the expedition loyal to Nolan said it was a purely commercial venture, planned for profit from trading with the Indians and capturing wild horses. This is probably true, but other expedition members, possibly buying favor by telling the Spanish what they wanted to hear, said Nolan was bent on conquest.

A Spanish patrol from Nacogdoches "discovered" the camp, surrounded and captured the rustlers and killed Nolan. To prove Nolan dead, William Barr, an Irish businessman travelling with the Spanish troops as guide and interpreter, cut off Nolan's ears and sent them to the Viceroy in Mexico City.

ERECTED
IN MEMORY OF
PHILLIP NOLAN
BORN IN IRELAND,
FIRST CAME TO TEXAS, AND
ESTABLISHED RESIDENCE AT
NACOGDOCHES IN 1791. WHEN
KILLED, WAS A RESIDENT OF
NATCHEZ, MISS. KILLED NEAR
THIS SITE MARCH 21, 1801 BY
THE SPANIARDS. WAS BURIED
HERE BY HIS NEGRO SLAVES
CAESAR AND ROBERT. NOLAN'S
DEATH AROUSED A WAVE OF
INDIGNATION THAT LED TO THE
INDEPENDENCE OF TEXAS.

Barr had a vested interest in the capture of Nolan and his men. He arranged with his friend, the Spanish governor Miro, to be the only merchant licensed to trade in Texas, and Nolan was encroaching on his territory. It is unlikely troops from Nacogdoches would have found Nolan's expedition without William Barr's guidance, however it is also unlikely that the death of Nolan had anything to do with the start of the Texas Revolution, no matter what this marker says.

During the Civil War, Edward Everett Hale wrote the fictional short story, "Man Without a Country" and named his main character Philip Nolan because the name was well known at the time. Other than the use of his name, Philip Nolan, the "filibuster," had nothing to do with that story.

The word filibuster now calls to mind a long-winded speech attempting to block some legislation in the U.S. Senate. In 1800, it was a name applied to outlaws that fomented revolution and took territory unlawfully. Philip Nolan was the first of many filibusters or "land pirates" to operate in Texas, but not the only one with direct ties to General Wilkinson.

George Washington called Wilkinson out of retirement in 1796 and appointed him as Commanding General of the United States Army, where he served until 1798. Two years later, in 1800, he was reappointed to this position by President John Adams, and served through the terms of Adams, Thomas Jefferson and James Madison. He was ousted in 1812, amid charges of incompetence. Wilkinson was court-martialed but acquitted. During all this time he was a paid agent and citizen of Spain.

Spain, because of serious financial problems, ceded Louisiana to France in 1800, under the condition that Napoleon would never let the territory fall into the hands of an English-speaking nation. Three years later, Napoleon, not one to let a promise stand in the way of a profit, abruptly sold the whole territory to the United States for 15 million dollars. Now, Spain was forced to define borders, draw up treaties, and disperse troops to defend her territory.

The greedy and treacherous Anglos were right next door to Texas and cash-strapped Spain was nervous.

President Thomas Jefferson appointed his trusted Commanding General of the Army, James Wilkinson, as the first governor of the newly acquired upper Louisiana Territory, which included all of the territory except the city of New Orleans, and effectively put the fox in charge of the henhouse. Wilkinson immediately entered into a conspiracy with Aaron Burr to establish a new country by taking control of Kentucky and the Louisiana Territory. The general also wanted to include Texas, and perhaps a part of Mexico in his new nation.

When the plot began to unravel, Wilkinson proclaimed innocence, blamed the whole incident on Burr, and testified against him at the trial. Aaron Burr was a perfect scapegoat. Having recently killed Alexander Hamilton in a duel, he was out of favor in Washington, and any charges he made against General Wilkinson would result in self-incrimination. He remained silent and was acquitted on a technicality. Wilkinson, as usual, evaded blame, although the head of the grand jury that investigated the incident characterized him as "the only man I ever saw, who was from the bark to the very core, a villain."

With his dual roles as commander of the army and governor of Louisiana, Wilkinson was extremely powerful. He declared martial law and became outright ruler of the Louisiana territory. He dispatched a protégé, Captain Zebulon Pike, on a mission into New Spain—Texas and New Mexico—supposedly to find the sources of the Red and Arkansas Rivers. Privately, Wilkinson wanted to gauge the strength of the Spanish army and discover the best route to invade Texas. Pike built a fort for the winter near the southeastern Colorado mountain that bears his name and posted an American flag there, even though he knew he was in Spanish territory. He and his men were arrested and taken to Santa Fe where Pike was wined and dined by uneasy Spaniards, then escorted back to the Louisiana border and released. His troops were imprisoned in Mexico, but because of the risk of an unwanted war with the United States, Spain treated Pike with great courtesy.

In his duties as governor of Louisiana, Wilkinson made an agreement with General Herrera, commander of the Spanish forces in East Texas. Although neither had authority to speak for their governments, they decided to set up a neutral zone between Louisiana and Texas. The Spanish army would not move east of the Sabine River and the American forces would not go west of the Rio Hondo, which paralleled the Sabine in Louisiana. This effectively moved the border seven miles east and surrendered some American territory, but it prevented border clashes and possible armed hostilities between the two countries. President Jefferson approved the idea and commended General Wilkinson on his initiative.

Because neither army patrolled the zone, this "Neutral Ground" quickly became a haven for outlaws, cutthroats and thieves. When Mexico started to rebel against the Spanish King, Mexican political refugees fled into the area. Disturbed by the increasing lawlessness, General Wilkinson obtained Spain's permission to enter the space with American troops and remove the criminal element.

The general sent a young lieutenant, Augustus Magee, into the Neutral Ground with orders to "clean it out." Magee graduated third in his class at West Point, this was his first duty station, and he was eager to prove himself. He was very efficient, if perhaps a bit brutal. Some of the outlaws were killed in battle and others were hanged. The lieutenant routinely had men tied to trees and flogged to make sure they understood the rules. The Neutral Ground grew quiet and peaceful.

Augustus William Magee

In 1810, an obscure priest in Guanajuato, Father Hidalgo, issued the grito or "cry" and called for an end to the Spanish Rule in Mexico. The Mexican people took sides, with Republicans on the side of revolution while Royalists remained loyal subjects of the King of Spain. The Republicans looked to America for support, financial and otherwise, and some aligned themselves with American soldiers of fortune to fight against the Spanish. Father Hidalgo's head was soon hanging on display in Guanajuato, but the seeds of revolution were sown. The civil unrest in Mexico fermented for more than a decade before the Spanish were driven out.

Lieutenant Magee became very interested in Texas, a not unusual malady among General Wilkinson's associates. Magee's good friend, Captain Zebulon Pike, had reported that the Spanish army was ill-equipped, poorly trained, and, in his opinion, could easily be defeated. Magee felt that the only thing needed to remove Texas from Spanish control was good military leadership. Knowing he could provide that, he contemplated invasion of Texas.

Two things, which may have been coincidental, but more likely were arranged by General Wilkinson, helped Augustus Magee make up his mind. First, in spite of his good record, he was passed over for promotion to captain. Second, Wilkinson put him in touch with a Mexican Republican, Bernardo Gutierrez de Lara, who was in Natchitoches, Louisiana, raising capital and troops for an expedition into Texas. Magee resigned his commission and joined Gutierrez. They agreed Gutierrez would provide funds and political savvy and Magee would command the army.

Magee went to New Orleans, the gathering point for adventurers, outlaws, revolutionaries, mercenaries and misfits looking to go to Texas for fun and profit. He soon raised an army—mostly Americans but also Mexican rebels, Louisiana Frenchmen, and even some adventurous Indians. Many of these recruits had been run out of the Neutral Ground by Magee, and one day he might regret enlisting them.

Young American patriots, looking to free Texas from the yoke of Spanish oppression, made up much of the group, and the promise of forty dollars a month and a league of Texas land helped fill the ranks. Magee's army was a melting pot of races, nationalities, moralities, and persuasions, with only one consistent feature—most all the officers were Americans.

These officers included Samuel Kemper, who fought the Spanish in Florida, Henry Perry, a former quartermaster in the American army, and James Gaines, a Louisiana sheriff who, twenty-four years later, signed the Texas Declaration of Independence. Rounding out the officers' corps were James Carr, Reuben Ross, a man named Locket from Virginia, and John Davis Bradburn from Kentucky. Bradburn, a mercenary, would play a pivotal role in the Texas Revolution as an officer in the Mexican army. Rezin Bowie, an older brother of James, also joined the group and became the first of the Bowie clan to visit the interior of Texas. The Bowies dealt with Jean Lafitte, slave trading on Galveston Island.

In August of 1812, the army moved west with Gutierrez de Lara and Augustus Magee at the head. At Nacogdoches, the undermanned Spanish guards took one look and headed south. The local citizens welcomed Magee and his men as liberators. Magee moved his army, now some 800 strong, west toward Bexar and La Bahia, the other chief settlements in Texas. Alerted by the fleeing Spanish troops from Nacogdoches, Governor Manuel Maria de Salcedo of Bexar sent 1500 troops to hold Magee's army north of the Guadalupe River. Magee showed his mettle by outflanking the Spanish troops, moving south, surprising and capturing the lightly defended Presidio at La Bahia.

The Presidio at La Bahia—later called Goliad—was by far the finest fortified position in Texas. The Spanish Army moved the fort to this location in 1747 and replaced the wood fortifications with stone over the next twenty years. For almost a hundred years, it was the only Spanish fort defending the Gulf Coast from the Rio Grande to the Mississippi River. With stone walls ten feet thick, several cannon, ample ammunition, a good water supply, and comfortable barracks, it was difficult to assault and easy to defend.

Magee moved his men into the presidio and prepared to hold his position with captured Spanish cannon and munitions. He paid his troops with Spanish coin liberated from the war chest he discovered at the fort. When Governor Salcedo, furious that he had been out maneuvered, arrived and demanded surrender, Magee and his "Revolutionary Army of the North" laughed at him. A four-month siege began, during which young Colonel Augustus Magee suffered an untimely death.

Colonel Magee's death is one of the mysteries in Texas history. At twenty-four years of age, he raised an army and captured two-thirds of the territory in Texas and was well on his way to taking the remainder away from the Spaniards. This kind of ability, drive, and ambition creates enemies; some of them very dangerous men with long memories. Magee fell ill early during the siege of La Bahia and, after suffering for months, died. Samuel Kemper, the American rebel from Florida, took over command of the forces.

Some think Magee committed suicide; others believe he died of malaria or another disease. Mirabeau B. Lamar, who interviewed many participants of this campaign for his book on Texas history, was convinced Magee was poisoned by his own men. Many of these men had been flogged or otherwise abused at Magee's order when he cleared out the Neutral Ground. Some of his officers disagreed with his conduct of the war and were jealous of his accomplishments, and, toward the end, he had serious philosophical differences and violent arguments with Gutierrez de Lara, his Mexican political partner. Mexican political partners were inherently dangerous creatures

Disagreements between Mexican revolutionaries and American volunteers were predictable. The Mexicans assumed all conquered territory would be ruled in the Spanish mold, a sort of "we're the bosses and you're the peons" approach, while the Americans intended to set up a democratic form of government and vote on major issues. The Mexicans knew nothing about democracy and didn't want to confuse the lower levels of society with such Anglo foolishness. They planned for Texas to remain a part of Mexico. The Americans insisted it should become a part of the United States. These alliances, although initially attractive, were doomed from the start.

Word of Magee's success spread North and dozens of idealistic young Americans headed to Texas for adventure, free land, and, in their minds, the opportunity to free an enslaved and oppressed people. Most of these men saw themselves as patriots, some were looking for adventure, and some were looking for a place to hide from the long arm of the law.

A few days after the death of Magee, Governor Salcedo launched a full-scale attack on the Presidio at Goliad, with disastrous results for his army. Kemper's troops easily defended the fort and inflicted heavy casualties on the Royalist forces. Salcedo gave up and withdrew back to San Antonio.

New volunteers from the north swelled Kemper's ranks, and, in late March of 1813, he trailed the Spaniards to San Antonio.

The "Republican Army of the North" defeated Governor Salcedo's forces in short order. The terms of surrender called for the Royalist Army to be disbanded and the officers paroled. San Antonio was occupied, all prisoners were released, and the victorious soldiers were rewarded with captured Spanish booty. It was a stunning victory. For the first time in history, Texas was rid of all Spanish forces and in the hands of "land pirates" from the north.

As soon as the military danger was past, Bernardo Gutierrez de Lara and the Mexican politicians took control and informed the Americans that Texas was Mexican soil and subject to Mexican laws and customs. The Mexicans would dictate the form of government and Texas would remain a territory of Mexico. Even though they had been promised freedom, Governor Salcedo and several of his loyal officers were taken out and murdered. Gutierrez de Lara ordered their throats cut, the customary Spanish method of dealing with political enemies.

The idealistic young Americans were devastated. Kemper, many of his officers, and the bulk of the American idealists resigned in protest. They made their way back to the United States, leaving Texas to the deceitful Mexicans, and the filibuster army loosely in the command of Henry Perry, the former quartermaster. Gutierrez de Lara surrendered his position to Alvarez de Toledo, a Spanish idealist who had joined the revolution and was more palatable to the remaining Americans.

The army that was left in Texas was filled with cutthroats and knaves. It included Mexican rebels, Louisiana Frenchmen, a few Indians, and about 800 Americans. Even though many of the remaining Americans were competent soldiers and had good Kentucky rifles, they were freebooters that lacked the revolutionary zeal of Magee's troops. More importantly, they lacked Magee's leadership.

General Joaquin de Arredondo was sent from Mexico City with 2,000 men to deal with the rebels. He engaged them in battle at the Medina River, a few miles south of San Antonio, on August 18, 1813. Without Magee, confusion ruled the ranks of the filibusters, with Perry in command of the American troops and Toledo now heading the Mexican revolutionaries. General Arredondo, a professional soldier and competent commander, lured the rebels into an ambush and, after a fierce battle, defeated them. This battle, and the carnage that followed, was the single bloodiest episode in history on Texas soil. Over 1300 rebel soldiers were killed outright, including most of the remaining Americans.

To the Spanish government in Mexico City, these men were pirates and, as such, deserved to be put to the sword. Consequently, anyone who was captured or surrendered was unceremoniously slaughtered. Fewer than a hundred Americans escaped. Two of the escapees were Henry Perry and John Davis Bradburn, mercenary idealists who had joined Magee in New Orleans. The two managed to slip away through the woods and eventually make their way back to Louisiana. They joined the militia and fought the British under Andrew Jackson at the Battle of New Orleans.

Arredondo planned to remove all Anglo settlers from Texas. Spanish troops went into San Antonio and arrested everyone suspected of collusion with the rebels, which included most of the Anglos. Several hundred men were put to death without trial and their wives and daughters suffered the proverbial "fate worse than death." Even in remote Nacogdoches, those Americans who did not flee were treated in the same fashion. Arredondo effectively removed the bothersome Anglos from Texas. With rare exception, everyone left alive in Texas spoke Spanish, practiced the catholic religion, and professed loyalty to the King of Spain. This lesson was not lost on a nineteen-year-old lieutenant in Arredondo's army — Antonio Lopez de Santa Anna.

During the time of Magee's filibuster, General James Wilkinson, while no longer Commander of the United States Army, was away from home during the War of 1812, serving as a major general in command of troops. Difficulties occurred. Wilkerson was relieved of command but found not guilty of wrong by a board of inquiry. Historian Robert Leckie called him "a general who never won a battle and never lost a court-martial."

Wilkinson returned to Mississippi and lived for a time near Natchez, on land provided him by his employer when Spain owned Louisiana, Governor Miro. Relatives moved nearby and the general helped rear Jane Herbert Wilkinson, the daughter of his deceased brother. In 1815, Jane married a young doctor, James Long, who was a favorite of Andrew Jackson. Dr. Long served under Jackson at the Battle of New Orleans. Long was very industrious and founded a medical practice, operated a plantation, and worked as a merchant in the Natchez area. He also developed a deep interest in Texas, as earlier mentioned, a not uncommon condition among young men associated with General Wilkinson.

The Secretary of State for the United States, John Quincy Adams, and Spain's Foreign Minister, Luis de Onis, negotiated the Adams–Onis Treaty in 1819. Also called the Florida Treaty, it ceded Florida to the United States and established the border between the U.S. and New Spain, which included Mexico, Texas, and all the current Southwestern United States. The treaty was widely considered a master stroke of diplomacy by Adams. Spain was reeling from the disastrous Peninsula War, in fear of losing all her American colonies, facing bankruptcy and civil unrest at home, and in a poor negotiating position. The treaty was very favorable to the United States, but it was not generally welcomed in the American South.

General Wilkinson, Dr. James Long, and almost every other landowner in Mississippi and the Deep South felt that Adams had given away Texas. The Texas/Louisiana border was established at the Sabine River, but the southerners felt that it should have been set at the Rio Grande. They wanted the cotton land in Texas and set about to get it.

The irate citizens of Natchez decided to raise money and an army and take Texas by force. General Wilkinson and his nephew-in-law, Dr. Long, were especially outspoken in their opposition to the treaty and support of the invasion. They promised it would not be much of a problem; everyone knew the Spaniards couldn't fight. In their view, any comparison of the races demonstrated that Anglos were much superior. The intelligent and articulate young Dr. Long was put in charge of the expedition and soon a war chest of over half a million dollars was collected.

Following the footsteps of Augustus Magee, and likely the guidance of General Wilkinson, Dr. Long travelled to New Orleans. The city still offered a ready supply of idealistic young men anxious to go to Texas in search of adventure, free land and easy profit. In addition to the idealists, the usual array of profiteers, fugitives, opportunists, and hardened criminals was also available.

Long met Jose Felix Trespalacios, a Mexican Republican, fighting to free Mexico from Spanish rule. The men joined forces with Dr. Long leading the expedition and Trespalacios providing political insight and some financial support. As already demonstrated, different goals doomed this arrangement from the start, but such partnerships were not unusual.

Ben Milam, a thirty-one-year-old adventurer, joined the group in New Orleans. Milam had just returned from his first trip to Texas, where he traded and lived with the Indians. He had become close friends with David Burnet, who was suffering from consumption and living with the Indians in an attempt to restore his health. Milam had planned to return to Texas, and this expedition offered free land. Trespalacios and Long recognized talent, and Ben Milam became a colonel in their army.

Jim Bowie also joined the volunteers in New Orleans. He was twenty-three years old and involved with his brother Rezin in a slave-trading venture with Jean Lafitte. Jim Bowie had been to Galveston Island, Lafitte's headquarters, and wanted to see more of Texas.

Long's little army moved out in June of 1819 and occupied Nacogdoches. Against the advice of Trespalacios, the rebels wrote a "Declaration of Independence," and established "The Republic of Texas." Dr. Long was elected president, and they published the first English language newspaper in Texas, the *Texas Republican*. The group planned to award ten square miles of Texas land to each member of the expedition.

The newspaper was published only during the month of August, 1819, then closed for lack of support. Many of the soldiers, including Jim Bowie, drifted back to Louisiana, bored and suspicious of the "free" land. In November, Spanish troops sent by the Viceroy in Mexico City arrived and scattered Long and his men. Some of the filibusters were captured but most escaped back to Louisiana.

Doctor Long moved to Point Bolivar, on the coast, where he was joined by his young wife, Wilkinson's niece Jane, their five-year-old daughter and a twelve-year-old slave girl, Kian. There, he tried unsuccessfully to recruit Jean Lafitte to his cause. Lafitte, a paid informant of the Spanish, delayed Long and kept the Spanish in Mexico City informed of his activities.

In September of 1821, James Long left his little family to lead an attack on the Presidio at La Bahia. He promised Jane he would return, and she, six months pregnant, promised to wait "as long as it takes." Jane, alone with her daughter and Kian, the slave girl, delivered a baby girl on December 21, 1821, during an ice storm. Only determination, raw courage, and raw oysters kept the women from starving during the long, cold winter.

Jane Long later styled herself the "Mother of Texas," based upon the idea that her baby was the first Anglo child born in Texas. This claim was easily disproved by census records dating back to 1806, but Jane steadfastly defended the claim and had the title put on her tombstone.

Jane Long

James Long had learned, from his failed filibuster in Nacogdoches, not to establish a Republic of Texas in New Spain. This time, his plan followed the ideas of Trespalacios. He would help the Mexican rebels win their independence from Spain, and then work to free Texas from the new Mexican government. When Long left to capture Goliad, his partner, Trespalacios, and Ben Milam sailed with a contingent of men to attack the Spanish at Vera Cruz. Long failed to take La Bahia and was captured by the Spanish and sent to prison in Mexico City.

Trespalacios and Milam arrived at Vera Cruz to discover the revolution was over, the Spanish had been dislodged, and Mexico was free. The Mexican revolutionaries greeted them as heroes.

Long, very popular with Iturbide and the new Mexican government, awaited release from the Spanish prison. It was rumored that Long might receive a high appointment from the new government, perhaps even the coveted governorship of the Texas territory. Trespalacios was jealous of Long's popularity.

While waiting for the Mexican bureaucracy to grant his freedom, James Long was "accidentally" shot and killed by a guard in the prison. Mexico was in turmoil at the time, and evidence indicates that Long's death was arranged and paid for by his old friend, Jose Felix Trespalacios. Ben Milam believed Trespalacios guilty and threatened to kill him over the incident. Milam was imprisoned for his threats.

Milam was eventually released and became a citizen of Mexico. He was appointed a colonel in the Mexican Army but resigned to go back to Texas. With James Long out of the way, Trespalacios was appointed the Governor of Texas. He and Milam patched up their differences.

Meanwhile, General James Wilkinson retired from the U.S. Army and arranged to have himself appointed U.S. Envoy to Mexico. He moved to Mexico City in 1822 and, ignoring most of his other duties, began to actively seek land grants in Texas. Also in Mexico City at the time were Stephen F. Austin, Haden Edwards, Robert Leftwich, Ben Milam, and others seeking Texas land. These Americans knew each other and spent time together socially. With the exception of General Wilkinson, who died before any grants were issued, all of them eventually were allotted land grants and became empresarios in Texas.

Wilkinson, after all his illegal schemes, finally attempted to legally obtain a part of Texas. He died in Mexico City at age 68 and is buried there. His death, in December of 1825, was blamed on a combination of climate and opium. The general supported and helped finance three major filibusters, but it is doubtful he ever set foot inside Texas. His thirty-eight years of treason were not fully known for three-quarters of a century, finally exposed by Spanish records captured in Cuba in 1898, during the Spanish/American War. Theodore Roosevelt, after studying captured documents in Havana, said, "In all our history, there is no more despicable character."

# CHAPTER FIVE

# Juan Davis Bradburn and William Barret Travis

John Davis Bradburn did not believe he lacked moral fiber. Oh, he had changed his mind at times during his career, but those reversals were more due to the learning curve than any lack of fortitude on his part. Except, maybe, that time in 1816, at Perry's Point on the Texas coast, when he left Henry Perry and joined Francisco Javier Mina. Mina's plan to invade Tampico and help the rebels in Mexico win their independence from Spain was fairly simple. Some might consider that move a little opportunistic, but Bradburn was not yet thirty years old, Perry wasn't very well organized, and Mina had a much more comfortable and sea-worthy ship.

Perry had saved Bradburn's life back in 1813, when they were with Gus Magee's bunch, filibustering in San Antonio. General Arredondo caught their army at the Medina River and the battle turned into a bloodbath. The Spanish set about to kill every single American in Texas. Perry took off into the woods and Bradburn followed. They escaped the massacre and walked back to New Orleans. Sure, he owed Perry, but Bradburn felt safer going with Mina—Perry's boat leaked.

The Spanish considered Bradburn an American filibuster, even though he wasn't actually fighting for Texas. He had joined the Mexican rebels and was trying to free Mexico from Spain, so the change at Guanajuato wasn't really because of any lack of courage. When Colonel Young was killed, Bradburn was suddenly left in sole command of the American filibusters and he ordered a retreat. Three-fourths of Bradburn's troops were killed, so anyone could see Bradburn's leadership saved the lives of one fourth of his men.

The change he made in December of 1820 may have looked indecisive to someone not familiar with the details, but the rebels were losing. He left the rebels and went over to the Spanish Army, under the command of General Agustin de Iturbide, a really good general. That could have been misinterpreted, but Iturbide renounced Spain and took over Mexico as dictator, so everything worked out fine. John Bradburn became a Mexican citizen, changed his name to Juan and was made a colonel in the Mexican army. Bradburn's friend, Antonio Lopez de Santa Anna, did the same thing and he came out a general.

Emperor Agustín de Iturbide

Emperor Iturbide sent Bradburn to the United States as an envoy and Bradburn returned from Washington to report that the U.S., no friend of Spain, recognized Mexico as an independent nation. A pleased Iturbide arranged Bradburn's marriage to a Mexican heiress, Maria Josefa Hurtado de Mendosa y Caballero de los Olivos. John and Maria's only child, a son, became a priest.

Life was good for the American, turned Mexican, turned Spaniard, turned Mexican, until 1823, when his patron, Iturbide, abdicated the throne and was exiled by the Federalists. Bradburn was a Centralist, believing that all government power should be centralized. The Federalists allowed American settlers to immigrate into Texas, issuing land grants to Stephen Austin, Richard Leftwich, Haden Edwards, Ben Milam, and others.

General Arredondo, now the Texas governor, changed his opinion of Anglo colonists. He decided annihilation might not be the best route. American immigrants could be useful building a buffer zone between the dreaded Comanche and loyal Mexican citizens. They could also establish a tax base where none existed. Taxes dried up after 1813, when Arredondo forced the Anglos from Texas. Empresario grants had worked very well for Spain when she owned Missouri. Moses Austin, a mining engineer, brought in dozens of families who quietly mined lead, worked their land, and paid their taxes. Moses' son, Stephen, along with other empresarios, set up shop in Texas and thousands of American citizens poured in.

So many Americans flooded in so quickly, the Mexican government became nervous that the Americans might take Texas away from Mexico. American colonists were squeezing Mexicans out and making noises about human rights, democratic elections, religious freedom and other silly Anglo notions. The colonists considered themselves superior to the Mexicans and made no effort to learn the Spanish language or worship in the Catholic Church. Even though slavery was against Mexican law, they owned slaves. Mexico was in a perpetual financial bind and the colonists were not paying their share of the tax burden. Most paid no taxes at all. To combat these problems, the Mexican government passed a series of laws on April 6, 1830.

These laws prohibited immigration from any adjacent country. The reasoning here was transparent, because the United States was the only adjacent country. The empresario grant for any colony with less than 150 colonists was cancelled. The property tax law, which exempted colonists from property taxes for ten years, was rescinded. The Mexican Army was instructed to enforce harsh penalties for slave owners. Custom houses were to be constructed to collect tariffs on goods coming into and going out of Texas.

To balance the ratio of Mexicans to American colonists, provisions of these laws encouraged Mexican citizens to move to Texas, with the government offering free land and paying all moving expenses. European colonists were encouraged to help dilute the overwhelming American presence. Mexican prisoners were moved to Texas and used as labor for building roads and infrastructure. American colonists woke up on April 7, 1830, on Mexican soil with Mexican officials enforcing Mexican laws. They were less than happy about this turn of events.

Colonel Juan Davis Bradburn was sent to Texas with soldiers to enforce these laws and establish the first custom house on Galveston Bay. He felt he was picked for this duty because he was out of favor with the current government, but he was a logical choice. He was bi-lingual and familiar with the country around the bay. He chose to erect the first custom house and collect tariffs at Perry's Point, where he and Henry Perry had conspired against the Spanish years before, when he was still John and when he was still American.

Bradburn, as instructed, named the settlement "Anahuac" after the Anahuac Valley, the ancient home of the Aztecs in Mexico. He began building the customs house, and soon had his soldiers and workmen at wits end, allowing construction one day, and having it torn down as substandard the next. He did not choose to be indecisive; it seemed to be his nature. His job was difficult and complicated, his troops were lazy convicts, the American colonists were plotting against him, and no one understood how lonely it was at the top.

Because the laws forbade new colonists, Bradburn refused to allow immigrants to come ashore. In a short time, Trinity Bay was teeming with anchored ships holding Americans who had paid for their homesteads and were understandably frustrated. Bradburn was very courteous, but firm—he said they could wait in the harbor until Mexican laws changed, or they could go back where they came from.

American colonists ashore were doubly upset with Bradburn because he was from Kentucky—to them, an American enforcing Mexican law—they felt he was a traitor. He upset his troops as much as he angered the citizens of Anahuac. The troops deserted and the citizens verged on rebellion. The two camps in Anahuac eyed each other with suspicion—the colonists wanting America style justice and the army expecting Mexican style submission. Into this turmoil came a pimpled, debt-ridden, idealistic, twenty-one-year old Alabama lawyer—William Barret Travis.

Travis was born August 9, 1809, in South Carolina. His family moved to Alabama when he was nine. Young William disliked the idea of becoming a farmer, so he applied himself diligently to his education. He read voraciously, worked tirelessly at his studies, and became a teacher, lawyer, and newspaper publisher. The intelligent, ambitious young man also became a Mason, fathered a child, and married one of his students, in that order, all before he was twenty.

Travis attained the standing of Master Mason during August of 1829. Because Masons were required to be twenty-one years old, it is probable that he lied about his age, something that did not seem to bother the young man—he lied when it suited him, about a lot of things.

Even though Travis was a talented writer, his newspaper suffered from lack of advertisers. Claiborne, Alabama, needed a newspaper, and Travis wanted the prestige of being the editor of a successful paper. The paper floundered. His law practice floundered. His marriage floundered. William and his lovely young wife, Rosanna, were not getting along. No matter how hard Travis worked, debts continued to mount and lawsuits were pending. The industrious young man was miserable.

William and Rosanna Cato Travis were living beyond their means. They were supporting themselves, little Charles Edward, and three slaves.

The slaves were borrowed from Rosanna's parents, but had to be fed and maintained. Perhaps Travis endured this expense to cater to the beautiful Rosanna's need to be "the lady of the house." In truth, she was barely eighteen years old, a poor housekeeper, spoiled, immature, promiscuous, and pregnant with her second child.

Travis had no quarrel with the idea of fidelity in marriage, so long as it applied to the female partner. He could stray if he wished, but his male ego would not allow his wife to seek satisfaction elsewhere. Rosanna was very friendly with a man named Samuel Cloud, and Travis questioned their relationship. He worried the child Rosanna carried was not his. Life was complicated in Claiborne, Alabama.

In April of 1831, eight months after his twenty-first birthday, William Barret Travis kissed the pregnant Rosanna goodbye, mounted his horse, and rode toward Texas. The Alabama court ruled he must pay his debts or go to jail, and he left before a warrant could be issued for his arrest. He promised to return for his wife and children when he could afford to support the family. He rode out of Claiborne, took the ferry across the Alabama River, and headed west. He planned to never return.

William Barret Travis had much time to think on his trip west from Alabama. All his life he had read romantic novels, Sir Walter Scott, Shakespeare, and stories of bigger-than-life heroes, doing good and righting wrong. Travis felt he had another chance at life and he would do it right this time. He would be a dashing, romantic character. Naturally, he would become wealthy. He would live and dress flamboyantly, ride the finest horses, seduce every available woman, play cards and gamble. In his mind, he would be welcome at every party, telling stories and weaving tales that held his audience spellbound. Travis would fascinate people with his vast knowledge, deep intellect, and quick wit. He would have the love of beautiful women and the respect of honest men. He would remain single and he would be called "Buck." He may have over estimated his abilities, but he was twenty-one-years old and these dreams were achievable. His mistakes were left behind in Alabama, and there was no reason to return. Texas was the perfect place to start a new life.

Travis went directly to San Felipe, the bustling capital of the colony founded by Stephen F. Austin. Although he had no intention of living on or working the land, Travis's view of a successful professional gentleman involved owning property. He listed himself as a lawyer, technically true, and as twenty-two years of age, a small lie. Travis also said he was single, a bigger lie and evidence that he intended to abandon his family in Alabama. Had he admitted his marriage, he could have applied for a league of land, but instead, in a telling move, asked Austin for the standard one-quarter league allotted to single men. On May 23, 1831, he received title and signed a promissory note for ten dollars, due in one year. His one quarter league (eleven hundred seven acres) was located near Harrisburg, in present-day Houston, and he paid something less than one penny per acre. Austin recorded the transaction, even though the laws of April 6, 1830, made it illegal. American colonists continued to do business as usual, picking the Mexican laws they chose to obey.

As was his habit, Travis did his homework. He rode over to see his land near Buffalo Bayou and continued east until he came upon the settlement at Anahuac. A new customs house was under construction there, and work would be available for lawyers. He had already begun to study the Spanish language and Mexican Law. The ambitious Travis knew if he was to succeed in this new land, he must learn both.

Travis settled into the community at Anahuac and moved into a boarding house where he met Patrick Jack, a young lawyer from Georgia. They had much in common, became friends and shared an office, helping each other with legal issues, and, in the manner of twenty-somethings then and now, challenging authority. For sport, they teased and baited the local military.

Travis asked his friends to call him "Buck," a more appropriate name for his new persona.

Things were tough for Juan Davis Bradburn in Anahuac. Construction on the customs house was lagging because the convicts were lazy and kept deserting. The settlers in the area refused to obey orders, thought they were still in America, and kept grousing about their rights. These people didn't understand that the "Bill of Rights" stopped at the Sabine River. They arrogantly thought they carried American rights with them, no matter where they settled. Colonel Bradburn would teach them a thing or two about arrogance.

Bradburn's biggest problems with the settlers revolved around the two young lawyers, Pat Jack and Buck Travis. Pat Jack had organized a local militia, even though such organizations were prohibited by Mexican law. Jack declared the militia necessary for defense against raids by Comanche and Tawakoni Indians, which Bradburn didn't buy. The nearest hostile Indians were at least two hundred miles away, and there had not been a raid near the Gulf Coast in years. Santa Anna was leading a revolt in Mexico at the time and Bradburn suspected the settlers would declare themselves *Satanistas* (followers of Santa Anna) and attack his troops. He trumped up a charge and arrested Pat Jack, the captain of the militia. After a flurry of activity by Jack's friends, especially his office mate, William B. Travis, Bradburn was forced to release Jack. The Americans were yelling about "due process" and other such Anglo nonsense.

Two runaway slaves from Louisiana applied to Bradburn for amnesty. He allowed them to stay at his camp and refused to release them to their owner, William Logan. Logan hired Travis to arrange their return and when Travis asked Bradburn for the release of Logan's property, Bradburn lied, saying the slaves had enlisted in his army and had applied for Mexican citizenship. Travis was furious. The Constitution held that slaves were property of their owners, just as livestock. Travis, and the other settlers, ignored the fact that the American Constitution had no legal status in Mexico.

As the spring of 1832 unfolded in Anahuac, a young female settler was raped by a drunken soldier, a local thief was tarred and feathered, and a semi-riot broke out between the settlers and the soldiers. Buck Travis was very vocal in his criticism of Colonel Bradburn, and Bradburn was losing control of his command. He was concerned about the effect that would have on his military career, so he did what incompetent officers always do. He overreacted.

On May 17, 1832, Juan Bradburn sent a squad of soldiers to the law offices and had Travis arrested. Patrick Jack walked along with Travis and taunted the guards. At the fort, Jack engaged Bradburn in a cussing match. The Colonel had him arrested and threw both lawyers into the stockade. Now, he had the two chief troublemakers under lock and key.

News of William Travis and Patrick Jack's arrests spread through the colonies. Soon, local militias were gathering, perhaps using the excuse that Indians had been sighted in the swamp. Bradburn arrested other "troublemakers," and threatened to kill Travis and Jack at the first sign of trouble from the militia. The Texians, now some three hundred strong, blockaded Anahuac, cutting off all supplies and communications from Bradburn and his men.

To give the appearance of legality, the Texians declared themselves *Santanistas* and stated they were faithful Mexican citizens joining Santa Anna in rebelling against the current administration, as Bradburn had predicted. They presented a list of grievances called the Turtle Bayou Resolutions, basically asking for the repeal or revision of the laws of April 6, 1830 and return to the Mexican Constitution of 1824. This typically American response to the problem dumbfounded the Mexicans.

Colonel José de la Piedras, commander of the post at Nacogdoches, hurried down with troops to help Colonel Bradburn. When he saw the size of the opposition, Piedras decided to negotiate. After a few days of talk, it was resolved that the prisoners would be released to civilian law, the colonists would return to their homes and lay down their arms, and Colonel Bradburn would be replaced by a more understanding and cooperative officer.

The civilian courts at Liberty could find no laws broken by Travis or Patrick Jack, so both men were released. The two had been confined for fifty days inside a brick kiln, two of those days chained to the floor while a guard stood, primed and ready, with orders to shoot them if any attack was made on the fort.

Immediately upon his release, Travis wrote a series of editorials about his captivity, the brutality of Colonel Bradburn and the Mexican army, and the lack of proper protection for individual rights that existed in the Mexican colonies. Colonial newspapers hungrily published these articles, and American newspapers quickly picked them up. The American public listened with keen interest to any news from Texas. Travis became a favorite hero of idealistic young men, longing for the riches and adventure that surely awaited in Texas.

*Judge Robert McAlpin Williamson*
Courtesy Texas Highway Department

A new friend of Buck Travis, "Three-Legged-Willie" Williamson, gave him ample space in the *Mexican Citizen*, the San Felipe paper Williamson owned. As a child, Williamson had a muscle disease which left his right leg permanently bent at the knee. He strapped on an artificial leg from the knee down, and appeared to have three legs. Travis was gaining a reputation in the Texas Colonies. Some saw him as a patriot; others thought he was a troublemaking "War Dog," but no one questioned his courage. He demonstrated that on the floor of Colonel Bradburn's brick kiln as he berated the guard assigned to kill him.

Juan Davis Bradburn, still in Anahuac, but without a command, kept a low profile. His little army sided with the *Santanistas* and sailed without him for Mexico soon after Travis was freed. Unable to gain passage on a ship, (his blockade had alienated the captains), and in fear for his life, Bradburn left for Louisiana in the dead of night, and once again, made his way overland from Texas to New Orleans. It was a more difficult trip than the one he had made with Henry Perry, but he had been twenty years younger back then.

Bradburn reported to the Mexican Embassy in New Orleans, where he learned Travis' slanted editorials had been published in Louisiana. Based on the American newspaper accounts of the "Anahuac Disturbance," the colonel was not exactly welcomed with open arms. He made his way back to Matamoros, retired from the army and farmed vegetables in the Rio Grande valley near present-day McAllen for two years. In 1835, he went back into the Mexican army during the Texas Revolution and served without distinction under General Urrea during that general's successful sweep of the Texas Gulf Coast. After the war, Bradburn returned to Matamoros and died there in 1842 at age fifty-five.

Buck Travis decided it was time to relocate his practice. Anahuac was a nice place, but with his new celebrity, he felt he needed to take his act to a larger stage. In Texas, at the time, only two places qualified: San Antonio (Bexar) or San Felipe. The choice was easy—San Felipe was an American town and Bexar was a Mexican city. Even though he chose San Felipe, unlike most American colonists, Travis never indicated any prejudice toward the Mexican people. In all his dealings and writings, he treated the race as equals. Especially the women.

San Felipe, the capital of Austin's Colony, was forty miles due west of present-day Houston, just off the Atascocita Trace. It consisted of about fifty log buildings and sat on a bluff on the west bank of the Brazos River. Most of the colonists lived on their own land outside the village, while the busy town of San Felipe contained inns and boarding houses, a general store, two saloons, a weekly newspaper, gambling halls, dirt streets, and some wooden sidewalks. Stephen F. Austin lived there in a typical dog-trot cabin with dirt floors. He conducted business on one side and slept in the other.

San Felipe was more like Claiborne, Alabama, where Travis had his family, than Anahuac had been. Several lawyers in the bustling community divided their time between real estate, debt collection, and civil matters. Travis knew some of them and, because of the Anahuac disturbance, they were all familiar with him. A new celebrity in town, he enjoyed the attention. The decision to stay was easy. Travis, now barely twenty-three-years-old, paid one dollar a night for room and board for himself and his horse. He rented an office, and on September 1, 1832, announced that William B. Travis, Attorney and Counselor at Law, was open for business.

Young Travis kept a journal with notes about his daily activities, business dealings, and gambling profits and losses, Also in this diary, as any other twenty-four year old male might have done, he catalogued his sexual encounters. The sexual entries were kept in Spanish, for he was becoming fluent in that language. An entry in September of 1833 stated the number of women, (fifty-six), he had sex with. The entry did not qualify the number as to whether it meant total sexual encounters or encounters with different women. The accepted interpretation of the statement is that he had sex with a total of fifty-six different women to that point in his lifetime.

Other entries were written in English. Travis' law practice became prosperous and he gambled frequently, sometimes winning and sometimes losing. He never lost enough to hamper his lifestyle, and he carefully and promptly paid all his debts.

The law business often took Travis to the growing community of Brazoria, where he stayed in the boarding house of Jane Long. Jane had returned to Texas, and, as James Long's widow, convinced Austin to sell her a "league and a labor" of land. With slave labor, she operated a successful cotton plantation in addition to the boarding house. The fact that women usually did not own land, or operate plantations, did not deter the strong-willed, self-styled "Mother of Texas."

Travis stayed at her boarding house often enough to pay a reduced rate, the same as her permanent guests. Rumors circulated about a romance between the twenty-four-year-old Travis and the forty-three-year-old Jane, but that is doubtful. Had Jane indicated even the slightest interest in a sexual liaison, young Travis would most certainly have made himself available, and catalogued the event in his journal. The rumors were likely spread by Jane. She also imagined romances with Ben Milam, Sam Houston, and Mirabeau Lamar, but after a long and eventful life, she died in 1880, still the widow of only one husband, Dr. James Long. She insisted that "Mother of Texas" be engraved on her tombstone.

Buck Travis' frequent sexual encounters tended to be paid romps with Mexican whores, or quick trysts with house maids who shared their charms to augment their income. Although he most often paid for sex, he did seduce a few local belles, carefully staying away from any long-term commitment. With a wife back in Alabama, that sort of thing could get a bit awkward.

Travis corresponded with his wife Rosanna and her brother, but sent no money or other support, and gave no indication that he ever intended to return to Alabama or reunite with his family. He did arrange for his son, Charles Edward, to live with a friend in Texas, so he could be near. William

Travis never spoke of the breakup of his marriage, but he obviously held some animosity toward Rosanna. He may have never seen the little girl, Susan Isabella, because he suspected he was not her father. If the marriage dissolved because of infidelity on Rosanna's part, which is certainly possible, the damage to his ego could explain his anger, embarrassment, and silence.

Travis arranged to pay off all the Alabama debts, working through a friend who travelled to Claiborne, but shared none of his new-found wealth with Rosanna or the daughter. Rosanna, now living with Samuel Cloud, filed for divorce, stating abandonment as the cause.

Travis did not contest the proceedings—in fact, time and a lovely young woman had altered his views. He was engaged to Rebecca Cummings, the daughter of one of Austin's "Old Three Hundred," a wealthy innkeeper at Mill Creek near San Felipe. The Alabama divorce was granted in January of 1836, and Rosanna immediately married Cloud, but Travis made no move to marry Miss Cummings. Her ardor may have cooled because Travis had given her a dose of the clap, but more likely he was caught up in the revolution and preparation for the defense of the Alamo. It is possible he died never knowing his divorce was final.

Pressure from the Texians and the internal turmoil in Mexico allowed the Mexican military an excuse to quietly withdraw until the Mexican political morass could be untangled. After Jim Bowie led a minor revolt in East Texas in August of 1832, Colonel Jose de la Piedras and the garrison at Nacogdoches withdrew, and there were no Mexican soldiers east of San Antonio. The Texians imported and exported goods without tariffs, welcomed boatloads of new colonists, speculated in land, paid no taxes, and generally enjoyed themselves, feeling that no government was good government. A flood of adventurers and opportunists, smelling easy money and free land, poured into Texas, looking for profit and spoiling for a fight.

The resolution of the Anahuac Disturbance and the reception of the Turtle Bayou Resolutions emboldened the colonists and they continued to press for their "rights." While some wanted independence, most were willing to remain colonists of Mexico. They wanted to be separated from Coahuila, deal directly with the national government in Mexico City, and have more say in their government.

By 1835, Santa Anna gained a strangle-hold on the Mexican Government and prepared to re-enact the harsh controls of April 6, 1830. He reneged on his promise to return to the Constitution of 1824, and instead, instituted martial law. Santa Anna declared himself emperor and set about quashing all opposition and executing all captured rebel leaders. He sent a small force to Anahuac to re-open the customs house there, and to impose and collect taxes as the law required.

Buck Travis had accomplished most of the things he thought about on the way to Texas. He was making more money than he ever dreamed, he was a landowner and respected member of the community, enjoyed frequent games of chance and was more active sexually than ever. He dressed lavishly, rode beautiful horses, and pictured himself a welcome guest at every party. He was not especially quick-witted or engaging in conversation, so it is likely he overestimated his charm. His countenance tended to be dour and his personality was just short of dull. His sense of humor was so strange it seemed almost warped. Travis accomplished his goals with hard work, preparation, and intense study, not with a dazzling personality or flashes of intellectual brilliance.

With enough free time to dabble in politics, Travis organized a group to capture the new custom house at Anahuac and send the soldiers back to Mexico. After a skirmish at Velasco, Travis and his men accomplished the first goal—they captured the thirty Mexican soldiers guarding the installation. By dawn, most of Travis' men had sobered up, and they couldn't decide what to do with their prisoners. With almost no support from the colonists, after some discussion and examination of options, the Texians released the soldiers and sheepishly went back to San Felipe.

Travis failed to gain the support he needed to repeat his earlier triumph. Cooler heads among the colonists considered Travis' foray to be foolhardy over-reaction at best and blatant piracy at worst. Travis, instead of being the hero, was considered an irresponsible War Dog, anxious to plunge the colonies into a war they didn't want and could not win.

Colonel Ugartechea, commandant at San Antonio, issued orders for the return of a small cannon on loan to the city of Gonzales. The citizens were to bring the cannon to San Antonio and turn it in. When Ugartechea's orders were ignored, he sent a troop of soldiers to pick up the cannon. Captain Castaneda, in charge of the detail, allowed his men to camp a few miles outside the city on the banks of the Guadalupe River, planning to do a little fishing that afternoon, and routinely pick up the cannon in the morning, then ride back to San Antonio.

Volunteers from all over the colony heard of the coming showdown and hurried to Gonzales to help out. By nightfall, about one hundred men gathered. Someone made a flag out of a bed sheet, depicting a cannon with the "Come and Take It" slogan. Most of the men busied themselves drinking. The more they drank, the braver they became. A boy reported that he had seen a group of Mexican soldiers camped on the river, about seven miles west of town. The Texians decided to have a few more drinks, then ride out after midnight, slip up on the Mexicans, and attack at first light.

Early the next morning, October 2, 1835, the Texian rebels located the camp of the Mexicans, but didn't quite manage to slip up on them. A dense fog descended during the night and at three am, the Gonzales boys were stumbling around in the woods, drunk, lost, and most likely whispering, "Shhh! They's Mezkins out here." One of the drunk rebels fell off his horse and broke his nose.

The Mexican captain's orders did not include fighting, so he quietly gathered his troops for a hasty retreat to the safety of San Antonio. By dawn, the fog had lifted about two feet, so the drunks could lie on the ground and see the legs of the Mexican horses. After a parley with the confused Captain Casteneda, the Texians attacked, firing muskets, long rifles, and the little cannon through the fog into the camp. The cannon was not very accurate. Captain J. C. Neill, an artillery officer during the War of 1812 could almost always get it to fire north or south, but hitting a barn or any other such sharpshooting was out of the question. Lt. Almaron Dickinson helped Neill with the little cannon, and later accompanied him to San Antonio to help defend the Alamo.

During the battle, two Mexicans got shot. The shooting was undeniably accidental—the Mexicans happened to be in the wrong place at the wrong time. The final tally at Gonzales was: Mexicans—2 dead; Texians—one bloody nose.

The Texians, to celebrate their victory, decided to go back to Gonzales and have a little drink or two. This incident is largely reported as the first battle of the Texas War for Independence, but it was preceded by the two "Anahuac Disturbances" and a skirmish at Nacogdoches instigated by Jim Bowie. The Gonzales battle was, however, a point of no return. It was too blatant to be ignored—Santa Anna was coming and he knew how to deal with rebels.

William B. Travis hurried to join the group at Gonzales but arrived a day after the battle. He stayed there for a few days, posturing, re-living the incident, and generally acting as a War Dog. Buck was not fond of strong drink, but he enjoyed hanging around a saloon, playing a little poker, telling war stories, and perhaps getting lucky with an accommodating barmaid.

# CHAPTER SIX
# The Texas Revolution

The Texian colonists, for the most part, did not want a revolution. The early settlers, especially Austin's original "Old Three Hundred" were busy tilling the soil on their prosperous farms and plantations. They were happy being colonists of Mexico. Most of them would rather have been colonists in America or some other country that they could admire and "look up to", but, all in all, Mexican rules were not that hard to live with. The tariffs and taxes were mostly deferred, import and export duties were not being collected, and the Mexican officials usually ignored the travelling Methodist and Baptist preachers who were holding sporadic camp meetings in spite of the ban on all but the Catholic religion.

Rumors of impending change worried the settlers. It was said that Santa Anna was reneging on his promise to revert to the more lenient rules of 1824, and the colonists decided to petition the government for guarantees of freedoms, much like they had enjoyed in the United States. It was perfectly logical to an Anglo mind that the people gathered and voted and made the government aware of their concerns. Otherwise, how could the government know the wishes of its people?

In October of 1832, delegates were elected and a provisional government set up at Washington-on-the-Brazos to manage the affairs of Texas in Texas. The Texians wanted to separate themselves from the Mexican state of Coahuila and deal directly with Mexico City. They desired a return to the liberal colonization policies of the Mexican Constitution of 1824. The colonists wanted freedom to govern themselves as they had done in the United

States. The name they chose for their new capital city spoke volumes about what they wanted.

Mexicans did not understand the American mindset. Any change in government initiated by the people in Mexico always worked the same way, as if the script had been prepared hundreds of years before. When a regime became so oppressive that the people could no longer tolerate it, a "grito" or "cry" was made by a leader, perhaps a local politician, priest, or army officer, asking for relief. If the "cry" was popular and the people agreed, a group of leaders would compile a list of grievances called "pronunciations" and ask for redress. If there was sufficient support for the pronunciations, a "plan" to enable their enactment was presented. Actual bloodshed usually started right after the "grito", and by the time of the "pronunciations", full scale war was in progress.

At the October 1832 meeting, the colonists sent Stephen F. Austin to Mexico City with a list of grievances to place before the government. This was, in the minds of the Anglo settlers, a perfectly logical, sane and proper way to address the problem. In the minds of the Mexicans, however, this was the second phase of a revolution, the list of "pronunciations," and all-out rebellion was in progress. They arrested Austin and placed him in solitary confinement in the old inquisition prison in Mexico City. Austin was not charged with any crime, but was held incommunicado for over two years, as a hostage to ensure Texian cooperation. He was released in 1835, during a "general amnesty," another concept foreign to the American mind. Austin met briefly with Santa Anna and returned to Texas. For years, Austin had preached loyalty to the Mexican government, but his imprisonment changed all that. He was now convinced that Texas must separate from Mexico and become a part of the United States.

With the skirmish at Gonzales on October 2, 1835, the die was cast. Texians were rebelling against the Mexican Government. The Anahuac and Velasco disturbances had been easy enough to explain away for the colonists, especially with Mexico's government in turmoil, but Gonzales was a point of no return. The only question, and there was a difference of opinion, were the Texians bent on independence, or were they trying to revert back to the laws under the Mexican Constitution of 1824?

Volunteers poured in from all over Texas and from the United States. Colonists could taste revolution in the air. Stephen Austin, not fully recovered from his years in the Mexican prison and with no military experience, was appointed commander of the Texian Army by Governor Smith. Three hundred volunteers arrived at San Felipe and Austin led them to join the rebel army at Gonzales.

General Martin Perfecto de Cos, Santa Anna's brother-in-law, landed at Copano Bay with 1200 troops and occupied the presidio at Goliad. He left a small force to hold the fort and moved his troops into San Antonio, relieving Colonel Ugartechea and taking command. Cos's troops were regular army, well trained, disciplined soldiers who should have no trouble defending the city and putting down the rebellion.

On October 10, 1835, Captain George Collinsworth and forty-seven militiamen prepared to attack the fort at Goliad. As they scouted the fort at night, they stumbled upon Ben Milam hiding in a grove of mesquite. Ben had recently escaped from his third imprisonment in Mexico. He joined Collinsworth and they killed one guard, broke down the front door and captured the sleeping Mexican officers and the presidio. They took 300 stands of small arms, two cannons and about $10,000.00 in much-needed cash. It was not a great victory, but it emboldened the colonists and dealt a blow to the morale of General Cos and the Mexican army.

Milam wrote after the battle, "I assisted Mexico to gain her independence. I have endured hot and cold, hunger and thirst; I have borne losses and suffered persecutions; I have been a tenant of every prison between this and Mexico. But the events of this night have compensated me for all my losses and all my sufferings."

The only Mexican soldiers left in the colony were in San Antonio, so the group at Gonzales decided to go on to San Antonio. Following the inexperienced General Stephen F. Austin, they headed toward Bexar, a disorganized crew with a homemade flag, dragging a silly little cannon with solid wooden wheels. Noah Smithwick, one of the volunteers, wrote:

"Words are inadequate to convey the impression of the appearance of the first Texas army as it formed in marching order…it certainly bore little resemblance to the army of my childhood dreams. Buckskin breeches were the nearest approach to uniform and there was a wide diversity even there, some being new and soft and yellow, while others, from long familiarity with rain and grease and dirt, had become hard and black and shiny....Boots being an unknown quantity, some wore shoes and some moccasins. Here a broad-brimmed sombrero overshadowed the military cap at its side; there the tall "beegum" rode familiarly beside a coonskin cap, with a tail hanging down behind, as all well-regulated tails should do. Here a big American horse loomed above the nimble Spanish pony…there a half-broke mustang pranced beside a sober, methodical mule…in lieu of a canteen each man carried a Spanish gourd …A fantastic military array to the casual observer, but the one great purpose animating every heart clothed us in a uniform more perfect in our eyes than was ever donned by regulars on dress parade."

If the little army was not pretty, it was deadly. Everyone was armed with a long rifle and most had razor-sharp hunting knives, many patterned after the popular "Bowie Knife." These Texians knew little about military discipline, walked rather than marched, and came and went much as they pleased. Firing their long rifles, they could consistently break a dinner plate at a hundred yards. Mexican muskets were mostly useless at anything more than fifty yards, even when their powder was dry and potent enough to fire.

The Texians were not trained soldiers. They would not dare march out into an open field, squat and fire at an entrenched enemy, then stand and re-load. Instead, they hid behind trees or rocks, aimed carefully and, when the enemies were near enough, shot them in the head. Because most of them had to depend upon skill with a rifle to eat and feed their families, they did not waste ammunition by missing. Hunting rifles didn't come with bayonets. If Mexicans were foolish enough to force them into hand to hand combat, the larger Texians used rifle butts and razor-sharp Bowie knives with deadly efficiency.

This late fall and early winter campaign had other advantages for the colonists. For the farmers, the harvest was over and there was not a lot to do on the farm until spring planting. It was a good time for a revolution and volunteers kept joining the ranks, spoiling for a fight. Much of the army consisted of Texians, mostly farmers, but that was changing.

Volunteer companies of young patriots were forming across the southern United States. In Macon, Georgia, the Georgia Battalion was formed, consisting of three companies from Macon and two companies from Columbus. The battalion commander, Colonel William Ward, obtained rifles and other supplies from the armory of the state of Georgia. This is one of the few instances of arms being provided for Texas by an existing state in the union. Alabama may have loaned some weapons to the Red Rovers, and the city of Cincinnati donated the "Twin Sisters," two little cannon that Houston used effectively at San Jacinto. The state of Georgia, incidentally, billed Texas for the rifles after the war. That bill, along with many others, was never paid by the cash-strapped Republic.

As the Macon Grays marched toward Columbus to join the Georgia Battalion, they camped near the Troutman Inn at Knoxville, Georgia. Joanna Elizabeth Troutman, the talented and romantic seventeen-year-old daughter of the innkeeper, was enchanted by a young lieutenant and moved by the plight of the Texians fighting tyranny. She attended a "Texas Rally," listened to the fiery speeches and decided to do something to help.

Late at night, from the porch of her family home, she saw a single prominent star in the sky which reminded her of Texas, alone in its battle for independence. The next day, with the help of three girlfriends, using fabric from some of her petticoats, she sewed a flag with a white silk field and a single five-pointed blue star. The inscription "Liberty or Death" appeared on one side and a Latin phrase, translated as "Where Liberty Dwells There is My Fatherland," on the other.

Miss Troutman presented the flag to Col. Ward in a ceremony on the steps of the Troutman Inn. She instructed the flag be given to the care of a dashing young West Point graduate, Lieutenant Hugh McLeod of nearby Macon, who would resign his commission in the U.S. Army to join the fight for Texas independence. Col. Ward and the "Macon Grays" carried the flag to Texas and it first flew over Velasco, then over Fannin's troops at Goliad. In what could be considered an omen, the flag tangled in its lanyard and was destroyed while flying over Fannin's command. Although single star flags were popular at the time, Miss Troutman's flag is credited with the origin of the lone star as the symbol of Texas.

Hugh McLeod wrote a thank you letter to Miss Troutman, promising to bring honor to the flag she had created and adding, "Your flag will yet wave over fields of victory in defiance of despotism." Whether or not they continued to communicate is unknown, but McLeod went on to a long, if not particularly distinguished, military career in Texas and three years later,

Miss Troutman married a Georgia plantation owner and lived out her life on Elmwood Plantation in Crawford County, Georgia.

After the victory at San Jacinto, Sam Houston arranged to send an oversized silver salad fork and spoon from Santa Anna's expensive dinnerware to Miss Troutman. The family still cherishes the silverware, and the letter from Thomas Rusk that accompanied it.

As word of the Gonzales confrontation spread, young idealists from all over the south joined together and headed for Texas, many spurred on by Travis' writings. In late October, two companies of New Orleans Grays headed west. In November they were joined by two groups from Alabama, the Red Rovers from Courtland and the Mobile Grays. The Kentucky Mustangs were formed in Nacogdoches, Texas, of immigrants from Kentucky and Tennessee. Davy Crockett led a dozen volunteers from east Tennessee into Texas, and Mirabeau B. Lamar, an old friend of James Fannin and a hero of Hugh McLeod, came with others from Macon, Georgia.

The young men who made up these companies were not land speculators or real estate developers as were many of the original War Dogs. Many of these volunteers had friends or family members already in Texas and went to join them in the struggle. Most were idealistic young patriots who were willing to put their lives on the line to stop the Mexican government from taking what was considered God-given rights for all Americans. They conveniently ignored the fact that the colonists had voluntarily signed away those rights when they settled in Texas.

Seventeen-year-old Herman Ehrenberg came with the New Orleans Grays as a drummer boy. His company happily joined Fannin at La Bahia. Others came alone, or in groups of twos or threes, and simply joined the army or militia wherever they found an available unit. The army was officially created by the rebel government at Washington-on-the-Brazos. While under Mexican rule, most communities had established their own voluntary militia, using "protection from the Indians" as an excuse to bear arms.

As the Gonzales rebels, now officially the Texas army, moved toward San Antonio, they finally abandoned the unwieldy little cannon at Sandy Creek. Lacking lubrication, the wooden wheels locked up and burned the axle. The rebels buried the cannon and moved on without artillery.

Stephen Austin, the reluctant general, dispatched Lt. William B. Travis as head of a cavalry unit to harass the Mexican army and sent a group of ninety-four men, under Jim Bowie and James Fannin, to reconnoiter the missions along the river south of San Antonio. Austin asked that they avoid any engagement with the enemy.

James Bowie had proved himself in battle on more than one occasion. He had no formal military training but was known to be without fear. Before coming to Texas, he had developed a reputation in duels and knife fights, and since settling in Texas, had led men in several successful battles against Tonkawa and Comanche.

James Bowie

In 1831, Bowie married Ursula Veramendi, the beautiful daughter of the very influential Juan Martín de Veramendi, Mexican vice-governor of Texas. Juan Veramendi liked Bowie and financed him in some business ventures. James and Ursula lived in the Veramendi mansion and had two children.

In November of 1831, Bowie, with his father-in-law's support, organized an expedition in search of the lost Spanish San Saba Silver Mine. Accompanied by his brother, Rezin, and ten adventurers, Bowie made his way to the Menard area, near the ruins of the 1758 Santa Cruz de San Saba Mission. Bowie's group was attacked by 160 Indians, mostly Tawakoni. Bowie cooly organized the defense, and after a thirteen hour battle, the Indians withdrew. Bowie lost one man, and his troops killed about 40 Indians.

Ursula Veramendi Bowie

Friendly Indians had carried the word to San Antonio that Bowie's expedition, outnumbered more than twelve to one, had been attacked by Indians. There was little hope of survival, and Ursula Bowie began to wear widow's black. Bowie's growing reputation was enhanced when he and his troops paraded into San Antonio on December sixth.

A cholera epidemic struck San Antonio in the summer of 1833, and the Veramendi family insisted Ursula and the children accompany them to the family home in Monclova where they would be safe. Unfortunately, Ursula, her parents, and both Bowie children were stricken and died. In addition to the loss of his family, Bowie lost his father-in-law's influence, counsel, and finance in business matters. After these losses, he began to drink heavily, lost pride in his appearance, and became unreliable. Nonetheless, Sam Houston trusted Bowie implicitly. Most other Texas leaders, including Austin, respected his military ability but were bothered by his drinking. Houston had no problem with that. Houston drank with him.

Near the Mission Concepcion, as nightfall approached, Bowie took charge of the troops and arranged them in the trees along the San Antonio River, between two fords, with their backs to the stream. The riverbank was six feet high and formed a perfect breastwork for the shooters. Bowie was aware General Cos was in the area with four hundred men and cannon, so he chose his position carefully. Any attack would have to come from the level plain immediately in front of his position. Fannin, whose military experience consisted dropping out after two years at West Point, quietly watched and learned from Bowie. Ben Milam, a private, also watched and waited his turn at history.

A heavy fog moved in during the night, and just after daylight on October 28, 1835, General Cos' Cavalry, trying to bait Bowie's men into pursuit, advanced across the plain, fired a harmless volley into the trees surrounding the Texians, then hurriedly retreated into the fog. The Mexicans were not overly concerned. They had the Texians virtually surrounded, backed against the river, and outnumbered four to one. Bowie's men held their fire and waited. The Mexicans, using standard cavalry tactics, advanced to a position about 100 yards from the entrenched Texians, fired another harmless volley, and, with lances forward, charged, spurring their horses to full gallop. No Texians fired until the Mexicans were 80 yards away, when Deef Smith, at Bowie's orders, dropped the lead officer with a well-placed rifle ball.

At that signal, the rebels commenced steady rifle fire with deadly precision, individually picking a target and hitting it. Bowie arranged his men so that half were in firing position and half were behind the bluff reloading, allowing for a continuous, deadly rate of fire. As a substantial number of their comrades fell to the ground, dead or wounded, the confused Mexican cavalry turned and raced for cover in the fog.

The Mexicans, to their credit, did not give up. They attempted two more assaults, and each failed, never getting within forty yards of the rebels. The tried and true cavalry tactics simply did not work against the methodical fire of these concealed farmers. General Cos slipped a troop of infantry and a cannon across the river at one of the fords.

The first load of grapeshot from the eighteen-pounder went high, showered Bowie's men with pecans, leaves, and tree limbs, but otherwise did no damage. Bowie immediately assigned three sharpshooters to take out anyone who touched the cannon. When the battle was over, a dozen dead men surrounded the cannon and no Mexican would go near it.

Several Texians had chosen to sleep in a grove of trees away from the river and were stranded there when the Mexican cavalry attacked early that morning. They decided to lie low and watch the battle. Now, as the Mexican infantry formed a skirmish line to charge the Texian position, the rebels found themselves on the left flank, looking right down the line. They began to fire the long rifles, taking their time, picking their targets carefully, and efficiently killing Mexicans.

Cos' infantry, thinking they had been outflanked by a much larger force, panicked. Privates threw down their weapons and ran, officers shouted in vain, Texians fired, and soldiers fell. Adding to the confusion, two or three Mexicans mounted each of the mules that had pulled the cannon into place and charged past the troops, hardware and harnesses dragging and bouncing behind.

The whole force bottle-necked at the river. Texians mercifully withheld their fire and allowed the beaten Mexicans to escape across the river. Under a flag of truce, General Cos received permission to gather his dead and wounded and return to San Antonio. The Mexicans lost at least sixty soldiers killed and many more wounded, all at the hands of a group of sodbusters who now had one of their cannons.

The Texians suffered their first casualty of the war in this battle. A big, heavy-set young man called Big Dick Andrews was so excited by the battle that he defiantly stood waving atop the river bank, completely exposed to enemy fire. He was shot in the torso and died in Noah Smithwick's arms, the first Texian casualty of the revolution and the only rebel casualty of the battle. A few Texians were slightly wounded.

Over all, the Texian forces had much to rejoice about, but some disturbing results of the battle cannot be ignored. The Texians developed an unhealthy contempt for the fighting ability of the Mexican army and too much confidence in their own long rifles and tactics. Not all the Mexican generals were as inept as Cos, and not all the Texian officers were as competent as Bowie.

Another negative consequence of the battle had to do with Colonel Fannin. With no previous combat experience, his first exposure to battle was under the superb leadership of Jim Bowie. Even half drunk, Bowie's instincts and experience guided him, and his tactics were simple, direct, and effective. He was fearless, confident and decisive. Fannin, arrogant and conceited, considered himself Bowie's equal. Regardless of his polished manner and supreme self-confidence, Fannin was an indecisive novice, a fact that would cause irreparable harm to the Texian cause.

Stephen F. Austin

Within an hour of the withdrawal of General Cos' troops, General Stephen F. Austin brought up the main body of Texians and camped across the river. Austin was peeved. Not only had Bowie disobeyed orders about engaging the enemy, Lt. William Barret Travis and his cavalry, also contrary to orders, had harassed Cos' troops as they made their way back to San Antonio, under a flag of truce.

Austin, uneasy that his orders were not being followed to the letter, felt that if Bowie had waited until his army was in position, General Cos and his troops could have been captured and the city of San Antonio taken without a pitched battle. Bowie, who had spies inside the city, knew how well the Mexican Army was dug in and disagreed with Austin's contention.

Unaware of the tension among their leaders, Bowie's men relaxed and quietly breakfasted on pecans provided by the Mexican cannon. General Cos and the Mexican army made their way back to the relative safety of San Antonio, their ranks depleted and their morale in shambles.

The rebels surrounded San Antonio but, as time went by, indecision over the next move robbed them of morale and supplies. The Texian leadership, relying on information provided by friends of Jim Bowie in the city, believed Cos' troops too well dug in to risk a frontal assault. The Mexicans had no stomach for fighting the Texians outside in the open. As this stalemate continued, Texian troops started to go home. Many of the farmers had only joined the militia for one or two months. It was cold and wet now, food was scarce and poorly prepared, and army life was boring. The farmers went home to snug dog-trot cabins and woman-cooked meals. They were replaced by a steady stream of volunteers from the American south.

With his lack of military training, Stephen Austin much preferred negotiation to battle. He engaged in negotiation with Cos as a means to free San Antonio from Mexican dominance. General Cos, aware of his brother-in-law Santa Anna's wishes, was not about to give up without a fight. Negotiations took precious time, and supplies and morale in both armies ran low. Austin, nervous in his new position, tended to make decisions by consensus, after much discussion. He appeared indecisive to his men.

In late November, the fledgling Texas government at Washington-on-the-Brazos, perhaps with prodding from Sam Houston, asked Austin to resign as commander of the Texian army, go to New Orleans and assume new duties as good-will ambassador and fund-raiser in the United States. Austin welcomed this transition to duties for which he was much better qualified, and the grateful army elected the experienced and competent Edward Burleson its new commander.

Austin left for his new duties on November 25, 1835. The next day, Deef Smith rode into the bored camp with word that a loaded mule train was approaching San Antonio under heavy guard. Jim Bowie, always on the lookout for profit, believed the train contained the Mexican army payroll, and had no trouble gathering a hundred volunteers to attack.

The rebels found the mule train several miles outside San Antonio and attacked the surprised Mexicans immediately. The mules stampeded, along with the guards, and the Texians waged a running battle all the way into San Antonio. Bowie's men killed fifty Mexican soldiers and suffered only two wounded. They captured about half the mules and took them back to camp, only to find them loaded with hay for the Mexican horses. Many of the pastures around San Antonio had been burned by Travis and his cavalry and others were watched by the rebels, so the Mexicans were forced to bring hay from remote locations. The battle became known in history as the "Grass Fight."

Bowie, on orders from Sam Houston, left the little army at San Antonio and travelled to La Bahia at Goliad. Houston wanted Bowie, his old friend and drinking buddy, to lead, or at least plan, an attack on Matamoros at the mouth of the Rio Grande. Bowie went to La Bahia to inventory supplies, evaluate officers and men, and help plan the expedition. Houston, meanwhile, was busy as an elected delegate at Washington-on-the-Brazos, attempting to establish order, protect military interests, and create harmony in the inexperienced, confused, jealous, and spiteful Texas Legislature. Buck Travis, who had been leading a troop of cavalry around South Texas, went to San Felipe to spend some time attending to his bustling law business. Travis was also elected a delegate to the legislative body, so he travelled the additional thirty miles to look in on the disorganized proceedings.

A week later, Burleson and his staff decided to abandon the siege of San Antonio and withdraw until spring. Farmers in the army were leaving with increasing frequency and food was scarce and ill-prepared. Most of the soldiers had enlisted during the late summer and had no warm clothing. The army now consisted of possibly five hundred men, many of them untrained recruits from the American south. Sam Houston urged Burleson to leave San Antonio to the Mexicans and join his army, training near the Brazos River. Even though many felt that this move would forfeit all chance of capturing San Antonio, the order to withdraw was given and wagons were loaded. The voluntary army did not like the idea of siege, nor did it like the idea of withdrawal. These men came to fight. Some rode hundreds of miles to fight for Texas Independence. There were plenty of Mexicans in San Antonio, but the opportunity to fight them was being denied.

Benjamin "Ben" Milam

"Who will go with Old Ben Milam into San Antonio?" Shouted Milam, a forty-seven-year-old private, scouting for Burleson's army. The shout echoed through the camp and over three hundred men stepped forward, demanding to be included. Burleson, having no choice, agreed to support an attack of volunteers and the group was divided into two forces, one under newly appointed Colonel Ben Milam and the other commanded by the respected Colonel Frank W. Johnson. Captain J. C. Neill would create a diversion at the Alamo with his captured Mexican cannon, and Burleson would hold the balance of his troops in reserve outside the city.

The battle started at three a.m. on the morning of December 5, 1835. Neill and his squad fired away at the Alamo, creating the diversion while across town, three hundred and one Texians moved into San Antonio to attack almost twelve hundred well-entrenched Mexican regulars.

Deef Smith, already well known for his exceptional marksmanship and unflinching bravery, and his son-in-law, Hendrick Arnold, both residents of San Antonio, agreed to guide the troops into the city. Smith guided Colonel Johnson's forces, and Arnold, a highly regarded free black man, guided Ben Milam's group. "El Colorado" (the redhead) Smith, no relation to Deef Smith but also a resident of San Antonio married to a Tejano woman, helped Arnold with Milan's group.

As Deef Smith led Colonel Johnson's men down Soledad Street toward the Veramendi House near the square, a Mexican sentry fired at them. Deef Smith took out the guard with one shot and led the men into the Veramendi courtyard. The Texians quickly overpowered the soldiers in the Veramendi house, but the noise roused the sleeping Mexican Army and constant rifle and cannon fire kept Johnson and his men inside the fort-like home of Bowie's father-in-law.

Meanwhile, Hendrick Arnold and El Colorado Smith led Milam and his men, undetected, to the de La Garza House, diagonally across the street from Veramendi's home. Milam's men set up a barrage of sniper fire, along with occasional grapeshot from a six-pounder they had dragged along.

The Texians were adept at house-to-house fighting. Sharpshooters kept the enemy pinned down while others used battering rams to crash through doors or even walls to engage the enemy in hand to hand combat. The demoralized Mexicans had no taste for this type of fight. Their muskets were not accurate enough to keep anyone pinned down, their grapeshot had little effect on the adobe walls the Texians used for cover, and the smaller Mexicans were at a disadvantage in hand-to-hand combat.

The third day of the battle, December 7, Colonel Milam stepped out into the courtyard of the Veramendi house to confer with his officers, or, as some historians insist, to relieve himself. A sniper, firing over the wall from a huge Cypress tree on the riverbank, shot him in the head and Milam died instantly. The sniper was shot, but the damage was done. Ben Milam was buried that afternoon with proper ceremony by Masonic brothers in Veramendi's back courtyard. He became an instant legend.

Benjamin Rush Milam was known and respected all over Texas and Mexico. He had fought with the filibusters to help Iturbide take Mexico from Spain. He was rewarded with Mexican citizenship and was appointed a Colonel in the Mexican Army. He met and sided with Santa Anna when the *Satanistas* successfully rebelled. He was rewarded for his efforts with at least two empresario grants. Milam and a partner put the first steam-powered riverboat on the Red River. Jane Long says that Milam asked for her hand in marriage, but Jane said that about most everyone. By any measure, Ben Milam was a great man and deserved to be honored as a Texas hero.

Within four days, the 300 Texians moved, house to house, through San Antonio, taking the main square and forcing Cos and his army to take shelter in the old church called Alamo. Cos did not feel that he could properly defend the presidio with the 1100 men he had left. He posted a white flag and asked for surrender terms. With the withdrawal of Cos and his troops, the Texians kept all the military supplies—cannons, ammunition, livestock, wagons, and provisions—J.C. Neill, newly appointed Lt. Colonel, took charge of the Alamo and all the supplies. There was no longer any Mexican military presence in Texas, but any celebration was premature.

The surrender of his brother-in-law infuriated Santa Anna. Moving much quicker than anyone expected, he was in Saltillo, staging over 6,000 troops for the invasion of Texas. He dispatched General Ramirez y Sesma, with fifteen hundred troops, to San Antonio as an advance guard. General Don Jose Urrea, with six hundred men, including Juan Davis Bradburn, was sent to defend Matamoros, and Santa Anna commanded the main body of four thousand troops and marched on San Antonio. Santa Anna knew how to deal with rebellion—General Aredondo taught him—rebels were pirates and he would give no quarter.

Governor Henry Smith and the elected officials in the Texas legislature were embroiled in a senseless, time consuming, and costly "amateur hour" at Washington-on-the-Brazos. No funds were available to pay expenses and donations came with strings attached. Land speculators and lawyers wrangled for advantage, working with hidden agendas.

The legislature appointed four different generals as supreme commander of the Texas army, all at the same time. Henry Smith vetoed the appointments. The legislature impeached Smith. Smith refused to leave office and threatened to "shoot any son-of-a-bitch" who tried to make him. The group could not even agree to declare independence—most favored a return to the Mexican Constitution of 1824.

Sam Houston, the elected delegate from Nacogdoches, planned to be the head of the Texas army. On a recent trip to New Orleans, Houston, always the flamboyant dresser, had purchased a general's uniform, complete with a sash, metals, and plumed hat. He kept the uniform packed away while he attended to his duties as a delegate to the convention, but when the fighting commenced he would be dressed for the part.

Governor Smith ordered Sam Houston, his choice for commander of the Texian Army, to mount a force and take the Mexican city of Matamoros, a seaport at the mouth of the Rio Bravo (Rio Grande). Matamoros was a rich city, collecting tariffs from all imported and exported goods that went through the port. It was lightly defended and Texas desperately needed the gold coin available there. Houston evidently concurred in this plan, because he took steps to obey Smith's orders.

Smith also ordered his friend, William B. Travis, to gather a hundred volunteers and go to San Antonio and help Colonel Neill defend the Alamo. Travis may have been the only officer left in the Texian Army who would obey orders from Smith, but he began immediately gathering volunteers to head for San Antonio and the Alamo and his appointment with destiny.

After issuing these orders, Governor Smith "hunkered down" with a loaded pistol, in case any "son-of-a-bitch" tried to unseat him.

## CHAPTER SEVEN
# Antonio Lopez de Santa Anna and the Alamo

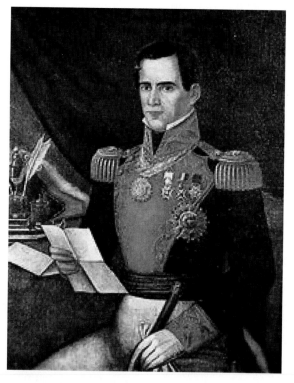

Antonio Lopez de Santa Anna

Antonio Lopez de Santa Anna was born in Jalapa in 1795. His father was Spanish and his mother was Criolla--of pure Spanish parents, but born in Mexico. In the caste system of Mexico, this would place Santa Anna on the lower level of the highest rank. He went into the Spanish Army at age sixteen and did very well, receiving a battlefield commission and several promotions fighting during the revolution of 1810. Santa Anna was an excellent soldier and loved to campaign. He first came to Texas when he was eighteen, as a young lieutenant under General Arredondo. The young officer learned tactics from the wily Arredondo and, in 1813, after the Magee filibuster, participated in the brutality that virtually removed all Anglo settlers from Texas.

Santa Anna was especially impressed with the speed and ease of the depopulation. Arredondo killed a few prisoners and hung a few settlers, spread the word that more executions would follow, and the Anglos disappeared. Most everyone who stayed in the territory professed loyalty to the King of Spain, faithfully attended the Catholic Church, and spoke Spanish.

In 1821, Captain Santa Anna, fighting for the Spanish under Iturbide, switched sides and survived when Iturbide renounced the Spanish and became emperor of Mexico. At age twenty-seven, Brigadier General Santa Anna was a favorite of the new emperor, but felt the ruler's power waning, and moved to the Federalist side, supporting the Constitution of 1824.

Power in Mexico was spread among three factions—the church, the military, and the aristocracy. Santa Anna had an uncanny ability to understand the whims of power and predict the winning side. He learned being a good soldier was important but choosing the correct side in any confrontation was more important.

In 1829, the young general became a national hero when he commanded troops that stopped a Spanish invasion attempt at Tampico. At thirty-four, the hero of Tampico wisely withdrew to his hacienda at Jalapa. He read and studied history, war, and politics as he waited while the factions in the Mexican ruling class fought for control. Three years later, in 1832, in a mostly bloodless revolution, Santa Anna came out of exile and took control of the government. He promised return to the principals of the Constitution of 1824, power to the poor, and a liberal government in Mexico. His liberal policies made him vastly popular in Mexico and Texas, as well as in England and the United States.

At age forty, in 1835, Santa Anna used the army to take control of the government, reversed his position, established a centralist system, and declared himself emperor. He watched as the Texians took more and more latitude while Mexico was in turmoil. The problems at Velasco and Anahuac could no longer be ignored as "growing pains" or other such Anglo nonsense. The incident at Gonzales was open rebellion. Santa Anna was taking his army to Texas and he was furious. His own brother-in-law, General Cos, allowed the Texians to take over San Antonio. Santa Anna was angry and embarrassed. This time, it was "No More Mr. Nice Guy."

Throughout his career, Santa Anna had little regard for the welfare of his troops. He was egocentric and considered underlings so many "chickens." Soldiers were expendable, to be used as needed and replaced when necessary. He moved his army to Texas, but he did so without doctors, medical supplies or equipment for use in the care of sick or wounded. He provided the troops with short rations only and expected them to fend for themselves. Living off the land was no easy matter as they crossed the deserts of northern Mexico. The Mexican troops suffered from poor nutrition, inadequate medical care, and lack of proper clothing.

On the other hand, the self-styled "Napoleon of the West" provided luxuries for himself. The wagon which carried his provisions was stocked with the finest French wines, champagne, brandy, opium, chocolate and fine foods from all over the world. He wore silk shirts with diamond studs and slept between silk sheets in a silk tent. His staff included a personal chef and physician.

As Santa Anna moved his army north, William Barret Travis, on orders from Governor Smith, attempted to gather a hundred men and go to San Antonio to help Lt. Colonel Neill defend the city. Travis managed to attract only thirty volunteers and offered to resign in embarrassment.

Governor Smith refused his resignation and urged Travis to take his men to San Antonio to assist Neill. Travis assumed he was to take command of the Alamo. He relished the opportunity. He felt the hand of destiny on his shoulder.

The legislative council gave Dr. James Grant, a real estate promoter, permission to invade Mexico and take Matamoros--disregarding the fact that such orders had already been given Sam Houston. Doctor Grant, a newcomer with no military experience, had never been a resident of Texas and owned nothing north of the Rio Grande. His substantial Mexican holdings had been confiscated, and he fled north to Texas to become an ardent war dog.

Grant had considerable financial interest in seizing Matamoros. He promised his troops "the first spoils taken from the enemy." "General" Grant went to San Antonio and recruited his troops from the garrison there. With "General" Frank Johnson's consent, he stripped Colonel Neill of all the military supplies, wagons, and equipment that had been taken from the Mexicans when General Cos surrendered. Neill was left to defend San Antonio and take care of eighty wounded men with meager supplies, little food, and no equipment.

"Generals" Grant and Johnson proceeded to Goliad to join "General" James Fannin. Sam Houston, the only one of the four "supreme commanders" with a proper general's uniform, hurried to join the other three. There was glory to be had if Matamoros was captured, and Houston wanted a share.

Tejano ranchers and other Mexican sympathizers, including a substantial number of American colonists, furnished Santa Anna with a vast and reliable spy network in Texas. He was aware of the plan to capture Matamoros and dispatched the supremely competent General Don Jose Urrea with orders to intercept and dispose of any troops headed there, then retake Goliad and sweep the coastal bend clear of rebellious Texians. Urrea would be joined at Matamoros by a battalion from Campeche, giving him a total of 1200 men.

When General Houston arrived at Goliad, the other three "generals" and their troops were gone. Fannin was nearby at Copano Bay, with about twenty-five Texian colonists and over four hundred volunteers from the "Georgia Battalion." He was trying to arrange for a ship so his men could attack Matamoros from the sea. He had orders from the council to do so.

Grant and Johnson, with three hundred men between them, also had orders from the council to attack Matamoros. They were close by in Refugio, trying to locate Fannin. Houston had a general's uniform and orders from Governor Smith, but the other generals had soldiers. No one was interested in taking orders from Sam Houston, even if he was dressed for the part. Houston decided not to push the issue. He asked Jim Bowie, who was at Goliad, to take whatever men he could find and go to San Antonio. Houston wanted an honest military assessment of the fortifications there from someone he trusted, and he had great respect for Bowie. Houston expected to order the Alamo abandoned, but wanted to see what Bowie thought. Jim Bowie left for San Antonio, planning to take command of the Alamo. Houston went to San Felipe, hoping to wield some influence on the delegates at Washington-on-the-Brazos.

Santa Anna's army was near Laredo, fighting a blue norther that brought snow and freezing temperatures into Mexico. The soldiers, not accustomed or outfitted for a Texas winter, suffered, and many of the *mestizos* froze to death. Santa Anna did not care. He only brought the peons along for cannon fodder. The supreme ruler stayed warm in his silk tent.

Houston, washing his hands of Matamoros, returned to the convention at Washington-on-the Brazos. Grant and Johnson argued, split their troops and started independently across country toward Matamoros, not realizing that they would have to fight General Urrea to get there. Fannin, uniquely able to fail at almost anything he tried, was unable to commandeer a ship, so he moved the Georgia boys back to the presidio at Goliad. Bowie and his small group joined Neill and Travis at the Alamo. Santa Anna and the

Mexican Army suffered in the cold as they neared Laredo, marching toward San Antonio.

The face of the Texian army had changed. Many of the colonists in Texas returned to their farms and volunteers from America replaced them. Some of these soldiers were mercenaries or criminals, but most were idealistic young men from the American south, burning with a desire to fight injustice and establish freedom in the territory of Texas. Their grandfathers fought in the American Revolution; their fathers and uncles fought in the War of 1812; this was their war. No one doubted that Texas would become part of America when the battle was won.

Many of the Texas colonists were not so keen on the revolution. Mexico had been good to them. They had all the land they could work, almost no interference from the government, deferred taxes, warm homes, and honest Anglo neighbors. Stephen Austin had counseled patient obedience to the unstable Mexican government until he returned from his recent imprisonment. His new message of revolt was slow to take hold with the conservative colonists.

Bowie and Travis arrived at the Alamo within days of each other, in late January. Both expected to take command. They found Lt. Col. Neill with 104 men, only nine of which were Texians. Volunteers from almost every state in the Union, some from Great Britain, and several from other parts of Europe manned the fort. A dozen of the defenders were from Ireland. The men with Travis and Bowie, almost all Texians, brought the total to about 140.

Neill took a furlough in mid-February to attend to family matters, and left Travis in charge. Travis and Bowie clashed but worked out a compromise—Bowie would command the volunteers and Travis would command the regular army. They carefully worked in tandem until Bowie became so ill that Travis took over.

Travis, at twenty-six, was born for this command. He spent his time inspecting the fortifications, discussing, recommending, and approving changes with the engineer, Green Jameson. He arranged for supplies and ammunition. He wrote letters asking for help from any quarter and postured for the enlisted men. The men preferred Jim Bowie as a leader, but slowly accepted Travis. He was aloof and kept to himself, but his will was strong and his patriotism was unquestioned.

Travis developed great respect for the engineer, Green Jameson, the guide, El Colorado, and the scout, Deef Smith. Smith moved ghost-like, in and out of San Antonio and became the eyes and ears of the Texian army. In addition to his work at the Alamo, Travis spent a lot of time in his nearby quarters, thinking, planning and writing. His personal needs were attended by Joe, his young slave.

On the day Col. Neill left the Alamo, February 12, Davy Crockett and a few volunteers from Tennessee rode into town. Crockett, a former U.S. Congressman and living legend, immediately lifted the spirits of the hungry, weary troops. He refused any leadership role and asked only to be considered a "high private." His presence and outgoing personality entertained the men and his stories took their minds away from their troubles. Crockett and his Tennessee Volunteers raised the number of defenders in the Alamo to 150.

On February 22, the Texians celebrated Washington's Birthday with a fandango in downtown San Antonio, ignoring reports by friendly Tejanos that Santa Anna and the Mexican Army were near. They partied with warm and willing senoritas until the wee hours, dancing, singing, eating, and drinking. On the morning of February 23, most were nursing hangovers when the Mexican army came into town. Only ten men were inside the Alamo when the enemy was sighted.

General Ramirez y Sesma and his advance guard of fifteen hundred men were the first to arrive in San Antonio. The plaza was alive with activity as dozens of Tejanos fled the city. The Mexican troops stopped on the outskirts of town and seemed content to loiter there, being no apparent threat to the Texians. In the weeks that followed, Sesma was roundly criticized by many fellow officers in the Mexican Army. Had he simply attacked when he arrived, he could have overpowered the ill-prepared garrison at the Alamo, saving the siege and the lives of hundreds of Mexican soldiers. His hesitancy was labeled cowardice and he was viewed with disgust by many of his peers.

The Texian troops were scattered over San Antonio, a few living with families and others finding shelter wherever they could. Travis ordered everyone into the Alamo. "Generals" Grant and Johnson had stripped the garrison of its provisions, but Travis's men found twenty or thirty head of cattle abandoned by fleeing Tejanos, and discovered eighty or ninety bushels of corn, all of which they moved into the makeshift fort. Travis and his "boy," Joe, abandoned the house downtown and moved into quarters inside the walls. Travis watched from the roof of the old chapel as the Mexican Army moved unchallenged through the streets of San Antonio.

Sesma's army occupied the city without firing a shot. Santa Anna and the bulk of his forces were approaching, only a day or two behind the advance guard. Travis and his command hunkered down inside the Alamo, with seventeen small cannon and one eighteen pounder, but precious little powder and shot.

During the next week or so, Travis hurriedly scratched out pleas for help, including one to Fannin at Goliad, and another to the people of Gonzales. He dispatched El Colorado and others with these letters. He sent Deef Smith with a letter for Sam Houston. .

Inside the fort huddled Susannah and Angelina Dickinson, the wife and baby daughter of Lt. Almaron Dickinson, the cannoneer from Gonzales. Also seeking refuge were perhaps a dozen Tejano women and children (some were relatives of Bowie's wife,) and at least one slave, Travis's manservant, Joe. A hundred and fifty able-bodied men stood ready to defend the old church that Cos had abandoned, feeling that 1100 men were too few for a proper defense. Travis was convinced help—men, equipment, food, and supplies—was on its way.

James Walker Fannin

Lt. Col. James Walker Fannin, upon receiving the plea for help from Travis, acted with uncharacteristic dispatch. He ordered supplies and equipment loaded onto wagons, assembled three hundred troops and started them toward San Antonio. It was a tough trip. The wagons stuck in the mud. His troops were unable to make decent headway, their powder was wet and an ox fell in the ditch. After struggling for two long miles, he gave up and returned to the warmth and safety of the presidio at Goliad, secure in the knowledge he had done his best. The boys at the Alamo were on their own.

Santa Anna established headquarters in San Antonio and planned his assault, even though there was no good reason to waste the resources. The Alamo did not guard the only road into Texas. The shoddy little fort offered no strategic value. Santa Anna's army could have easily bypassed it, ignoring it altogether or leaving a small force to keep the Texians penned inside until they starved, while the rest of the army marched on to deal with Houston's rabble group. A quick Mexican sweep through the colony could have rid Texas of rebels, but Santa Anna was determined to make a statement.

Santa Anna wanted the troublesome Americans out of Texas. In 1813, when he first came to Texas with General Arredondo, he had seen the results of a terror campaign. A few well-placed killings and the whole uprising evaporated. Santa Anna stopped in San Antonio for that reason—he wanted to make an example of Travis and his command. He planned to grind the Alamo into dust and annihilate the defenders while all of Texas looked on. He knew the value of terror and intended to use it to sanitize Texas and immortalize himself. But the supreme ruler had other needs.

The women of northern Mexico were known to be more beautiful, more desirably shaped, and more attractive than Mexican ladies farther south. As Santa Anna's men occupied the city, General Castrillon reported to him the presence of a beautiful teenage girl living nearby with her widowed mother. The young woman was beautiful, high-born and well educated, but had lived in poverty since her father died. Santa Anna was immediately intrigued and asked the General to bring the girl to him. Castrillon refused, feeling he'd been asked to act as a pimp. Another officer, one of many yes-men Santa Anna kept on staff, had no problem being a pimp, and volunteered for the duty.

The young officer presented the proposition to the girl's mother. One of the most powerful men in the world desired to honor her daughter by taking her into his bed. This was not unusual—in fact, it was a national pastime—but the mother was incensed and would have none of it. If Santa Anna wanted to deflower her precious daughter, he would have to marry the girl in the Catholic Church. The mother was adamant. No church wedding, no precious daughter.

The young officer reported the bad news to Santa Anna, who was overcome with desire for the lovely girl. The local priest refused to perform the wedding; it was common knowledge that Santa Anna had a dutiful wife back home in Jalapa. The emperor, however, was deeply in lust and the young apple-polishing officer worked out a compromise.

In the barracks, a well-educated fellow officer masqueraded as all sorts of people. He was hilariously funny and did a great impression of a priest. The comedian borrowed some priestly robes, performed the wedding ceremony in a local church, and Santa Anna happily honeymooned with his young bride as the siege continued. After the fall of the Alamo, his Excellency sent the girl, in a carriage with a military escort, home to Jalapa. She moved into a house near the town square, not far from Santa Anna's home and his real wife. She may have delivered Santa Anna's illegitimate child.

This incident affected the attitudes of Mexican officers and men. No problem having a girlfriend—either a quick fling or a more permanent arrangement—that was expected, even admired, but the devout Catholic officers could not condone flaunting the sacraments of the church. Santa Anna was losing what little respect he had from his subordinates. At the same time, he was surrounding himself with a group of yes-men who lacked the imagination or courage to disagree.

The Mexicans, on the afternoon of their first day in San Antonio, unfurled a blood-red flag from the bell tower of the San Fernando Cathedral, indicating that Santa Anna would give no quarter. Travis, watching from the chapel roof, immediately ordered Lt. Dickinson to fire the eighteen-pounder in answer. The cannon ball bounced noisily but harmlessly down the street and wasted powder. It did no harm to the Mexicans but may have harmed the Texian cause. Travis had acted rashly, defiantly, on the spur of the moment without consulting anyone, even his co-commander, Jim Bowie.

Bowie quickly sent Green Jameson, the engineer, under a flag of truce, to parlay with the Mexicans. Jameson said the cannon fired accidentally and asked for surrender terms. The only terms offered were "at discretion," meaning unconditional surrender. Santa Anna wanted the glory of a great victory, not a bunch of Anglo prisoners. Given Santa Anna's mindset, it is doubtful the outcome of the siege would have differed had Travis not fired the cannon.

Travis was defiant. He still expected help, but the outlook was not good. He wrote to his fiancée, Rebecca Cummings, and to his son. The tone of the letters indicated he knew that he must die. He had resigned himself to that fact and planned to do so in a blaze of glory. The next day, on February 24th, he wrote one of the most eloquent, courageous, and defiant letters in history. It is obvious that he meant this letter for the citizens of the United States, not just the rebels in Texas. He wrote:

*Commandancy of the Alamo ,*

*Bexar, February 24th, 1836*

*To the People of Texas and all Americans in the World—*

*Fellow Citizens and Compatriots:*

*I am besieged with a thousand or more of the Mexicans under Santa Anna. I have sustained a continual Bombardment and cannonade for 24 hours and have not lost a man. The enemy has demanded surrender at discretion, otherwise, the garrison is to be put to the sword, if the fort is taken. I have answered the demand with a cannon shot, and our flag still waves proudly from the wall. I shall never surrender or retreat. Then, I call on you in the name of Liberty, of patriotism, and everything dear to the American character, to come to our aid with all dispatch. The enemy is receiving reinforcements daily and will no doubt increase to three or four thousand in four or five days. If this call is neglected I am determined to sustain myself as long as possible and die like a soldier who never forgets what is due his honor and that of his country. VICTORY OR DEATH.*

*William Barret Travis*

*Lt. Col. Comd't.*

*P.S. The Lord is on our side. When the enemy appeared in sight, we had not three bushels of corn. We have since found in deserted houses eighty or ninety bushels and got into the walls 20 or 30 head of Beeves. Travis*

William Barret Travis sketch by Wiley Martin (3 months before Travis was killed)

Travis was not sorry he fired the cannon. He bragged about it. He was at center stage, defiant, playing the part he always dreamed. He was a bigger-than-life hero. If the Alamo must fall and he could do nothing to prevent it, he would make it costly for the Mexicans and publicize it to Americans everywhere. The fall of the Alamo would be a small price to pay for his place in history.

William Barret Travis suspected his life would be short, regardless of the outcome at the Alamo. He was suffering from gonorrhea, and had given it to his fiancée, Rebecca Cummings. He recently made a will which provided for the care and education of his children, including the daughter he did not claim and had never seen. His relationship with his fiancée was strained.

Rosanna, his abandoned wife in Alabama, had filed for divorce, but Travis had no idea it had been granted. He might well have simply decided to trade his miserable existence for the opportunity to die a glorious death for his country and become a hero for all time.

Rebecca Cummings had given Travis her cat's eye ring that he wore on a string around his neck. Her ardor may have cooled, but Travis loved Rebecca deeply and placed the ring around the neck of little Angelina Dickinson. He hoped the toddler would survive the battle and the ring would prove to Rebecca that his love was true.

When it was too late to matter, reinforcements arrived. At one in the morning of March 1st, thirty-two men, twenty-nine volunteers from Gonzales, led by "El Colorado" and two other scouts, threaded their way through the Mexican lines and entered the fortress through the south gate. They had come without provisions, with little ammunition, with only the clothes on their backs. Travis didn't need more hungry mouths to feed, but the reinforcements momentarily lifted the morale of the defenders and provided much-needed optimism. These twenty-nine volunteers, mostly farmers from around Gonzales, were the only help Travis would get, and they would all be dead in less than a week.

The contentious delegates of the Texas legislature, with a document obviously copied from Thomas Jefferson, finally declared Texas independence on March 2nd. The next day, March 3rd, El Colorado delivered Travis' victory or death letter, asking for support. They argued most all day but, in the end, did nothing.

Santa Anna's spies told him that Travis was running low on food and ammunition and might be planning to surrender. A rumor circulated that the rebels might try to sneak or break out of the Alamo. The Mexican ruler could not let any of this happen. For his plan to succeed, he must attack and wipe out Travis and his men. His generals pleaded with him to wait three days, until larger cannon arrived. With heavier guns, the Alamo's walls could be breached at will. Only one day's bombardment would leave Travis and his men standing around in an open courtyard, but that would not suit Santa Anna's needs.

The Supreme Emperor refused to wait. General Urrea had defeated and killed two of the appointed "generals," Grant and Johnson, and was moving, unmolested, along the coast. He would certainly take Fannin and the fort at Goliad soon.

General Jose de Urrea

Mexico City newspapers were singing his praise. Urrea was effectively stealing the limelight from Santa Anna. Only a great victory could stop this erosion of power, and Santa Anna felt it must be stopped. Blood, a lot of blood, must be shed, otherwise, there was no glorious victory.

Travis may have offered the defenders of the Alamo an opportunity to leave the fort before the battle. A persistent story goes that on March 3rd,

Travis drew a line in the sand with his sword and asked those willing to stay and fight to step across. Only one man, Louis "Moses" Rose, refused to cross. Rose, 51, nicknamed "Moses" by his fellow soldiers because of his comparative old age, was allowed to slip out through an open window that night, and made his way to a friend's ranch in Grimes County. Rose later operated a butcher shop in Nacogdoches, where he defended his desertion by saying simply, "I was not ready to die."

Although Rose never told the story of Travis' line in the sand, he indicated that he had chosen to leave with Travis' blessing. Susannah Dickinson didn't mention the story for twenty years. When asked about it in the 1850's, she said she thought it was true. The story became so popular, she added it to her standard set of recollections on the battle of the Alamo. Susannah had fallen on hard times, with promiscuity, a string of abusive husbands, venereal disease and poverty contributing to her dismal life. She wallowed in prostitution and sank into alcoholism. Who could blame the girl for embellishing a bit on her fifteen minutes of fame?

Joe, Travis' slave, could have verified the "line" story, but he was not available. He stole a horse and disappeared on April 21, 1837, on the first anniversary of Texas Independence. He chose to hide and pose as a free man, rather than continue as a slave. He was reported to be in Alabama. He was seen in Austin in 1875 or 1876. He may have lived out his life in the Austin vicinity, hiding in plain sight. Joe, as a slave, was listed as an asset in Travis' estate, but the lawyers handling the disposition failed to locate him.

We may never know whether Travis drew a line in the sand, but it is exactly the kind of dramatic gesture he would embrace. In his mind's eye, he was a lonely and courageous commander, drawing a line in the sand and convincing his troops to fight to the death. Travis was certain this was to be his destiny. He was prepared to die for it.

On March 5th, Santa Anna ordered a dawn attack for the next day. His best troops were to lead the attack, a great honor, but a virtual death sentence.

He had a late dinner that evening with General Castrillon, the genteel older commander who tried to convince Santa Anna to wait on the artillery and save the lives of Mexican soldiers. According to one of his aides, Santa Anna picked up a chicken leg, shook it at Castrillon, and said, "What are the lives of soldiers more than so many chickens? I tell you, the Alamo must fall, and my orders must be obeyed at all hazards."

The Mexicans came in hordes. Before daylight, at about five in the morning, they attacked from all sides at once. Lt. Almaron Dickinson repeatedly fired the eighteen-pounder filled with grapeshot, chains, spikes and nails into the masses with devastating effect. The smaller cannon fired the same deadly mixture from their positions. The attackers saw their fellow soldiers dismembered, disemboweled, and killed outright, but still they bravely moved forward. The deadly long rifles lay down a withering fire. As the troopers approached the walls, the Texians threw down grenades and rocks, followed by withering shotgun and pistol fire. Still they came, too many to stop. On their third attempt, the Mexicans reached the north wall, climbed over the bodies of their comrades and managed to get a toehold up and over. Some gained access at the fort's southwestern corner, near the chapel, and started to flood into the courtyard.

The defenders, in desperation, fell back and used their rifles as clubs. They slashed with swords and Bowie knives. The Mexicans, pouring in from several breaches now, fought with bayonets, sabers, and pistols. Both sides used shotguns, but reloading was impossible. The Texians fell back into the barracks, fighting defensively, killing many before giving up their lives. Three groups of defenders managed to break out near the stables on the east side and tried to cross the field to the safety of some trees. Mexican Calvary, stationed there to prevent retreat by their own troops, cut them down with lances and sabers.

William Barret Travis, when the alarm sounded, rushed to the north wall, and Joe, his slave, followed. Joe heard him shout his only order during the battle, "Come on boys, the Mexicans are upon us, and we'll give them hell!" Then Travis turned and fired his pistol down into the advancing Mexicans. Joe saw him shudder, then fall backwards with a rifle ball half-buried in his forehead. Travis sat up with his sword in hand, looked around quizzically, then fell dead and rolled down the dirt ramp. He was one of the first Texians to die in the battle. Joe ran to hide in Travis' quarters.

The Mexicans went into a blood frenzy. They stormed into the adobe quarters and moved from room to room, searching out and bayoneting the occupants, blindly re-stabbing dead men. Some of the officers tried to stop the slaughter, but to no avail. The killing lasted until there was no one left to kill and all was quiet. It was full daylight now—the battle lasted barely an hour and a half.

Despite conflicting stories, most believe Jim Bowie died in his bunk, bayoneted while shivering with typhoid under his blanket. His mother, when told of his death, calmly stated, "I'll wager no wounds were found in his back."

Almaron Dickinson died near the eighteen-pounder he fired with such murderous precision. Green Jameson, James Bonham and the twenty-nine family men from Gonzales died. All the defenders died. Deef Smith survived because he was delivering a letter to Sam Houston and Travis had El Colorado sneak out with the letter to the convention at Washington-on-the Brazos. Both scouts lived to fight at San Jacinto.

Much of what is known of the battle, especially from the Mexican perspective, comes from the writings of Lt. Jose Enrique de la Pina who was with Santa Anna's forces at the Alamo. De la Pina kept a daily journal during his time in Texas. His papers were published in Mexico in 1837, but not translated into English until 1955. As with many historical documents, well-educated, learned, intelligent, and honest scholars disagree vehemently as to their authenticity. The fact that these diaries were translated at almost the same time Walt Disney and Fess Parker re-invented Davy Crockett and the Alamo gives fuel to one side of the argument. The substance, consistency, and style of the entries speak well for the other.

The main point of contention with De La Pina's diaries has to do with the death of Davy Crockett. The popular vision of Crockett dying in battle in front of the chapel, surrounded by a dozen dead Mexicans, is sacred to some historians. A version of this story was told by Susanna Dickinson. A similar rendition (with a different location) was told by Joe, Travis' boy slave. Walt Disney sold millions of coonskin caps with this story.

De la Pina was a great fan of General Urrea and missed no opportunity to praise the young general's actions. By the same token, he had nothing but disdain for Santa Anna, Filosola, and Sesma, among others. He considered generals Sesma and Filosola to be brown-nosing cowards and Santa Anna to be out of touch with reality.

De la Pina claims, after the battle, Davy Crockett and six other survivors were brought before Santa Anna under protection of the intelligent and sensitive General Castrillon, who asked the Emperor to spare these few so they could spread the word that the Mexicans were invincible. Santa Anna was incensed—his orders were clear—no quarter. He ordered the men killed and turned his back. Immediately, several officers of his staff fell upon and murdered the defenseless prisoners. De la Pina said honor did not allow him to name the officers who participated in the slaughter, but honor aside, he let slip that one of them might have been General Sesma.

Susanna Dickinson and her daughter, Angelina, were brought before Santa Anna, who was much taken with both. He offered to adopt the toddler and see that she received the finest education available in Mexico. Susanna declined the offer, unaware that she was dooming her child to a life of misery. Santa Anna released the Dickinson women along with Joe, Travis's black servant, a few Tejano women and children (relatives of Jim Bowie's wife), and Ben, a black cook who had traveled with the Mexican army as General

Sesma's chef. Santa Anna wrote a letter to the remaining citizens of Texas and asked the little group to deliver it to the Texians.

Santa Anna's reasons for releasing the black men probably had to do with his desire to create unrest among the slaves of the colonists. The letter he sent with Susannah promised fair treatment of all colonists faithful to Mexico and death to all rebels. The idea that all Americans were believed to be rebels was clear and the letter created the desired panic in the colonies.

Santa Anna ordered all the bodies of the rebellious Texians stacked and burned. One of his young officers, Francisco Esparza, asked that the body of his brother, Gregorio, be released to him for a proper burial. Francisco convinced Santa Anna that his brother was a prisoner of the Texians and had died at their hands. His request was granted and Gregorio was the only defender of the Alamo buried in a proper grave with a proper ceremony. His body now rests near Ben Milam's gravesite, in a little park in downtown San Antonio.

Travis's records list 182 defenders killed at the Alamo. De la Pina said he personally counted 242 bodies in the stacks before they were burned, and others put the total at something over two hundred. Santa Anna, in his official reports, claimed 600 to 700 Texians killed and seventy Mexican soldiers lost, both absolute lies. Historians agree that Mexican losses must have been 400 to 600 killed and at least that many wounded. A large portion of the wounded died slow, painful, unnecessary deaths due to lack of medical supplies.

In 1837, Juan Seguin headed a detail of soldiers who collected the bones of the Alamo defenders and buried them near the old chapel, "in a peach orchard." In conjunction with the Texas Centennial in 1936, some of the bones recovered were interred in a marble sarcophagus in the San Fernando Cathedral, in downtown San Antonio. Although the remains are identified as Crockett, Travis, and Bowie, no one knows which of the defenders may be buried there.

The ring that Rebecca Cummings gave Travis was somehow recovered from Angelina Dickinson and is currently on display at the Gift Shop/Museum adjacent to the Alamo.

Ben, the free black man who cooked for General Sesma, joined the Texian Army and finished the war as Sam Houston's chef.

De La Pina's writings angered powerful men in the Mexican government. He spent a short time in prison, and after his release he was murdered on the street in Mexico City in October of 1840. His killer was released from prison in 1842, on the authority of an unnamed, high-ranking Mexican politician.

## CHAPTER EIGHT
# Sam Houston and San Jacinto

Sam Houston was in a bind. He promised Chief Bowl of the Cherokee that he would visit and smoke the peace pipe. Travis was posturing at the Alamo, even though Houston had asked him to abandon the old church-turned-fort. Bowie was too drunk most of the time to make much sense, and the idiots in the convention had appointed four different supreme commanders of the Texas Army.

Houston was one of the supreme commanders, but he was at a disadvantage. He had a custom-made general's uniform from a tailor in New Orleans, but the other three generals had troops, equipment and ammunition. He felt his presence was critical at the convention in Washington-on-the-Brazos, but he wanted to inspect the fortifications in San Antonio first-hand. Amateurs were in command of the planned assault on Matamoros, and his meager army desperately needed discipline and training.

Houston did the only thing he knew how to do. He kept his word. He left the bickering delegates in Washington-on-the-Brazos and made his way to Nacogdoches to palaver with the Cherokee. Texas could not afford to let the Indians join the Mexican side in this confrontation, and Houston knew that was a definite possibility.

Chief Bowl was an old and trusted friend and Sam returned with Bowl's word that the Cherokee would stay out of the fight. In return, Houston promised Texas would give the Cherokee people title to their lands after the revolution. Houston made this promise never doubting the Texas government would honor his word.

Over six feet, two inches tall (some claim he was six feet six) at a time when most men were less than five-eight, Sam Houston was an imposing man. He dressed flamboyantly, wearing colorful vests and, at times, Indian blankets. He never failed to stand out in a crowd. He was seriously wounded fighting the Creek Indians in the War of 1812 and had only partial use of his right arm. Before coming to Texas, Houston studied law and passed the bar, served as a U.S. Congressman, and was elected governor of Tennessee. Houston's friend and mentor, U.S. President Andrew Jackson, wanted Texas. Evidence suggests he sent Houston to deliver it.

General Sam Houston--About 1840

Sam had been in Texas, living in Nacogdoches, three years when he was elected delegate to the second convention at Washington-on-the-Brazos. The convention's stated purpose: to remain loyal subjects of Mexico, establish local government in Texas, and negotiate grievances, both real and imagined, directly with the central government in Mexico City. This was perfectly logical to the Anglo-American colonists, but the Mexicans considered any disagreement with the central government treasonous. This difference in mindset complicated the relationship.

Houston, a good lawyer and a consummate politician, tried to guide the disorganized, ill-prepared convention delegates toward intelligent, well-thought-out decisions, but little was accomplished. Lack of funds contributed to inaction, but secret agendas, constant bickering, fragile egos, and blatant self-dealing among the delegates made progress next to impossible.

Returning from his visit with the Cherokees in late February, Houston went back to work in Washington-on-the-Brazos, this time pushing for an American-style Declaration of Independence from Mexico. He convinced the delegates, many of whom wanted to abandon their deliberations and join Travis at the Alamo, that it was more important to stay and finish the work of establishing a government. After signing the Texas Declaration of Independence on his forty-third birthday, March 2, 1836, Houston made his way to Gonzales, where he took command of the 374 men in the Texas Army.

Erastus "Deef" Smith joined Houston at Gonzales, delivering Travis' last letter requesting men and ammunition and vowing to fight to the death. Houston sent the trusted New York-born frontiersman back to San Antonio, for definitive word on the condition of the Alamo. Houston was learning to depend more and more on the reliable scout. He knew Smith would return with a complete and accurate report or he would not return at all.

Houston ordered Fannin to abandon the presidio at Goliad immediately, march to Victoria and leave a token unit to guard the city, and then bring the bulk of his troops to join the Texian army at Gonzales. These orders didn't suit the ambitious, jealous, vain, and grossly incompetent Colonel Fannin, and were ignored.

Deef Smith returned from San Antonio leading a wagon with Susannah Dickinson and her baby daughter Angelina, along with Joe, Travis's young slave, and Ben, a free black man who had been chef for the Mexican General

Sesma. A few Mexican women and children, relatives of Jim Bowie's wife, also rode in the wagon.

Smith reported the Alamo had fallen on March 6, and the entire garrison had been put to death by Santa Anna. Mrs. Dickinson carried a letter from Santa Anna, promising a similar fate for anyone suspected of aiding the rebels.

Colonel Fannin, a victim of his own ineptitude, created excuses and postponed his departure for a week. When he ran out of excuses, he left the only secure fortress in Texas, marched about ten miles, and allowed his entire command to be surrounded by Mexican forces on the open prairie near Coleta Creek. The efficient Mexican General Jose Urrea promised mercy, if it was in his power. Fannin surrendered his army, having no choice but to trust the young general.

General Urrea had previously dispensed with two other factions of the little Texas army under "generals" Grant and Johnson. Both groups had planned to capture Matamoros, which was important because it was a major seaport and collected duties from merchant ships, mostly in hard currency. Texas desperately needed that money and the supplies it would provide. Santa Anna's network of spies informed him of the Texian's plan, and he sent General Urrea to protect Matamoros. Urrea easily located and defeated the amateur "generals" and their troops.

Urrea's forces fought and won skirmishes at Copano, San Patricio, Agua Dulce, Refugio, and Victoria before capturing the inept Col. Fannin's entire command at the battle of Coleto Creek. Contemporary accounts of a high-born woman rescuing Texian prisoners from certain death after these battles are well documented. In Victoria, she stood between the firing squad and a group of prisoners, telling the Mexican officer in charge that he would have to shoot her first to execute the Texians. The prisoners were spared. She was also instrumental in having many captives relocated to Matamoros before they could be executed. It is not unlikely that General Urrea allowed her activities because he agreed with her.

Later, she saved more than forty condemned men at Goliad by hiding them under the beds in the hospital. General Urrea arranged to be in Victoria when Santa Anna's orders to execute the prisoners at Goliad were carried out by Col. Portillo on Palm Sunday, March 27, 1836. The young woman harangued Portillo unmercifully as he marched almost four hundred remaining prisoners to their doom.

The young German boy, Herman Ehrenberg, managed to escape the massacre by running through the thick smoke and diving into the river in the confusion. He had been shot at, slashed with a saber, splattered with his comrades' blood, and shot at again, but he escaped into the river and the wilderness beyond. About thirty others escaped the slaughter in a similar manner.

Three weeks later, sunburned, disoriented, thirsty, and half-starved, Ehrenberg stumbled into a Mexican patrol at Matagorda and was re-captured. General Urrea recognized the young German and was delighted to see that he had survived. "Ah, my little Prussian," he laughed. Herman Ehrenberg lived a long and prosperous life in Texas, and his writings give us much insight into the Goliad Massacre and the disastrous Runaway Scrape that followed.

The lady in question was almost certainly Francisca (Panchita) Alavez, an absolute beauty assumed to be the wife of Captain Telesforo Alavez, the paymaster for General Urrea. The Mexican army allowed some troops to bring travelling companions, and Captain Alavez's lady generated a lot of attention. Barely twenty years old at the time and described as a "high-born, black eyed beauty," Panchita made quite an impression. Military records indicate Captain Alavez was present at all the locations where prisoners were spared. One survivor called her, "Senora Alavez," and another, "Madame Captain Alavez." Yet another referred to her as "Pacheta Alevesco, wife of Captain A." Some simply called her "the wife of a Mexican officer."

Francisca (Panchita) Alavez

For her efforts, Panchita earned the title, "The Angel of Goliad," and was revered by Texians everywhere. Even so, Captain Alavez abandoned her at the first opportunity. An ambitious young officer cannot afford an outspoken companion. She made her way to Matamoros and was taken in by friends who knew of her efforts. Panchita was then lost to history for a time.

At this same time, a dozen or so escapees from the Goliad Massacre hid in the woods near the Guadalupe River, a few miles west of Victoria. Like Herman Ehrenberg, they had run away during the confusion and Mexican partols roamed the area searching for them. Some of the men were wounded and all were starving, fearing that capture meant certain death. Margaret Theressa Wright, an abandoned woman with seven children, lived in a cabin near the river and discovered the captives on her way to the river for water.

Margaret had the prisoners make a list of their needs and hide it in a hollow tree. She picked up their notes when she carried water from the river, and risked her life by delivering what she could obtain on her next trip, all under the watchful eyes of the Mexican soldiers camped nearby. She carried food and supplies in her empty buckets on the way to the river. Margaret even managed to steal a gun from the soldiers and deliver it to the Texians hidden in the woods. All eventually healed, and with Margaret's help, managed to join Houston's army.

With the fall of Fannin at Goliad, General Urrea had killed or captured approximately seven hundred Texian soldiers, and three generals. Houston didn't need the generals, but he certainly could have used the troops. Santa Anna had killed almost two hundred soldiers in San Antonio. Houston, knowing that Mexican General Sesma was near, ordered Gonzales burned and started his little army east. He needed to put some territory between his soldiers and the Mexican army to buy some time for recruiting, training, and re-supply.

General Sam Houston had always imagined his army would be neat, disciplined, and efficient, with starched uniforms, spit-shined boots, and spotless, well-oiled weapons. He pictured himself riding in front of his troops, his general's uniform resplendent with bright ribbons, his polished ceremonial sword dangling at his side, catching the sun's rays and flashing in all directions. The dismal retreat from Gonzales did not resemble that picture. Houston, a soggy red blanket hanging off his shoulders, rode in the rain at the head of his ragged troops. The image in his mind's eye was not even close.

The little Texian army left well after dark and marched through the night, stopping long enough for breakfast about nine miles east of Gonzales, under what is now known as the "Sam Houston Oak," or the "Runaway Scrape Oak." Houston had breakfast, prepared by his new chef, Ben, and made a speech, a sort of Pep Rally, to his troops and the colonists who were following along. The resilient Ben remained as Houston's chef until after the battle at San Jacinto.

Sam Houston Oak, near Gonzales

Old, stately trees were often used as landmarks during the early days of Texas, and many were named for the part they played in Texas history. The "Treaty Oak" in Austin comes to mind, along with the "Which Way Oak" near Houston.

General Sesma's Mexican army was reported to be forty miles west of Gonzales, moving quickly toward the burning city. Many civilians followed Houston's army, fleeing their homes in terror. The so-called "Runaway Scrape" began in San Felipe and Gonzales and quickly spread through the colony.

Houston knew he could not afford to fight the Mexicans with untrained troops, even though many of them lusted for revenge, having lost friends or relatives at the Alamo. The rag-tag band had no combat experience, no sense of military discipline, little equipment, and almost no provisions. No one suspected Fannin's entire command would be captured, much less put to death, but Houston worried. He knew he must evade the Mexican forces and gain time to build, train, and equip his army. This group of ragged, tobacco-chewing, chicken thieves could talk a good fight, and handle themselves in a barroom brawl, but fighting the well-equipped, disciplined Mexican army was another matter.

With the burning of Gonzales many colonists abandoned their homes and headed toward the Sabine River and safety in Louisiana. Two weeks later, news of the massacre of Fannin and almost four hundred troops spread through the colony. Virtually all the brave volunteers that so stirred Elizabeth Troutman when they marched through Knoxville, Georgia, were shot down by their captors, along with the Alabama Red Rovers and many of the New Orleans Grays. A few had left Fannin and joined Houston's army and would live to fight another day. Lt. Hugh McLeod, Miss Troutman's flag bearer, had been delayed by army paperwork in Louisiana and was in Nacogdoches, working with the local militia to fortify the city, on his way to join Houston's army at Lynchburg Crossing.

Panic gripped the Texian settlers. The exodus intensified. When the Mexican army approached, colonists vacated their homes and farms with only the clothing on their backs. The Mexicans looted and burned dozens of homesteads and killed some civilians. Many soldiers in Houston's army took unauthorized leave, promising to return when their families were safe in Louisiana. Santa Anna's intent was to remove all Anglo-American settlers from the colony of Texas as his mentor, General Arredondo, had done in 1813. The plan was working perfectly.

The Runaway Scrape was complicated by bands of outlaws who rode into homesteads or settlements shouting that the Mexicans were coming. The frightened settlers grabbed what they could carry and joined the mad dash toward the Sabine River. The outlaws then took their time and ransacked the empty homes.

Only two main roads led east to Louisiana at the time, and both were clogged with fleeing colonists, mostly women and children. They sloshed through the mud in the constant rain and waited in line for days to board over-crowded ferries at every river crossing. Cholera, Typhoid, whooping cough, measles and dysentery ravaged the frightened mob. Hundreds of children and old people died and were buried in unmarked graves alongside the muddy roads. The population of Texas was estimated at just under 40,000, not counting Indians, in 1836. It is believed that well over ten percent of the Anglo population died during the six weeks of the Runaway Scrape.

After the slaughter at the Alamo, Santa Anna planned to go back to Mexico with his new "bride," but changed his mind when his staff pointed out how popular General Urrea had become with Mexican newspapers and politicians. The young, handsome Urrea had a string of victories to his credit, his troops worshiped him, and many colonists loyal to Mexico along his route were treating him as a conquering hero. Santa Anna needed to stay in the field long enough to put down this upstart and recapture the spotlight. He sent his trophy teenage wife, in a carriage with a military escort and a money chest, to Talapa, and settled her into an apartment across town from his faithful legal wife. With his personal problems resolved, Santa Anna turned his attention east, toward General Sam Houston and his pitiful little army

The Texian army moved daily for a week, and then camped from March 19th to the 26th at Beasons's crossing, on the Colorado River near present-day Columbus. It was cold, muddy, and wet, and the rain continued unabated. Volunteers arrived daily, but most were ill-equipped and unarmed. The army was growing, now almost a thousand men, and in spite of the rain Houston continued training as they evaded the Mexican Army. On the 25th, Peter Kerr arrived at the camp with the morale-shattering news that Fannin's entire force of over four hundred men had been captured and imprisoned at Goliad. Houston had counted on those men for reinforcements.

General Ramirez y Sesma and his Mexican troops arrived across the Colorado River from Houston's army. Houston moved east to the Brazos River. Captain Moseley Baker and Major Wiley Martin, disgusted with constant retreating, challenged Houston's leadership and refused to fall back, preferring to stand and fight. Houston left a hundred men with Baker and a smaller group with Martin to prevent the Mexicans' crossing the Colorado River. Baker and Martin's long rifles were effective and bought Houston needed time to move away from the Mexican army.

The Texian troops were disgruntled and the provisional President of Texas, David G. Burnet, ordered Houston to stand and fight. Houston ignored the order, making Burnet, who was no friend, into a dedicated lifelong enemy. In spite of increasing threats of mutiny, Sam continued his practice of retreat and train, and shared his plans with no one.

On March 30th, after moving north, camp was established in the cane-brakes just west of the Brazos River, across from Groce's Plantation, about five miles southwest of present day Hempstead. The camp had a small lake which provided ample fresh water, and was located on a high, easily defended ridge surrounded by muddy cane fields. Houston knew his men could hold out here against a much larger force.

Jared Groce, perhaps the largest landholder in Texas, welcomed Houston and his men. He arranged for a field hospital to be set up on his property, provided food and supplies, and opened all the facilities of his plantation to Houston's army. He even had the plantation's lead plumbing pipes melted down for rifle balls.

Ignoring the rain, Houston drilled his troops. Additional soldiers continued to join the ragged army that swelled to over twelve hundred men. The pressure for offensive action increased. Houston steadfastly stayed his course, knowing that when he fought, he must win or Texas was lost.

Houston asked Deef Smith to organize a group of scouts to spy on the Mexicans and keep him informed as to their numbers, location, and condition. Among others, Smith chose Robert McManus, the younger brother of Jane McManus Storm.

Morale in the Mexican army was low and the troops were miserable. Not accustomed to rain, especially prolonged rain, they suffered even more than the Texians. Their heavy wagons mired in the mud and they lost much of their equipment. The Mexican soldiers were unused to the cold and suffered mightily, far from home, sleeping on wet blankets in the mud with inadequate clothing, little to eat, and no hope of improvement.

Santa Anna decided on a three-pronged attack. He negated General Urrea by putting him under the command of General Filisola, an Italian mercenary he had chosen to be second in command. Their orders were to continue along the coast and clear any opposition in that area. General Antonio Gaona, a Cuban, took the northern route, with orders to drive the Anglos across the Sabine and out of Texas. The corrupt Ramirez de Sesma, another Cuban, took the center route and looted and burned the capital at San Felipe.

Santa Anna joined Sesma at San Felipe, hoping to engage the elusive Houston. At this time, less than twenty miles separated the armies, but Houston was hidden in the canebrakes and the Mexican scouts could not find him. Deef Smith and his scouts constantly provided Houston with valuable intelligence, and continually harassed the Mexican scouts, making them much less effective.

Against Houston's wishes, David G. Burnet, Lorenzo De Zavala, Thomas Rusk, and other Texian officials deserted San Felipe and set up a provisional government fifty miles away in Harrisburg. Houston felt their retreat added to the colonist's panic and contributed to the "Runaway Scrape." Santa Anna set out for Harrisburg to capture the temporary government and thereby end the revolution.

On April 3rd, Houston's camp learned that Fannin and all his men had been executed by order of Santa Anna. The initial disbelief was soon replaced by cold fury. The Texians faced the sobering realization that their fate was victory or death. Santa Anna executed all prisoners.

Thomas Rusk, the Secretary of War of the new republic, and the only friend of Houston in the provisional government, made his way from

Harrisburg to visit Houston and his troops on April 4th. Burnet had ordered Rusk to use his influence to get Houston to fight or to replace him if necessary. After several hours' discussion, Rusk agreed with Houston's strategy. This was not happy news for Burnet, or for the rank and file in the Texian army. Secretary Rusk understood the situation and remained with the army to become Houston's only confidant.

The "Twin Sisters," two six-pound cannon donated to the Texas cause by the city of Cincinnati, Ohio, arrived and were assembled, much to the delight of Colonel J.C. Neill. The artillery officer now had artillery. Neill heard of the fall of the Alamo as he returned from a furlough and joined his old friend Houston and his army on the march. Twenty years before, during the War of 1812, both he and Houston had been wounded fighting the Creek Indians under Andrew Jackson at the Battle of Horseshoe Bend, in Alabama.

David G. Burnet's brother was mayor of Cincinnati, and instrumental in arranging for the donation of the "Twin Sisters" to the Texas cause. Perhaps because of this, Burnet placed undue importance on his temporary office. He was not an elected delegate to the convention, but went there as an "observer," and was elected interim president as a compromise candidate. None of this prevented him from trying to force his will on Houston and the army. The five-foot-one Burnet obviously suffered from the mother of all Napoleon Complexes.

Finally, on April 12th, Houston issued the order to cross the Brazos, pressed the steamboat *Yellowstone* and a small yawl into service for that purpose, and began to move his army toward the east. Baker and Martin's long rifles were again effective, slowing Sesma's crossing the Brazos. They rejoined Houston a few days later at Donoho's plantation, vowing to stay with the army only if Houston fought.

Mirabeau B. Lamar, a Georgia newspaperman, politician, and lawyer, rode in from Harrisburg and reported that the provisional government was still there and in operation. He volunteered as a private, and, because he had a good horse, Houston assigned him to the cavalry. Lamar, an old friend of Fannin, immediately joined the growing number of soldiers that openly questioned Houston's competence and courage.

The Brazos River crossing was completed by mid-morning on the 14th, and the army, now grown to twelve-hundred men, moved five miles east, camping overnight at the Donoho plantation. Charles Donoho, unlike Jared Groce, was not sympathetic with the revolution and not cooperative to wishes or needs of the troops. He forbade chopping trees for firewood on his property, so the soldiers used his rail fences for firewood. Being properly dried, the fence rails were much better suited to the job.

Houston was under continual criticism from Texian politicians, who understood little about the army's circumstances. Burnet continued to order him to stand and fight. More bothersome to Houston was the criticism from his own officers and men. Major Wiley Martin, an old friend of Houston's, was so outspoken that Sam relieved him of his command and placed him in charge of the civilian refugees following the troops.

Some historians believe Houston was moving east to Louisiana to lead the Mexican army into a trap. Andrew Jackson had stationed General Edmund Gaines just across the Sabine River and Houston may have intended to create a "border incident" to allow the Americans an excuse to invade Texas, as Jackson had done in Florida. General Gaines insisted he was there only to protect American lives from hostile Indians, and, to that end, moved troops into the vicinity of Nacogdoches. The Americans were safe—Gaines was about three hundred miles southeast of the nearest unfriendly Indian. Chief Bowl and his neutral Cherokees were near Nacogdoches, but, thanks to Houston's visit, offered no threat.

On April 16th, the questions were answered. The little army approached the "Which Way Oak" at a fork in the road near Abraham Roberts' farm. Whether instructed by Houston or of its own volition, the army took the right fork, toward Harrisburg and the enemy. Ample evidence suggests Houston intended to take the left fork that led to Louisiana, General Gaines and safety. Houston's troops and his officers were spoiling for a fight and would not be denied. It is not unlikely that, in this case, the army led the general.

Santa Anna had broken away from Sesma and the main army, taking seven hundred hand-picked men. He hoped to move fast enough to trap the provisional Texas government at Harrisburg, on Buffalo Bayou in the present-day city of Houston. Narrowly missing Burnet and the others in Harrisburg, he sent Colonel Juan Almonte and his cavalry dashing ahead to New Washington, present day Morgan's Point, in an attempt to capture the Texian president before he could cross to Galveston Island. Santa Anna sacked and burned Harrisburg, then followed Almonte.

Once more, Deef Smith and his scouts proved their worth. On the 18th of April, Smith crossed Buffalo Bayou at Harrisburg and captured a Mexican courier with dispatches from Santa Anna telling the location, strength, and plans for movement of his forces. Houston and Secretary Rusk studied the captured documents and agreed upon a plan. Thomas Rusk was the only man Houston trusted enough to share his plans.

The next day, a temporary hospital was set up in burned-out Harrisburg, and a guard unit assigned to protect the sick and wounded. Houston, with 918 healthy men, crossed the bayou and moved his army toward the Lynchburg Ferry. Thanks to Deef Smith, he knew the location and strength of the enemy. He knew Santa Anna's plans. He knew that defeat meant certain death. He bivouacked his troops in an oak grove directly in the path of the Mexican army.

Colonel Juan Almonte and his cavalry rode up to the dock at New Washington as the Texian government, Burnet and De Zavala and their party, drifted away in a small boat. Burnet reportedly stood up in the boat and bared his chest to give the Mexicans a proper target, but, seeing Mrs. Burnet on board, the chivalrous Colonel Almonte ordered his men to hold their fire, allowing the provisional Texian government to escape to Galveston.

Santa Anna ordered Almonte and his men to sack and burn New Washington. Morgan and his family were spared. A young officer spotted an attractive Mulatto servant girl and pulled her up behind him on his horse. Such temporary arrangements were not uncommon in the Mexican army, and the girl was no worse off. Life was not easy for indentured servants in Texas in 1836, especially unmarried young women.

Just after noon on April 20th, Colonel Almonte's cavalry joined Santa Anna as the army marched toward Lynchburg Crossing to press the search for Houston. Their scouts discovered Houston camped in an oak grove a half mile from the crossing. The rebel army was concealed in the trees, so there was not an accurate estimate of numbers, but Santa Anna was not worried. He had nothing but contempt for Houston and his rabble. He ordered his troops to make camp where they were, on a difficult-to-defend stretch of flat, swampy ground across an open plain from Houston's camp.

Santa Anna's choice of campsite was flawed, and his staff officers asked him to reconsider. General Castillion, the experienced old veteran, simply shrugged his shoulders when asked about the location. The San Jacinto River lay across a marshland to the east. The camp was in a grove of trees, immediately in front of a swamp that surrounded Peggy Lake and blocked any escape toward the south. (Peggy Lake was named after Peggy McCormick, widow and owner of the property). Directly in front of the camp, an open plain stretched almost a mile north to the grove of trees where Houston camped, with his back to Buffalo Bayou. Beyond the open prairie that lay to the west, the country was crisscrossed with bayous, swollen and made impassable by constant rains.

Colonel J. C. Neill, the artilleryman, eager to use the Twin Sisters, rashly engaged the Mexican artillery in a duel. The larger Mexican cannon was damaged, and Neill was wounded. Against Houston's orders, Colonel Sidney Sherman took his cavalry forward in a foolish attempt to capture the damaged Mexican cannon. He was driven back by Mexican Dragoons.

Only the valiant effort and superb horsemanship of Private Mirabeau Lamar prevented the capture or death of Secretary Thomas Rusk. Mexican officers who witnessed the event applauded Lamar's horsemanship and bravery.

Houston was furious. He had not patiently waited until the conditions were in his favor to see all the preparation dissolve into an ill-timed and unplanned brawl. He ordered his troops to withdraw. Sherman was stripped of the cavalry, tongue lashed, and left in charge of an infantry unit. Lamar was given a battlefield promotion and took over command of the cavalry. The wounded Colonel Neill was replaced by Col. George W. Hackley, the Inspector General of the Texian Army. Santa Anna was waiting for rein-forcements—General Cos and five hundred seasoned troops were due in the morning—and he did not press the engagement. The two armies settled into their respective camps for the night.

Santa Anna had noticed the young Mulatto girl, Emily, in the company of one of his officers and ordered her brought to his tent. He decided a day of rest was in order, Cos' reinforcements would be here in the morning, and the 22nd was as good a day as any to dispense with Houston and his pirates. He ordered his staff to plan an attack for the day after tomorrow and retired to his silk tent to relax with an opium pipe and the dark-eyed beauty.

The Mexicans worked through the night, feverishly preparing for an expected dawn attack on the 21st. Breastworks were built with anything at hand—logs, pack saddles, sandbags, luggage—whatever was available. By morning, a flimsy, five-foot-high wall of debris extended along the front of their camp, with an opening in the center for their only cannon, the damaged twelve-pounder. The sleepy, exhausted troops manned the breastworks at dawn, expecting the Texian attack at any moment.

The Texians across the field had slept soundly all night and were enjoy-ing a breakfast of bread and beef, their first real food in days. The flour for the bread was from captured stores bound for the Mexican army and Peggy McCormick's cattle happened to be grazing in the wrong place at the wrong time. The troops were well fed and spoiling for a fight. Sam Houston, for the first time in months, slept late and did not awake until the sun was high in the sky. Some say he awoke to see an eagle, his Indian talisman, circling above. If so, it was a good omen.

About mid-morning, a commotion in the Mexican camp alerted the Texians to the arrival of General Martin Perfecto de Cos, Santa Anna's brother-in-law, with almost five hundred troops. The troops were dog tired—they had force-marched all night. Santa Anna was furious. He had asked that Cos bring veteran soldiers, and these were raw, untested recruits.

Houston sent the reliable Deef Smith with a squad of men to demolish the bridge over Vince's Bayou, cutting off any more reinforcements for Santa Anna, but also cutting off the only path of retreat for either army. The Texians knew the battle meant victory or death and they were ready. Houston instructed Smith to return promptly so as not to miss the fight.

The Texian officers under Houston were divided in their loyalties, but on this morning, in this place, the entire army was united. They had beef for breakfast and were hungry for a fight. Houston called his officers together at noon. Two voted to attack the following morning, while the majority wanted to wait for Santa Anna's expected attack. Houston's rank and file soldiers wanted an immediate attack. Although it just wasn't done in civilized warfare, Houston agreed, and planned the assault for that very afternoon. His people were ready now. Why wait until the Mexicans were prepared?

Houston spread his troops across the prairie in front of their position. They lined up single file, four feet apart, facing the enemy. Lamar and the cavalry were placed on the far right, with orders to stop any attempt to flank the attackers on that side. Sidney Sherman's infantry and the swamp on the left would serve the same purpose. The Twin Sisters were placed near the center of the file, under the command of Col. Hackley, who replaced the wounded Neill. Houston mounted his great white horse, Saracen, and took his place in the center, directly in front of the men. The line was almost a thousand yards long, and, at 3:30 PM, Houston signaled with his sword. A three-man fife and drum corps, pressed into service for the occasion, played the only song all three knew, a lusty version of the bawdy ballad, "Will You Come to the Bower." The Texian army stepped off toward the enemy, excited beyond description.

Santa Anna's troops were lazing about camp, resting for tomorrow's battle. Most were sound asleep, exhausted from having spent the night building defenses for protection. Cos' raw recruits had endured a forced all-night march. Santa Anna and Emily Morgan were asleep in his tent. In one of those unexplained quirks that affect history, no one had put out pickets or posted sentries to watch the Texians across the pasture, less than a mile away.

About two hundred yards out, a slight ridge crossed the open space in front of the Mexican camp and shielded the Texians as they made their way forward. When they stepped over the rise, they expected discovery, but not a shot was fired. Finally, about seventy yards out, at Houston's orders, Hackley turned the Twin Sisters toward the enemy and commenced fire, blowing gaping holes in the flimsy breastworks. Thank you, city of Cincinnati.

The Mexican gun crew, startled and shaken, fired a load of grapeshot well over the heads of the Texians. A few Mexican soldiers fired into the attackers, with little effect. The Texian riflemen fired a volley, and then hit the dirt expecting return fire as they reloaded. When no answering fire came they stood up and swarmed into the Mexican camp. The Mexican gun crew was killed within minutes.

The Mexicans awoke from a sound sleep with the noise of gunshots, bugles, and shouting everywhere. Enemy troops had them surrounded, shooting, clubbing, stabbing, and yelling. Shouts of "Remember the Alamo" and "Remember La Bahia" filled the air. La Bahia was not yet called Goliad. The Mexicans, confused, leaderless, sleepy, and terrified, threw down their weapons and ran. They hid behind trees and dived into the swamp. Some tried to swim away and were shot in the water. The Texians shot helpless, unarmed soldiers, then, out of ammunition and lacking bayonets, waded in using their rifles as clubs and slashing with Bowie knives. Houston and some of his officers tried to stop the carnage, but it was not possible. Weeks of retreat, frustration, hunger, suffering, and deprivation were fresh on the minds of the Texians. Many had some whiskey to bolster their courage before the battle. The invaluable Deef Smith, just returned from destroying the bridge over Vince's Bayou, was heard to yell, "Take prisoners like the Mezkins do."

General Castillion, Colonel Delgado, and the competent Colonel Almonte tried to marshal the troops for defense but were unable to gain order and stop the panic. Castillion, the kind old general who tried to save David Crockett and others, was shot dead as he lay wounded on the ground. Delgado was captured and saved from certain death, in his words, by "a noble and generous captain of the cavalry, Allen, who by great exertion, saved us repeatedly from being slaughtered by the drunken and infuriated volunteers." Colonel Almonte surrendered himself and 400 men at dusk, after the Texians had grown bored with slaughter.

At the beginning of the battle, Santa Anna was terrified. He ran around the camp, wringing his hands and shouting conflicting orders. He grabbed the horse of an aide, mounted, and escaped across the prairie to the west, past Lamar's cavalry. He was chased to Vince's Bayou, only to discover Deef Smith had destroyed the bridge. Santa Anna abandoned his horse and evaded his pursuers in the thick brush. He hid as the Texians killed stragglers until dusk. After nightfall, he got rid of his uniform and took the jacket and trousers of a dead private.

Whatever faults Sam Houston may have had, lack of courage was not among them. He rode alone at the front of his troops during the entire battle. Houston made a big target and he knew it. Saracen, his great white horse, was shot from under him. An aide provided another which was also killed. When the second mount was hit, Houston's ankle was shattered by a copper rifle ball. He had to be lifted onto his third horse. Still he remained in the forefront of the action, leading his men. According to Houston's pocket watch, the Mexican resistance lasted just eighteen minutes. The slaughter continued until dusk. Counts later revealed 630 Mexicans killed, 208 wounded, and over 700 captured, compared to the Texian totals of nine killed, and about thirty, including Houston, wounded. All the Texian casualties took place during the first few minutes of the battle.

Santa Anna, supreme emperor of Mexico, was captured late the next morning, wearing a private's uniform with a silk shirt, diamond studs, and red woolen slippers. As he was taken past other prisoners, his captors heard them say, "El Presidente," and some officers stood. The guards realized they had captured the self-styled "Napoleon of the West," and took him directly to Sam Houston.

The Surrender of Santa Anna by William Henry Huddle

Houston was resting on a pallet under the "Headquarters Oak" where he had planned the battle. His ankle was swollen and painful and his doctor had prescribed opium to help soothe the pain. The Mexican Emperor announced, "I am General Antonio Lopez de Santa Anna and a prisoner of war at your disposition."

Houston, a bit sleepily, said, "General Santa Anna! Ah, indeed! Take a seat, General; I am glad to see you; take a seat."

Santa Anna, very nervous, asked Houston's doctor for a bit of opium to ease his stress. The wish was granted, and the two generals smoked and visited for two hours, while young Moses Austin Bryan, Major Lorenzo De Zavala, Jr., and Colonel Juan Almonte interpreted. Santa Anna wanted his life and Houston wanted Texas. At the end of the day, Santa Anna sent orders for General Filisola to take all Mexican soldiers and march them to Victoria or San Antonio to await further orders. Houston asked Deef Smith to deliver the orders to General Filisola.

To Houston's great relief (and surprise), Filisola, hand-picked by Santa Anna for his lack of imagination, obeyed the orders and started five thousand well-trained soldiers back toward Mexico. General Urrea and several others vehemently opposed the plan, but eventually gave in to military discipline and followed orders. Any of the Mexican generals, with half the troops available, could have defeated Houston and his little army and kept Texas for Mexico. The Mexican government immediately announced that any agreement or treaty made by Santa Anna, a captive, would not be honored. International law agreed with their position.

Emily Morgan was unknown to historians until 1956. The papers of William Bollaert, an English journalist, were published that year and included the story of Emily West/Morgan consorting with the Mexican General as the battle started. Bollaert wrote in 1842, barely six years after the battle, that he heard the story from a stranger on a steamship cruise between Galveston and Harrisburg. The stranger named his source as General Sam Houston.

Historians pounced on this information and immediately scoured the records for any mention of Emily. They came up with two scraps of evidence. The first piece was a contract for indentured service for one year between Emily West of New Haven, Connecticut, and Colonel James Morgan of Texas. Emily was to perform housekeeping services at Morgan's hotel in

New Washington, Texas. Morgan was to provide transportation to and from Texas, room and board, and $100 cash for the year's work. The second item was an application for passport from Texas to New York City, dated 1837, after Emily finished her year of servitude. On the application, Emily stated that she had lost her "Free Papers" at the Battle of San Jacinto, where she was held by the Mexicans until freed on April 21st by Texian soldiers. This story was attested to by Judge Isaac Moreland of Galveston, who had served as a major of artillery under Col. Hackley with Houston's army at San Jacinto.

Emily's papers could have been lost when the Mexicans burned New Washington and her place of employment. The fact that she claims to have lost them at San Jacinto leads to the conclusion that she went willingly with the young Mexican officer, having taken the time to gather her belongings before climbing up behind him on his horse.

Was she forced into Santa Anna's bed? An indentured servant was all but a slave. She slept on a corn shuck mattress in homespun, scratchy underwear and was often "used" by smelly field hands. She was twenty-one years old and unmarried. A handsome, forty-two-year old Mexican General offered a long, hot bath with French soap, champagne, perfume, chocolates, and silk panties. All she had to do was be nice to the General.

Emily West moved back to New York City in 1837 and disappeared. She was lost to history for 120 years, until Bollaert's Journal was published in 1956.

A month after San Jacinto, on May 19, 1836, Parker's Fort in Central Texas was attacked by Comanche Indians. Several members of the Parker family were killed, and five hostages were carried off. Eleven-year-old Cynthia Ann Parker and her younger brother John were taken, along with a teenage cousin, Rachel Plummer and Rachel's son James. An aunt, Elizabeth Kellogg, was also taken. All the hostages except Cynthia Ann were released within a few years.

Somewhere, deep in Mexico, the descendents of a Mexican officer who died in the Texas Revolution tell stories of his bravery and are respected by their neighbors for the family's historical significance. An oil painting of the ancestor in full dress uniform hangs over their mantel. Would they be so proud of his memory if they knew he was the officer who decided to take a nap instead of set out pickets at San Jacinto on that day in 1836?

# CHAPTER NINE

# Houston's First Term as President of the Republic

After the victory at San Jacinto, Houston needed to be moved to New Orleans where he could receive proper medical care for his shattered ankle. His prisoner, Santa Anna, was turned over to David Burnet and the provisional Texas government so they could work out what would become the Treaties of Velasco, based upon the preliminary agreements between Houston and Santa Anna. These treaties, one public and one private, dealt with the details of Texas independence and Santa Anna's release.

The Mexican Army, under Filisola, followed Santa Anna's orders and straggled across Texas, slogging through endless mud along the Gulf Coast. Senior officers fought among themselves. Equipment and wagons were lost in axle-deep mire. Food was scarce and medical supplies were nonexistent. Perhaps Houston did not beat the Mexican Army, but Texas did. Sam Houston won a battle, but Texas won the war. Sticky black gumbo, relentless humidity, punishing mosquitoes, constant rain; the whole humid environment along the Gulf Coast was foreign to Mexican soldiers and they suffered much during the humiliating retreat.

By the time the Mexican Army crossed the Colorado River, a trail of lost equipment, stranded wagons, dead mules, and abandoned ammunition stretched through the quagmire all the way back to the Brazos. Generals Filasola and Urrea were openly hostile toward each other, and the will to fight was gone from the once-proud Mexican Army. They turned toward

Matamoros, and home, instead of following Santa Anna's orders to withdraw and await orders in Guadalupe Victoria or San Antonio.

The provisional Texas government operated out of Galveston. Enjoying the power, but knowing his situation was at best temporary, David Burnet surrounded himself with friends and avowed enemies of Sam Houston. Houston was widely considered a hero by the citizens of Texas, but this group, for various reasons, mistrusted him and felt he was a danger to the fledgling nation. Beyond stated public reasons, they knew he was a danger to some of their private ambitions. Houston was hampered by notions of honor which were of no concern to some of these men.

Regardless of the blind loyalty and hero-worship displayed by most Texas colonists, Houston deserved much of the animosity he aroused. His enemies were mostly intelligent, educated, competent individuals who had successful careers in other places before they came to Texas. The unimaginative Burnet was vindictive and obsessive, and the amoral Potter was without merit, but most of the others were level-headed, thoughtful men. Houston, vain, arrogant, willful, and impatient, was known to drink too much, too often. His past was shadowy. He was a known Indian-lover, a very unpopular state of mind in those times. More than half his officers mistrusted his judgment and second-guessed his decisions, and some even considered him a coward. Burnet placed four of Houston's most dedicated enemies in his cabinet.

Six years earlier, in 1830, David G. Burnet sought Houston's help in selling a land grant he owned. Houston was in Washington at the time and took Burnet and Lorenzo de Zavala to New York City and put them in touch with a financier who formed the Galveston Bay and Texas Land Company to purchase their grants. Burnet, a small-minded and miserly man, was not satisfied with the deal. Even though he and de Zavala were able to unload the grants before they defaulted, he inexplicably held Houston responsible for his loss, and carried a grudge that festered for the rest of his life.

Arrogant and vindictive by nature, Burnet grew obsessive in his hatred of Sam Houston. He took political differences and military disagreements as personal affronts, and spent his life attempting to get even with Houston for offenses real and imagined. In later years, on at least two occasions, he challenged Houston to a duel. Houston laughed off the invitations, saying a duel would serve no useful purpose—the people of Texas were already fed up with both of them.

Mirabeau Lamar had been a friend of James Fannin back in Georgia and visited Fannin at Velasco during his first trip to Texas. Fannin, who was jealous of Houston, might have colored Lamar's view of the Commander-in-Chief. Lamar may have felt Houston was partially to blame for the disaster which befell the indecisive Fannin and his troops.

Burnet was elected provisional governor by a narrow margin and clashed with Houston at Washington-on-the-Brazos. Houston wanted the government to remain in that area to help stabilize the colonies and avoid a feared panic if they retreated. When Burnet insisted upon relocation to Harrisburg, the move helped trigger the "Runaway Scrape," and validated Houston's position. The relationship between the two leaders was based upon mutual mistrust and grew worse with time.

Burnet did not understand the plight of the army, and continually ordered Houston to stand and fight. Lamar, Sidney Sherman, and John Wharton openly criticized and second-guessed Houston on the march during the retreat and around the campfires preceding the Battle of San Jacinto. It is a tribute to Houston's character, or perhaps his desperation, that on the eve of the battle he appointed Lamar head of the cavalry.

Sidney Sherman, recently arrived in Texas leading Sherman's Newport Volunteers, was a friend of Burnet's brother back in Cincinnati. No doubt he agreed with Burnet's opposition to Houston--especially after Houston stripped him of his cavalry and dressed him down for foolhardy actions on the eve of the San Jacinto battle.

Hugh McLeod, the West Point graduate who started to Texas to deliver the Troutman Flag, was delayed in Louisiana while his resignation from the US Army was processed. This delay saved his life, for he would have been with the Georgia Volunteers and Colonel Fannin at Goliad. He missed the battle at San Jacinto because he was working to fortify and defend Nacogdoches during the Runaway Scrape, but joined Burnet and Lamar in Galveston soon after the battle. Lamar made a place for him in the army and McLeod became a serious, dedicated and lifelong enemy of Sam Houston.

Robert Potter, whose entire naval experience consisted of three years as a teenage midshipman in the U.S. Navy, violently disagreed with Houston during the convention at Washington-on-the-Brazos. Potter wanted to provide funds to finance a Texas Navy, and Houston felt, with the convention so strapped for cash, a navy would drain resources needed by the army. Houston believed this war would be fought on land and a navy would serve no useful purpose. It was Houston's nature to aggressively attack any political opposition, and Potter's nature to take political differences personally.

It is probable that Potter and Houston also knew each other from the U.S. Congress, even though their terms did not overlap. Houston served in the U.S. House from 1823 to 1827 and Potter served there from 1829 until 1831. Houston returned to Washington as a representative of the Cherokee Indian Nation in 1830, while Potter was serving. Both men were southerners and Jacksonian Democrats, but Houston's argument with Jackson over the treatment of the Indians was well known. His return to the capital city created quite a stir. Houston dressed in outlandish Indian garb and called attention to abuses of the Native Americans that Congress would much rather ignore.

Most likely, Houston was aware of the circumstances which drove Robert Potter to Texas. Potter was convicted of surgical castration of two men, one a preacher and the other a teenager, both suspected of sleeping with Potter's wife. His conviction carried a light sentence, but a messy divorce, public distaste, and general disfavor forced him to move to Texas. He was thrown out of office in the Carolina legislature for allegedly cheating at cards. The details were not generally known, and Potter, with good reason, did his best to hide his past.

Despite Houston's opposition, three ships were donated and others captured or confiscated, and the Texas Navy was formed. Burnet immediately appointed his friend Potter Secretary of the Navy. After the battle at San Jacinto, the wounded Houston used most of the money in the captured Mexican war chest to pay his troops, which infuriated Burnet. The provisional government had planned to use the money and Houston disobeyed Burnet's orders. Houston took no money for himself, but for unknown reasons, donated $3,000.00 to the Texas Navy. It is possible he considered that payment for passage to New Orleans.

David Burnet showed his rancor by ordering that no vessel of the Texas Navy be used to transport General Houston to New Orleans, using the excuse that all navy ships were needed to protect Galveston in the event a Mexican force attacked the island. Robert Potter, Secretary of the Navy and newly appointed Commandant of the Port of Galveston, enforced the order. Both men hoped the delay in treatment would cost Houston his life.

The problem was solved when the captain of the *Yellowstone,* the riverboat Houston used to ferry his troops across the Brazos River, was ordered to New Orleans for supplies. He refused to sail without Houston onboard. The army doctor caring for Houston accompanied him and was stripped of his commission for defying Burnet's orders. Admiral Potter managed to transfer the entire group to the *Flora,* an old, dirty and slow-moving schooner. Houston made it to New Orleans, after an unnecessarily long and painful journey. As the schooner docked, Houston, feverish, frail, and sick, but ever the showman, propped himself upright against the rail and waved as the crowd along the river cheered. Somewhere in the crowd, seventeen-year-old Margaret Lea and her staunch Baptist parents cheered the famous general.

That was Margaret's first glimpse of Sam Houston. In a few years, Margaret would marry the general, and bear him eight children.

With proper medical facilities and care, the hero of San Jacinto recovered, but walked with a cane for the rest of his life.

Meanwhile, Burnet moved the seat of government to Velasco, where he and Santa Anna drafted documents to legalize the agreements verbally worked out with Houston. In a public document, Santa Anna acknowledged his defeat and the existence of the Republic of Texas. In a private treaty, he vowed to work for Mexican recognition of the new republic and set the border at the Rio Bravo. (Rio Grande.) Mexico immediately disavowed any treaty made by Santa Anna, a prisoner of war, and refused to recognize the Republic of Texas.

International law sided with the Mexican view, and Mexico took the position that it had simply lost a battle in an ongoing war. The central government planned to invade Texas and put down the rebellion, regardless of the consequences to their captured emperor. Through diplomatic channels, Mexico promised war if the United States tried to annex Texas, or otherwise interfere with Mexico's "internal problems." American President Andrew Jackson, with internal problems of his own, relaxed his efforts to annex Texas. He simply could not afford a war with Mexico, and "free" states in the union strongly opposed the annexation of Texas, or any other "slave" state.

With a tenuous hold on freedom, the fragile Republic of Texas set about to maintain its independence, protect its territory, and govern its citizens. Burnet operated the provisional government from Velasco (present day Freeport) and busied himself writing thank-you notes and making plans for the election of a permanent government. He also worked diligently on a book exposing Sam Houston as a liar, thief, and charlatan. The book project consumed most of Burnet's remaining years but was never finished.

On September 5, 1836, Sam Houston was elected the first president of the Republic of Texas with over seventy-nine percent of the vote, defeating

Stephen F. Austin, who was ill, and Henry Smith, the former convention president who was impeached but refused to leave office and vowed to "shoot any son-of-a-bitch that tries" to oust him.

Mirabeau B. Lamar, the fiery Georgian and Burnet man, was elected vice president. Burnet resigned early and allowed Houston and Lamar to take office in October of 1836, instead of waiting until December as the constitution dictated. Burnet did not resign out of the goodness of his heart. Texas had no money, no system of taxation to get any money, a large, cash-hungry army, Indian problems, and the constant threat of Mexican invasion. Burnet preferred to resign and second-guess Houston rather than deal with the problems himself.

The Texas constitution, unwieldy at best, set the first president's term at two years. Then, to prevent the formation of political dynasties, all future chief executives were allowed one three-year term. No Texas president was allowed consecutive terms in office. An incumbent was not allowed to run for the office, so being president of Texas more than one term was an "iffy" proposition at best. Houston would be the only politician to manage it.

During his first term as President of the Republic, Houston set about to cut costs, generate funds, establish a stable government, and gain a lasting peace with the Indians. Secondary, but still important goals included establishing permanent exterior borders and admission into the United States. Houston managed to insert friends into most cabinet posts, but still had powerful enemies in the administration and the military.

Even though Mirabeau B. Lamar was elected vice president, he was no ally of Houston. They had become bitter enemies, disagreeing on the treatment of the Indians, the issue of statehood, the slavery question, even the location of the capital. Houston had nothing for the vice president to do, no faith in his ability, and no use for his opinions. Lamar actively disliked Houston and mistrusted his motives. During his two-year term as vice president, Lamar travelled, took time off, and wrote poetry. Houston ran the government as he pleased, without the help of the vice president.

## CHAPTER TEN
# Mirabeau B. Lamar as President of the Republic

Mirabeau B. Lamar

Hugh McLeod led a charmed life. He grew up in Georgia and graduated from West Point at age twenty-one in 1835. He struggled a bit academically, but he was a polished public speaker, amiable, jolly, and well-liked. No one mentioned that he was last in his class at the Military Academy. After the red-headed and freckled McLeod delivered a fiery and persuasive speech at a Texas rally, Johanna Troutman chose him to carry her Lone Star flag to Texas with the Georgia volunteers.

Because he was so enamored with the Texas cause and the outlook for a career in the U.S. Army appeared bleak, the stocky young officer decided to resign his commission as a second lieutenant and cast his lot with the Georgia boys going to Texas. His resignation paperwork was delayed, so he entrusted the Troutman flag to Col. William Wood, and reported to Fort Jessup, Louisiana, for mustering out. That paperwork snafu saved his life. The entire Georgia battalion, including Col. Wood, was marched out and shot at Goliad. They were under the command of another Georgia boy, the former slave trader and inept commander, Col. James Fannin.

Following his release from the U. S. Army, McLeod hurried to join Houston's forces at San Jacinto, but arrived after the battle and proceeded to Galveston. There he joined his boyhood idol, Mirabeau Lamar, and the interim governor of Texas, David Burnet. Lamar, Secretary of War in the temporary government, found a place in the Texas army for young McLeod. Eight days after the Battle of San Jacinto, the twenty-two-year-old second lieutenant, whose only military experience involved almost flunking out at West Point and serving about six months in a peacetime army, was appointed a major and assigned to the command staff of the Texas Army.

McLeod looked on Lamar with blind hero worship, and Lamar, flattered, looked out for the young man. When Lamar became president of the Republic in December of 1838, the twenty-four-year-old McLeod was Adjutant General of the Texas Army. Lamar's attitude toward Native Americans was diametrically opposed to that of Sam Houston, and the new president immediately set about to remove all Indians from the republic. McLeod helped evict the peaceful Caddos and Kickapoos, and Lamar sent him to meet with the Cherokees in 1839.

Lamar decided to reclaim the land Houston had promised to deed the Cherokees for their help in the Texas Revolution. In July of 1839, he sent

McLeod and others to council with the Indians, who were peacefully farming their land in east Texas, north of Nacogdoches. The interested "others" included Lamar's vice president, David Burnet. That same land had been ceded to him by a Mexican Land Grant, he sold it to the Galveston Bay and Texas Land Company, Houston gave it to the Cherokees, and Burnet hoped for an opportunity to get it back.

After three days of peaceful talks, the Texans lost patience and attacked. The two-day Battle of the Neches resulted in the death of Houston's old friend, Chief "Bowl." Hugh McLeod was slightly wounded in the battle and the Cherokee were driven across the Red River into what was then Arkansas Territory. McLeod took Bowl's distinctive hat as a sarcastic gift for Houston.

President Lamar, pleased that the "Cherokee Problem" was resolved, turned his attention to the "Comanche Problem," a much more complicated and dangerous situation. Raiding parties of Comanche swooped in from the Llano Estacado, tortured, raped, and killed settlers, kidnapped children, burned settlements, and stole horses with impunity. After the raids, the Comanche disappeared back into the trackless high plains, where no white man would go.

An opportunity to resolve the problem presented itself in January of 1840, when a band of Comanche sent delegates to San Antonio to try and arrange peace with the whites. After long years of war, an especially hard winter, and a deadly epidemic of smallpox, this small group felt that peace might be a better course of action. They arranged for a council to be held in March.

The leaders of the Republic of Texas did not understand the Comanche. The Comanche Nation existed as a group of individual tribes, living, hunting, raiding, moving, and dying on a piecemeal basis, with no central control or government. The nation was made up of at least twelve distinct tribes, broken into as many as thirty-five separate bands. Each band chose its own leaders, made its own rules, lived where it wished, and did as it pleased. They warred with everyone except other Comanche. Sam Houston may have understood all this, but his advice was not welcome in Lamar's administration. Because of their many differences, the two leaders could not stand each other.

Some eight or ten bands of Comanche were involved in the peace initiative, but dozens of bands refused to hold council with the dishonest Anglos. Council was a sacred thing to the Comanche and not to be entered into lightly. Delegates from the starving groups truthfully told the powers in San Antonio that all the prisoners they held would be released, borders would be established and honored, and none of their band would break the truce. They did not, and could not, speak for the other tribes, but the elated Texans thought this meant the entire Comanche Nation would lay down its arms, release hostages, and go back to peaceful existence out on the high plains, away from settled areas. The Texans believed President Lamar's "show no mercy" policy with the Indians was working.

Two prominent chiefs of the Comanche, Peta Nocona of the Noconas and Buffalo Hump of the Penatakas, refused to council with the whites and refused to release any hostages. Peta Nocona married a captive, Cynthia Ann Parker. They may have been married at that time—she would have been fourteen and had been with his tribe for over four years. Their son, Quanah Parker, born over five years later, became one of the most famous chiefs of the Comanche. Buffalo Hump was especially vocal in his opposition to the meeting and predicted dire consequences. Both these respected chiefs were well acquainted with the treachery of the whites, and felt it was foolhardy to attempt any dealings with them.

In March of 1840, President Mirabeau Lamar sent his new Inspector General of the Texas Army, twenty-six-year-old Lt. Col. Hugh McLeod, to San Antonio. McLeod was part of a three-man team sent to negotiate the terms of a peace treaty and the return of hostages with the Comanche Nation. Lamar knew McLeod was not the shiniest penny in the bank, but felt the impatient young colonel was bright enough to make a reasonable deal with a bunch of hungry Indians. He also knew that if the talks stalled, the impetuous McLeod was likely to fight, which was not, in Lamar's opinion, all bad.

On the morning of March 19, 1840, sixty-five Comanche, including twelve chiefs, arrived dressed in their finest ceremonial regalia. The chiefs were accompanied for this festive occasion by their squaws and children. The meeting was held in the council house adjacent to the jail where present-day Market Street and Delarosa meet the Main Plaza in downtown San Antonio. The twelve chiefs sat on the floor, as was their custom, and the Texans sat in chairs on an elevated platform facing and looking down on the Indians, a not surprising white man tactic. The other Comanche, mostly women and children, remained outside, in the back of the building. Two companies of Texas infantry assembled in front of the building to provide "security."

The Comanche brought only one white hostage, sixteen-year-old Matilda Lockhart, and several Mexican children of little interest to the Texans. Miss Lockhart informed the group that she had seen fifteen captives in the main Indian camp, and she believed the Indians would bring them in, one at a time, after the ransom for her was paid. From her observations, she thought the Indians wanted to establish a high value for the hostages before they released any of them.

When asked about hostages, Chief Muguara, spokesman for the Comanche, said that he was sure they would all be released, but only after a large ransom was paid for each. When he finished, he asked, "How do you like that answer?"

Whether Muguara was being sarcastic or was seriously seeking an opinion, the Texans did not like that answer. They were furious. In their minds, the Comanche had reneged on their promise to free the captives. Lamar, always expecting treachery from the Indians, had prepared for such an eventuality. If the Indians failed to produce the captives, the negotiating team had been instructed to imprison the chiefs and hold them to trade for the hostages. The interpreter was instructed to inform the chiefs that they were under arrest.

Outside, one of the rifle companies moved around the building to watch the Comanche at the back of the structure. The other group crowded around the open doors and windows of the council house, to hear the exchanges as they grew more heated. The glare of the bright sunshine made it difficult to see into the dark interior of the building.

The translator refused to tell the Indians they were under arrest, knowing there would be a violent reaction. Lt. Col. Fisher, head of the Texas council team, ordered him to translate the message. The nervous interpreter edged toward the door, delivered the message, and lunged outside as the Comanche leapt to their feet, slashing with razor-sharp knives at everyone within reach, and pushing for the door. One of the officers may have given the order, it may have been pre-arranged, or the soldiers may have acted spontaneously, but in any case, the riflemen at the doors and windows fired point blank into the building, hoping to hit Indians.

The braves, squaws and children outside, hearing the commotion, began to shoot arrows at everyone on the street, while the Texan soldiers began to fire at the Indians. According to the soldiers, they aimed for the braves and did not shoot at women and children.

The "battle" lasted only a few minutes. Lt. Col. McLeod's official report, issued the next day, accounted for the sixty-five Indians as follows: Thirty-five dead—thirty adult males, including all twelve of the chiefs, three women and two children. Twenty-seven women and children and two old men were captured and held at Mission San Jose. One renegade Mexican who came in with the Comanche, slipped away in the confusion.

The Texans lost seven dead and ten wounded. Of the seventeen Texas casualties, perhaps a few were harmed by Indians. Most were killed or wounded by friendly fire.

The Texans, once again demonstrating their ignorance of the Comanche, decided to release one of the women hostages, give her a good horse and provisions, and send her to the Llano Estacado with an ultimatum for the tribe. The Texans would release the remaining women and children and two old men when the Comanche brought in the fifteen hostages Matilda Lockhart had seen. A two-week truce would be allowed to give the tribes time to deliver the hostages.

The Comanche were mourning the loss of the twelve chiefs and other members of their tribe when the squaw delivered the message from the Texans. Immediately, they began to torture the remaining captives in some of the cruelest, slowest, and most painful methods ever devised. Matilda Lockhart's six-year-old sister was reportedly roasted alive over an open fire. All the hostages were dead within a short time. Of the original fifteen, three hostages had been adopted by Comanche families and were not harmed as they were considered members of the tribe. The Comanche made no distinction between native-born and adopted members of the tribe—all were considered Comanche and treated equally.

Hugh McLeod and Lt. Col. Fisher made their way back to the primitive new capital at Austin to report to President Lamar. The citizens of San Antonio worried about Comanche retaliation, but within a few weeks, things returned to normal.

In most descriptions of this event, Matilda Lockhart, who had spent eighteen months in captivity, is said to have been horribly disfigured from abuse by her captors. Her slender young body was scarred from months of torture with hot coals, rawhide whips and knives. Beatings with heavy clubs left evidence of broken bones. Supposedly, her nose was entirely gone, burned off with hot coals, which left a grotesque hole in the center of her face. Her appearance reportedly so enraged the Texans that they could not help but take revenge on the twelve chiefs.

Matilda is mentioned in Lt. Col. McLeod's report of the incident, written the day after the battle. McLeod acknowledged her obvious intelligence but said nothing about any sign of abuse. It was common knowledge that she had been repeatedly raped, as were all female captives, but no contemporary report says anything about scars, burns, or other evidence of torture. The newspaper reporters described everything about the "battle" in great detail, but no mention was made of a sixteen-year-old girl with a missing nose. Matilda's sister-in-law, in a letter to her mother, reported on Matilda's condition, but mentioned no disfigurement.

The first mention of abuse occurred more than fifty years later. In 1890, Mary Maverick wrote that Matilda had been abused, was terribly scarred, and her nose was badly burned. Texas writers and the press quickly jumped on the story and expanded it. At the time, Texas' image was suffering at the hands of the Victorian press, both on the East Coast and abroad. A tortured, abused, and disfigured sixteen-year-old girl may have helped give the Texans an excuse for their brutal treatment of the Comanche.

Out on the Llano Estacado, Chief Pochanaquarhip, known to the Anglos as Buffalo Hump, was planning reprisal. The sacred council laws had been violated. The hated whites had murdered chiefs under a flag of truce. Pochanaquarhip was aroused. He was not one to go soft when faced with adversity. He quietly planned and gathered braves, supplies, and horses for his revenge. The Texans were well advised to worry—Pochanaquarhip in the Penataka dialect means "an erection that won't go down." Buffalo Hump was destined to become a legend in his own time.

Considering the year—1840—and the Puritan ethics of America and Texas at that time, it is not a mystery that Pochanaquarhip, was mis-translated by the press. After all, many women could read, and some of them would surely read about that Comanche's peculiar condition. In the eyes of the men who reported the news, it was better that some things not be shared with women folk, especially vulgar stories about Indian chiefs. So far as anyone knew, no white man suffered from such an affliction, and how it would be looked upon among the female population was a cause for concern. What if women liked the idea? A savage, walking around with a petrified member, was just better not talked about in mixed company.

The media, not much changed in almost 180 years, decided to protect the public. They chose to ignore the facts, ignore the Comanche language, and ignore the perpetual woody. For noble reasons based upon the protection of its readers, the press called the chief "Buffalo Hump."

Buffalo Hump was described by a German scientist, Ferdinand Roemer, in 1847 as follows: "The pure unadulterated picture of a North American Indian, who, unlike the rest of his tribe, scorned every form of European dress. His body naked, a buffalo robe around his loins, brass rings on his arms, a string of beads around his neck, and with his long, coarse black hair hanging down, he sat there with the serious facial expression of a North American Indian which seems to be apathetic to the European. He attracted our special attention because he had distinguished himself through great daring and bravery in expeditions against the Texas frontier which he had engaged in times past."

The description of a Comanche War Chief is likely to be more nearly accurate when it comes from a disinterested third party, such as a European scientist. It was difficult for a Texan to be objective when describing a cruel and vicious enemy. Dr. Roemer noted that Buffalo Hump shunned all type of European dress. This must have included belts and suspenders, which were unnecessary for him. To protect his loins from exposure, Pochanaquarhip had that buffalo robe when he walked around. As the German scientist inferred, the only thing that hung down was the chief's coarse black hair and a string of beads around his neck.

Beginning immediately after the Council House Fight, Buffalo Hump travelled among the Comanche tribes, telling of the murder of their brothers during council under the flag of truce, and asking the tribes to join him in a quest for revenge. Being well-respected and eloquent, he had no trouble getting volunteers and, by midsummer, was ready to move against the hated Anglos.

In early August, over 500 mounted warriors, accompanied by at least that many squaws and children, moved out of the Llano Estacado and followed the Guadalupe River Valley from the vicinity of present-day Kerrville into the heart of the Republic of Texas. Pochanaquarhip brought squaws and young people to do the work—a Comanche brave could not be expected to gather firewood, set up camp, or cook meals.

The Indians purposely avoided Waterloo (Austin) and San Antonio. It was foolish to attack cities that had army garrisons and newly formed Texas Ranger Companies for protection. Buffalo Hump wanted to strike at the soft underbelly of the Republic. His scouts had been busy for weeks, gathering information and choosing routes. Some reports insist that agents from Mexico aided in the planning. He eased his warriors around Gonzales and moved toward Victoria.

Moving over a thousand Indians through 1840 Texas without being discovered was not possible. A troop of fifteen Rangers struck the trail of the Comanche and followed, but there were too many Indians to attack. The Rangers stayed close and sent out scouts to warn the citizens and gather help. The warnings didn't get to Victoria in time.

On August 6, 1840, the citizens of Victoria were surprised when they looked across Spring Creek and 600 mounted Comanche warriors stared back at them. The Comanche, having already killed several slaves and farmers working in the nearby fields, charged into town. Townspeople barricaded themselves inside their homes and fired at the Indians from upstairs windows. Buffalo Hump's braves bolted back and forth in the streets, setting fires and killing anyone they caught outside. Never willing to attack a fortified position, the Comanche soon tired of the sport and withdrew, taking 1,500 horses with them.

After noon on August 7, the Comanche gathered their spoils and headed toward Linnville, at that time the second largest port in Texas. They contented themselves by killing a few isolated farm workers and some freight haulers, then spent the night camped on what is now called Placedo Creek, about twelve miles from Linnville. Early on August 8, they went into town.

Buffalo Hump's scouts and Mexican "guides" had done a good job. The town of Linville was the main port where goods from New Orleans and points east were off-loaded to be freighted overland to San Antonio and Austin. At the time of the raid, over $300,000.00 worth of merchandise bound for market was stored in the warehouses of Linnville. The people of Linnville heard that the Indians were coming but refused to believe it. Even when Comanche appeared on the outskirts of town, they were thought to be Mexican horse traders.

Comanche surrounded the town and began to kill people and plunder warehouses. The local citizens fled to the sea and stayed out of range on small boats while they watched their homes burn. Indians raided the storage buildings, delighted with their discoveries. Squaws and children squealed with pleasure as they gathered goods and tied them on pack mules. A storehouse of dry goods bound for a San Antonio merchant was discovered and emptied, along with a safe full of silver bullion. Braves in top hats, carrying parasols, smoking cigars and drinking whiskey, laughed and played like school boys as they rode up and down the streets dragging feather mattresses and bolts of brightly colored cloth behind their ponies.

All the pack mules in town were loaded with merchandise, all the horses and mules were gathered into one herd, and all other livestock was penned and slaughtered. When the braves emptied a warehouse, they torched it. The residents of Linnville watched impotently as their city was systematically sacked and burned.

When the Indians crossed the bayou to camp for the night, nothing of value remained. Fields around town appeared to be covered with new fallen snow, but it was white feathers from mattresses found in the warehouses, slit open, and dragged for sport. Townspeople returned to shore after the Indians left. During the next few months, the weary citizens relocated to Port Lavaca, three-and-a-half miles south, and Linnville ceased to exist.

Buffalo Hump and his braves moved out, slowed by 3,000 horses and dozens of unmanageable pack mules loaded with plunder. Texas Rangers gathered, followed, and waited for an opportunity to attack.

Comanche, when raiding, ordinarily move in quickly, attack, and move out quickly. Usually, they are content to kill a few settlers, burn a homestead or two, steal some horses, and hurry back to the safety of the high plains. Many times, raids are planned to coincide with the full moon, so the raiders can come and go at night, riding full speed across the prairie by the light of what is still known in Texas as a "Comanche Moon."

The Great Linnville Raid, as it came to be known, was different. It was the largest raid by any group of Indians on a populated city in the history of the United States—Texas was not technically a part of the U.S. at the time but would become so in a bit more than five years. Buffalo Hump was forced to surrender the tribe's mobility because of the sheer size of his war party. He did not expect organized resistance from the Texans, even the Rangers. He knew that a small group of Rangers would be foolish to attack so many Indians. He also felt that his group would move faster than it did.

Military-style discipline, never strong among the Comanche, broke down completely after the Linnville raid. The Comanche were herding 3,000 stolen horses, leading dozens of stubborn, heavily laden pack mules, and carrying bedding, food, and cooking supplies for over a thousand people. Braves, some still wearing top hats and carrying parasols, rode horses, while the squaws and children walked. They were travelling two or three abreast and the column stretched out for several miles. By August 12, they had covered less than a hundred twenty miles, and the Rangers struck.

John Coffee Hays, just starting a career that would make him a legendary Texas Ranger, fought with a company of Rangers headed by Edward Burleson. Hays' friend from Tennessee, Ben McCulloch, was chief scout and later took command of a unit. They were joined by some militia men from nearby communities, and volunteers from central and east Texas, all together less than two hundred men. Big Foot Wallace, who lived nearby, joined the Rangers for this battle, perhaps his first with the Comanche. The Texans engaged the tail end of Buffalo Hump's column as it crossed Plum Creek, just east of present-day Lockhart. A running gun battle ensued, with the Texans charging and firing at anything that resembled a Comanche. The squaws and children abandoned their pack animals and hurried forward for protection.

Some of the Texans discovered a chest of silver on one of the mules and they became distracted. The Indians continued to run away, and the Texans concentrated on recovering the mules and investigating their cargo. The attack disintegrated into a treasure hunt, and the Indians moved ahead toward the high plains and safety. A few captives were rescued, some merchandise was recovered, and the silver bullion was distributed among the attackers.

The Texas newspapers, hungry for good news, proclaimed a great victory. According to the militia members, some eighty Indians were killed, but only twelve Comanche bodies were found.

Pochanaquarhip, riding bareback at the front of the column, was little disturbed by the rangers' attack. He led his people back to the Llano Estacado and continued to lead the tribe, in war and in peace, for many years.

When Sam Houston regained the Texas Presidency, he and Buffalo Hump signed a treaty in 1844 that guaranteed peace. If the Anglo settlers stayed off the Edwards Plateau, the Penetakas would stay out of central Texas. Houston and the Republic of Texas legislature were sincere, as was Buffalo Hump, but unfortunately, the Texas Senate neglected to include the agreed-upon boundaries in the final version, angering the Indians. Anglo settlers moving west would not be stopped at the Edwards Plateau, and within two years the treaty proved worthless. The Penetakas went back to raiding.

In March of 1847, Buffalo Hump, Old Owl, and Santa Anna (also called Santana) negotiated a treaty with John Meusebach and the German settlers in the Fisher-Miller Land Grant, just north of present day Fredericksburg. The Comanche trusted Meusebach and called him "El Sol Colorado" (The Red Sun) for his flaming red hair and beard. When Buffalo Hump asked why he should trust the white colonists, Meusebach replied that the Germans were a different tribe. Satisfied, Buffalo Hump went ahead with the treaty.

The treaty allowed white settlers to go unharmed into the Penetaka lands, and the Comanche to freely visit and trade in the white settlements. Both sides were to report any criminal activity and were responsible for punishing their lawbreakers. White surveyors would be allowed into the Penetaka lands and the Indians would be paid at least a $1000.00 for this privilege. The agreement opened almost 4,000,000 acres to colonization and may be the only treaty with the Indians that was never broken by either side.

In 1856, Buffalo Hump led his tribe, on the brink of starvation, to a new reservation on the Brazos River, set up by the US Government and supervised by the Indian Agent, Robert Neighbors. Despite Neighbors' protection, the tribe was mistreated, underfed, and blamed for every offense that occurred anywhere near the reservation. Finally, in desperation, Buffalo Hump led his people back out onto the Llano Estacado, where they were eventually captured by the U.S. Army and forced to move into Indian Territory.

On the reservation in Oklahoma, Pochanaquarhip asked for a small plot of land and some tools, so he could teach his people to farm. He died in 1870, farming that plot of land and insisting that his people get an education if they planned to succeed in the white man's world.

The Battle of Plum Creek was the first meeting of Captain Jack Hays and Buffalo Hump. Hays successfully fought the Penetaka for many years, engaging bands led by Buffalo Hump or one of his war chiefs. The fact that both men stayed alive is a tribute to their abilities.

"Cap'n Yack" was held in high regard by all Indians. Chief Flacco, a Lipan-Apache guide, called him, "Bravo too much." Flacco said, "Me and Red Wing are brave--not afraid to go to hell together. Cap'n Yack more brave--not afraid to go to hell by himself."

Captain Jack Hays left the Rangers and moved to California in 1850 and became the sheriff of San Francisco. When his first son was born, the Hays family received a gift from Buffalo Hump—a tiny golden spoon, engraved "Buffalo Hump, Jr."

After the Battle of Plum Creek, in August of 1840, Mirabeau Lamar, then current President of Texas, still faced problems. He had been elected by an overwhelming majority of the votes, largely because both his opponents committed suicide before the election. His policies differed greatly from those of Sam Houston, who preceded him and would follow him as president of the republic.

Unlike Houston, Lamar mistrusted all Indians and felt that they should be forced out of Texas by whatever means available, up to and including extermination. Houston was against slavery and wanted Texas to become a state of the Union. Lamar wanted to continue slavery and did not want to be annexed by the United States—he wanted to build a nation that stretched to the Pacific Ocean and was recognized as a world power. Lamar, with some justification, felt that Texas, with all its land and its vast potential, would be foolish to become subservient to any other country.

Lamar wanted immediate recognition of the Republic of Texas by France, England, and other world powers, which he hoped would enable the republic to borrow money from world banking institutions. Texas was dead broke, unable to collect taxes and, even after formal recognition by Britain and France, unable to borrow. During Lamar's three year tenure, the republic generated a bit over one million in revenue, and spent almost five million.

To distract the public from these problems and as a first step toward expanding the empire to the Pacific, Lamar started a campaign to annex New Mexico, at least that part east of the Rio Grande, which Texas had claimed since San Jacinto. The trade along the Santa Fe Trail would go a long way toward alleviating Texas' financial situation and Lamar was convinced that the people of New Mexico were ready to join Texas and split from the despotic rule of Santa Anna, who had returned to power in Mexico. Lamar believed when he announced Texas was ready to assimilate New Mexico, the New Mexican people would jump at the chance to become Texans.

Lamar tried to get support, financial and otherwise, from the Texas Congress for his plan to send a "trade mission" to New Mexico. The legislature would have nothing to do with the idea, so Lamar, on his own, appropriated $89,000.00 to finance the mission. No doubt he exceeded his authority and went against the constitution, but he managed to get the expedition organized and funded. He chose his young friend, Hugh McLeod, now a 27-year-old brigadier general, to lead the military component of the expedition.

McLeod was lap-dog loyal to Lamar. He was red-headed, freckle-faced, a bit rotund and quite a jolly fellow. A lot of fun at parties. He was also dumb as a post. There was a reason he was last in his class at West Point.

The Santa Fe Expedition consisted of 21 ox-drawn wagons carrying about $200,000.00 in merchandise, several businessmen, four civil commissioners, one newspaper editor, five companies of infantry, and one artillery company. Including the soldiers, the expedition totaled 321 men. General McLeod was in command of the military forces, which were there to lead and protect the expedition, not for any aggression against New Mexico.

With Mexican guides, eighty head of beef cattle for food, provisions for ninety days and high hopes, the wagon train left Brushy Creek, in the vicinity of present-day Round Rock, on June 19, 1841. The guides must have been dandies. Six weeks later, heading for Santa Fe, they were closer to Oklahoma City. They made it to the vicinity of present-day Wichita Falls, and mistook the Wichita River for the Red River. After following the Wichita for twelve days, McLeod realized their mistake, tongue-lashed the scouts and sent them north to hunt for the Red River. The guides deserted.

McLeod eventually found the Red River and followed it west. His command was in trouble—supplies were running low, there was little food, and no one knew how far it was to Santa Fe. Progress was slower than anticipated, and Indians had stolen some of their horses and all of the beef cattle. When the little group found the Llano Estacado, McLeod split them up and sent a patrol west on horseback to find a route to the trading villages of New Mexico, while he and his group camped in the valley. They couldn't find a place to climb the Caprock with twenty-one wagons.

The men in both groups were starving. According to the reporter Kendall, they ate snakes, prairie dogs, toads, and anything else they could catch, and they didn't cook it long. Indians had stolen their cattle and most of their horses. They lost six soldiers fighting Comanche, and morale was non-existent.

On September 12, the advance patrol sent back a guide to lead McLeod and the wagons into New Mexico, where the Texans expected a hero's welcome. In the meantime, the Mexican guides who deserted made it to Taos and told of the expedition headed toward New Mexico. The Mexican authorities were less than pleased.

When Governor Manuel Armijo heard of the expedition, he considered it an armed invasion. He brought 1500 troops to San Miguel and captured the advance party on September 17th, then surrounded and captured McLeod's main force near Tucumcari on October 5th. Captain William G. Lewis, who spoke Spanish, convinced both Texas parties to surrender, which may not have been a difficult task. The troops were thirsty, hungry, tired, and unwilling to fight a much larger force. Captain Lewis lied when he assured them that the Mexicans would treat them kindly and send them back to Texas with full bellies. Whether or not he knowingly lied is a matter for debate.

Surrender to a friendly army may have appeared to be a good option to the starving troops, but Armijo's army was not friendly.

The Texan captives were bound and listened as the Mexican officers debated their fate. Governor Armijo was determined to execute all the prisoners, the accepted Mexican way of dealing with revolutionaries. When the officers' vote was taken, the prisoners were spared by one vote. Early the next morning, they were bound together by twos and started a march to Santa Fe, then El Paso, on to Mexico City and finally to Vera Cruz and Perote Prison, where they arrived in December of 1841. Many died during the march from Santa Fe to El Paso, but the sadistic commander (an officer named Salazar) was replaced by a more lenient individual in El Paso and the rest of the 1200-mile march was less strenuous. Most of the prisoners were released in April of 1842, after diplomatic pressure from the United States Ambassador, Waddy Thompson.

Governor Armijo confiscated all the trade merchandise for his own use and continued to rule New Mexico with an iron fist. He was known to be corrupt—stories persist that he started his fortune by stealing sheep from his employer and selling them back. In 1846, he was prosecuted for treason and cowardice during the Mexican/American war but was acquitted.

Captain William G. Lewis was released by Armijo and rewarded with his choice of items from the Texan merchandise wagons. He was widely considered a traitor and was shunned by both Texans and Mexicans for the rest of his life. His intervention resulted in the surrender of all the Texas troops without a shot being fired. He may or may not have been aware of Governor Armijo's plans.

Even though Hugh McLeod was popular with his men and with President Lamar, he was not a good choice to lead the expedition. His choice of guides was obviously flawed, he allowed the beef cattle and over eighty horses to be stolen by Indians, he had no idea where Santa Fe was located or how far it was from Austin. He split his troops and surrendered without a fight. All in all, not unpredictable results from an officer last in his class at West Point.

General McLeod was treated leniently while in prison, because of his rank in the Texas Army and the rumor (which he may have started) that he was a favorite of President Lamar. He returned to Texas and retired from the military when Sam Houston regained the office of president. McLeod, a lawyer, opposed Houston on every major issue for the rest of his life. He died of illness during the Civil War while serving as a Lt. Colonel in the unit that became Hood's Texas Brigade. In honor of his contributions, Hugh McLeod's grave was moved to the Texas State Cemetery in Austin.

Mirabeau B. Lamar was blamed for the failure of the expedition. A "Letter to the Editor" in the Austin newspaper of the time suggested that he be traded for the Texan prisoners in Mexico. His political opposition considered him a much better poet than President. Lamar truly believed that Texas should stretch from the Gulf to the Pacific and worked tirelessly toward that end. He believed strongly in education and introduced legislation that forced each new county to set aside three leagues of state land to finance a school system. His work resulted in the establishment of Texas A&M in 1871 and Texas University in 1876.

George Wilkins Kendall of the *New Orleans Picayune*, who went on the expedition and wrote a book-length report about it, wrote at the time:

*President Lamar's estimation of the views and feelings of the people of Santa Fe and vicinity, was perfectly correct. Not a doubt can exist that they all were, and are (1843), anxious to throw off the oppressive yoke of Armijo, and come under the liberal institutions of Texas; but the Governor found us divided into small parties, broken down by long marches and want of food; discovered too, a traitor amongst us; and, taking advantage of these circumstances, his course was plain and his conquest easy.*

Had this mission proved successful, Lamar would have been heralded a great hero and the history of Texas, Mexico, and the United States would have been drastically altered. Lamar was a dreamer, who, like his rival, Sam Houston, dreamed big dreams. History will remember him for his substantial contributions to education in Texas and no one will blame him for his grandiose dreams. That sorta comes with the territory...

# CHAPTER ELEVEN
# Statehood and Manifest Destiny

The election for president of the Republic of Texas in 1841 was hotly contested. The candidates hated each other, and their personal animosities spilled over into the election rhetoric. David Burnet, the sitting vice president under Lamar was opposed by Sam Houston, the hero of San Jacinto. Houston was the odds-on favorite, but the fanatically religious Burnet staunchly represented the loyal opposition.

Because of a clause in the Texas Constitution, a president could not succeed himself. Houston was running for his second term, which would give him three more years in office. He hoped that would be enough time to right the wrongs done by the Mirabeau Lamar administration.

Politics in Texas at that time was relatively simple. One either agreed with Houston or opposed him. If there was a middle ground, no one chose to occupy it. Houston was for joining the United States and worked tirelessly toward that goal. He was for just treatment of the Indians. He was for a balanced budget and, during his first term, disbanded the expensive military to help achieve that goal. Mirabeau Lamar's group, the loyal opposition, opposed him at every turn. Lamar had big dreams. He wanted Texas to remain a republic and stretch to the Pacific Ocean. To realize that dream, Lamar appropriated money without permission of the legislature to illegally finance the ill-fated Santa Fe Expedition. His Indian policy suggested only two possible solutions—removal or annihilation.

The vindictive Burnet first got involved with Houston in 1830, when Houston was in Washington representing the Cherokee Nation. Burnet and Lorenzo de Zavala obtained an empresario grant from Mexico near Nacogdoches and could not fulfill their obligation to settle the required number of families on the land. In danger of losing the property, they travelled to Washington, met with Houston and asked for his help. He took them to New York and introduced them to a real estate broker. The broker established the Galveston Bay and Texas Land Company and bought their land grants. When forced to sell his share for $12,000, the miserly Burnet felt he had been cheated and blamed Houston.

The Galveston Bay and Texas Land Company became an attractive investment opportunity for New York financiers. A young lady, Jane McManus Storm, did some clerical work there. Her family invested heavily in the company. She and her brother came to Texas in 1834 to buy land. She met Sam Houston, who represented the Galveston Bay and Texas Land Company in Texas, and Stephen Austin, William Barret Travis, Mirabeau Lamar and others actively involved in Texas real estate. She bought script to be redeemed for land in Texas. The Galveston Bay and Texas Land Company claimed over twenty million acres in East Texas by that time.

Jane McManus Storm had married at eighteen, had a son, and divorced by age twenty-four. She was very independent, and chose to be a single parent, a rare situation in that time. Jane spoke seven languages, and became interested in Texas while working as assistant to Aaron Burr, where she translated sales literature for the Galveston Bay and Texas Land Company into German. Mexico had outlawed settlers from America, so European settlers were being solicited.

Burr, a notorious womanizer, had an affair with Jane. His wife of one year filed for divorce, claiming Burr was squandering her fortune on foolish Texas investments and naming Jane McManus Storm as his mistress. Burr was seventy-six and Jane was twenty-six, so being his mistress could not have been a taxing proposition for Jane. Even so, Burr's maid told scandalous stories of sexual activities that she had witnessed between the two.

While in Texas, before the revolution, Jane lived with her family at Matagorda, selling Texas real estate. Because of the rumored affair with Burr, a group of vindictive women, wives of some of Jane's competitors, attempted to exclude her from a public dance, saying she was unfit to mingle with "decent" people. William Cazneau and two of his friends challenged any and all to a duel to defend Jane's honor. The competitors decided it was a small matter, not worth a duel. The beautiful Jane, supremely confident, danced every dance and had a wonderful time.

Jane McManus Storm (widowed) Cazneau

Jane returned to her literary career in New York, working for Horace Greeley. Her younger brother, Robert, stayed in Texas and established a plantation on the east bank of the Trinity River. He joined Houston's army and was one of four scouts chosen by Deef Smith to spy on the movements of Santa Anna. After the scouting duties, he fought with valor at San Jacinto. Texas won her independence, and Robert continued to operate his plantation, work as a surveyor, and trade in real estate. He became one of the largest landholders and one of the richest men in Texas.

During the 1841 presidential campaign, the five-foot-one-inch Burnet referred to Houston as a Half-Breed for his policies toward the Indians. Houston referred to Burnet as "Little Davy," and nicknamed him Wetumpka. When Burnet demanded to know what the Cherokee word meant, Houston said, "Hog Thief." Burnet challenged Houston to a duel, which the six-foot-two-inch Houston refused by saying that he didn't fight downhill.

Houston was ruthless in his treatment of political enemies, but managed to keep his sense of perspective, and his sense of humor. Once, as he passed a political rival on the street, Houston politely greeted the man. The rival said," I don't speak to scoundrels on the street!" Houston replied, "Ah, but I do."

When the votes were counted, Houston won handily, with 7915 votes to Burnet's 3616. Edward Burleson, a competent soldier and Lamar confidant, was elected vice president. The military and other departments were filled with Lamar appointees, and most were like Burleson, no friend of Sam Houston. As would be expected, Houston loaded the cabinet with friends and cronies.

Lamar, notwithstanding his grandiose plans, left Texas in dire condition. With no money in the treasury and deeply in debt, Houston was sworn in as president. Always the showman, he dressed in cheap, homespun clothing for his inauguration address and declared the country broke. He said, "There is not a dollar in the treasury. Not only are we without money, we are without credit…"

Houston immediately slashed expenses at every turn. He cut wages, including his own, eliminated or downsized departments, disbanded the army, and put the navy up for sale. He quietly continued efforts to obtain statehood and, to help with that effort, initiated a friendly stance toward Mexico.

Mirabeau Lamar, during his term as president, moved the capital from Houston to a little mudhole of a town, Waterloo, on the north bank of the Colorado River. Lamar envisioned a new capital city, laid out near the geographic center of Texas, and named for the father of Texas, Stephen F. Austin. He absolutely did not want the capital in any city named for the big drunk, Houston. Waterloo was deep in the heart of Comancheria, a hundred miles north of San Antonio, and almost two hundred miles west of Washington-on-the-Brazos. Houston was determined to move the capital city back to civilization in his namesake city on the banks of Buffalo Bayou.

In 1842, Mexico launched several "invasions" of Texas, sending troops to capture San Antonio on two occasions, and penetrating almost to Austin. This gave Houston evidence to bolster his claim that Austin was too remote to be safe and the capital should be moved back to Houston. He was cautious in his response to the invasions because he feared they were staged by Santa Anna to trick Texas into over-reaction. Striking into Mexico would give the Mexicans an excuse to attack Texas without fear of interference by the United States, England or other countries with ambitions that involved Texas.

In a measured response, Houston sent Alexander Somervall at the head of 500 volunteers, to push the Mexican invaders out of Texas and back across the Rio Grande. Houston insisted that the Texan troops not cross the border unless they were sure that they could win any conflict, and that such an effort would result in a significant gain for Texas. Somervall followed his orders to the letter and ordered his troops to disengage and return to their homes, by way of Gonzales. Less than 200 of his volunteers chose to follow his orders. The others, along with five officers, chose to attack Mier, a Mexican city on the banks of the Rio Grande. They intended to plunder the city and take whatever goods they could find.

The attack was a disaster. The Mexican army had moved into the city overnight, and the Texans were outnumbered ten to one. After a fierce, day-long battle, the Texans surrendered and were taken to a Mexican prison in Matamoros. Santa Anna ordered all the Texans executed, but the Mexican general in charge protested, and the emperor settled for execution of one in ten.

The Mexicans placed 159 white beans and 17 black beans in a jar, blind-folded the prisoners and had them draw one bean each. The 17 who drew black beans were allowed time to write a letter, then taken out, blindfolded, and shot, nine in one group and eight in another. The others were marched to prison in Mexico City. Big Foot Wallace and Samuel Walker both survived this episode and later became legendaryTexas Rangers.

William Alexander Anderson Wallace had moved to Austin in 1840 to help construct the new capital city. He was accused of burglary, but demon-strated that his feet were much smaller than the mocasines of the Indian that committed the crime. Wallace was six feet, two inches tall, and weighed 240 pounds, with almost no fat. His feet were eleven and a half inches long, com-pared to the Indian's fourteen inch footprint. Depending upon which story you believe, Wallace killed the Indian, or he didn't. In any case, the nickname stuck, and Wallace's exploits were celebrated in Texas for the next sixty years.

In December of 1842, Houston, preparing to move the capital, ordered the archives of the republic moved from Austin to Washington on the Brazos. As his troops loaded boxes of paperwork onto wagons, a local boarding house owner, Angelina Eberly, discovered the activity and set about to sound the alarm so the Committee for Safety could prevent the move. Her motive was as old as Austin itself. The citizens of Austin feared that loss of the archives would result in depressed real estate values.

In the street near her boarding house, the city had placed a cannon for protection from the Indians and other frontier dangers. Angelina tugged the cannon around to face the Land Office Building and fired. The resulting explosion made a lot of noise but did little actual damage. It chipped some paint and made the Citizens Committee aware that the archives were being stolen. They rallied, captured the wagons and returned the archives to the Land Office. Austin remained the capital city, and real estate values there continue to fluctuate.

During the three-year Lamar administration, Houston travelled, visited old friends, and made some new ones. His day job as a practicing attorney carried him to Mobile, Alabama, where he sought investors in The Sabine City Company, an organization to develop the city of Sabine Pass. At a garden party, he met a deeply religious twenty-year-old beauty, Margaret Moffette Lea. Despite the 26-year difference in their ages, both were smitten. After exchanging love letters for some months, and over the objections of his friends and many in her family, they married on May 9, 1840.

Margaret was deeply in love with Sam Houston and determined to bring out the best in him. Over the next few years, Houston stopped drinking, cleaned up his language, and was baptized into the Baptist church. Margaret presented Houston with eight children and managed the plantation while Houston was away in Austin or Washington, doing his job as a well-respected politician. A typical year would see Houston come home from Washington, meet his new child, look over the crops, impregnate Margaret, and go back for the next session of congress. They stayed in touch with long, detailed and heartfelt letters.

Back in 1836, when Houston was serving his first term as president, a nineteen-year-old boy, John Coffee Hayes, presented him with a letter of introduction from Andrew Jackson. Houston introduced the boy to a fellow Tennessean, Ben McCulloch and enrolled him in the Texas Rangers. Both Hays and McCulloch worked as surveyors when not on scout for the rangers. The Comanche knew that surveyors always preceded settlers, and they fought to keep surveyors out of their lands. "Jack" Hayes discovered that to survive as a surveyor, he must protect himself and his crew from the Indians. He set about to learn how to effectively fight Indians by learning their ways. It was a matter of survival.

In Jack's first battle with the Comanche, on August 12, 1840, he served under Ben McCulloch and Ed Burleson in the so-called Battle of Plum Creek. The rangers rescued several hostages, recovered some merchandise, killed a few Comanche, and had minimal casualties. The newspapers of the time, hungry for any good news, proclaimed it a great victory for Texas. The rangers lost eleven, including some hostages who were killed by the Indians. They claimed to have killed 75 to 85 Indians, but only 12 Comanche bodies were recovered.

In short order, John Coffee Hays became Capt'n Jack Hays, a captain in the rangers and the most effective Indian fighter in Texas. McCulloch and others who had previously outranked him now voluntarily rode under his command. He taught his troops to fight like the Indians. They slept on the ground, kept dry camps, rode all night and did whatever was necessary to even the odds. Capt'n Jack never directed his troops from a safe position on the sidelines. He led them. He went into battle at the head of his men and met the enemy face to face. No matter the odds, Capt'n Jack entered every battle with the same orders. "We can whip them boys, there's no doubt about that," he'd say. "Follow me."

Captain Jack did not inherit the fear gene. The Comanche, who admired bravery above all else, spread the name "Capt'n Yack" throughout the tribes. Hays had a slight build and stood about 5' 9", but he carried himself with a demeanor that commanded respect.

While other chief executives of American states were busy deciding whether to go to the opera or concert, Sam Houston was trying to pacify the Indians and pull his cash-strapped country out of economic depression. To cut costs, he disbanded the navy and attempted to sell the ships. Looking through the files, he discovered that the navy had ordered 160 funny looking guns, five shot revolvers called Paterson Colts. At the time, Houston was also meeting with young Jack Hays to establish a new ranging company. The new company would patrol the frontier, north and west of San Antonio. The 27-year-old Hays had earned the right to head it up.

When Houston offered the guns to Hays, the ranger was excited. He took a wagon to Galveston and personally picked them up at the navy warehouse. In San Antonio, he issued two Paterson Colts with extra cylinders to each of his rangers. (They were called 'Paterson' because Colt made them in Paterson, New Jersey)

Loading the .36 caliber Paterson involved removing the barrel, then the cylinder. A percussion cap was placed in each of the five cylinders, powder was measured and poured in, then a lead ball was pushed in to seal the cylinder before the pistol could be re-assembled. This took considerable time and required a quiet workplace, so a spare cylinder was also loaded to give each revolver ten shots for battle, before the time-consuming reloading was again necessary.

Captain John Coffee Hays 1857

In early June of 1844, Capt'n Jack and fourteen rangers left San Antonio on scout. Each carried the usual arms plus two Paterson Colt revolvers and two extra loaded cylinders. They explored the hills and canyons for nine days without finding any Indian sign. As they set up camp near present-day Sisterdale, on the banks of Walker Creek, one of the rangers climbed a bee tree. From his perch in the top of the tree, he said, "Jerusalem, Captain! Yonder comes a thousand Indians."

The Indians, in typical battles, had learned to hold back and feint until the rangers fired their rifles, then their pistols. When the second weapon was discharged, while the rangers were busy reloading, the Indians rushed in and shot their arrows from close range with deadly accuracy. This time, as the Indians confidently rushed in, the rangers calmly shot them with the repeating Paterson Colts. Soon, two hundred or so confused Indians were retreating at full speed through the woods with fifteen rangers hot on their trail.

Ben McCulloch, who was second in command of this scout, estimated that fifty Indians were killed or wounded, including their war chief, Yellow Wolf. The rangers lost one killed and five wounded, including Samuel Walker. Walker was gravely wounded, not expected to live, with an Indian lance through his body. He recovered and continued to serve with distinction.

The Paterson Colt, sometimes called the Texas Paterson Colt, changed the balance of power on the Texas frontier. The Comanche said the rangers had a shot for every finger on their hands, which negated the effectiveness of a quiver full of arrows. Capt'n Jack and his rangers fought engagements with larger groups of Comanche at Bandera Pass, and later at Enchanted Rock, both with similar results, because of the increased firepower provided by the Paterson Colt. After the battle of Walker's creek, the days of the Comanche were numbered. Even so, it was thirty more years before they were subdued.

With less than half of Texas settled and civilized, Houston worked toward statehood for his entire first term as president. His friend, Andrew Jackson, favored annexation of Texas but was stymied in his efforts because of the certainty of war with Mexico, and the opposition of abolitionists in the American government. These circumstances made even recognition of Texas as a sovereign state very dangerous politically for Jackson.

Recognition of Texas by the United States was important on the world stage. It would allow Texas to borrow money, issue bonds, and establish diplomatic relations with European countries, who were waiting upon America, the closest neighbor, to verify its existence. Even land titles within the country could not be finalized, which hampered colonization. New colonists were desperately needed to maintain growth of the Texas economy.

With the election of Martin Van Buren, Jackson was freed from much of the political pressure causing the delay, and on March 3, 1837, his last day in office, Jackson formerly recognized Texas as a sovereign state. This was a far cry from annexation, and nothing had been done about relations with Mexico, or the slavery question. If Texas came into the union, it would come as a slave state, and the northern abolitionists would not allow that.

The whole matter was put on hold when Mirabeau Lamar was elected President of Texas, to follow Houston. Lamar did not want to be a part of the United States or any other country. He felt that Texas, with its vast lands and wealth of resources, would be foolish to become subservient to any other country. He believed Texas was destined to stretch from the Gulf of Mexico to the Pacific Ocean, and he set about to achieve that goal. Any Texas ambitions for statehood were abandoned during the three years of the Lamar administration.

In his first term as president, to pressure the American Government, Houston sent J. Pinckney Henderson to England and France as a sort of roving ambassador. In his second term, he sent his friend, Dr. Ashbel Smith. Smith's job was to establish friendly diplomatic relations, explore opportunities for trade, and perhaps arrange a long-term loan. Houston had no desire to become an English or French colony, but so long as that possibility existed, he would use it to push Washington for annexation. Smith worked effectively and stayed abroad until 1844.

Regardless of Houston's efforts, statehood for Texas was out of his hands, and depended on the political climate in the United States. If Texas was admitted to the union, war with Mexico was almost certain. Also, if Texas was admitted as a slave state, which was a given, then some form of appeasement would have to be worked out for the abolitionists. Houston finished his second term in 1844 nearer to that goal.

Anson Jones, a Houston man, defeated Ed Burleson in the election of 1844. Jones, the new president, continued to work for statehood. The United States presidential election took place in November of 1844, and the Democratic platform included the annexation of Texas. Henry Clay, the Whig candidate, spoke against annexation of Texas, based primarily on the slavery issue. James K. Polk was elected by a narrow margin, but the Democrats considered that a mandate for Texas annexation. They paired Texas, a slave state, with Oregon, a free state, to appease the abolitionists.

John Tyler, the sitting president, chose not to wait for Polk to take office, and asked congress to approve a joint resolution to annex Texas. The resolution allowed Texas to keep its public lands but did not assume its debts. It also stipulated that the U.S. would take over all dealings with Mexico. Tyler signed the resolution on his last day in office, March 3, 1845.

Texas elected a governor, approved a state constitution, and accepted the joint resolution in a special election in October of 1845. President Polk signed the annexation into law on December 29, 1845. On February 19, 1846, Texas President Anson Jones officially recognized the annexation by resigning as president, taking down the Texas flag flying over the capitol in Austin and replacing it with the American flag. In his speech at the ceremony, Jones said, "The Republic of Texas is no more." After the ceremony, J. Pinckney Henderson, who had been elected governor in the special election, assumed his duties as governor of the State of Texas.

Late in 1845, a nine-year-old boy, Charles Goodnight, left Illinois with his family and rode a white-faced mare named Blaze 800 miles to Texas. The family settled in the cross-timbers area, and Charles began to learn the cattle business. He later bragged that he was born the same year as Texas, and "joined" Texas the same year that Texas "joined" the Union.

Mexico, from the time of the Texas Revolution, had maintained that the Rio Grande River designated in the treaties as the border between Texas and Mexico was the Nueces River, not the Rio Bravo. Texas claimed the Rio Bravo was the Rio Grande. Upon annexation, President Polk moved to establish the international boundary at the Rio Grande. Polk believed in Manifest Destiny—the idea of a United States that stretched from the Atlantic to the Pacific---and moved to make the idea a reality.

Polk sent John Slidell, an American diplomat, to Mexico City with an offer. America would pay $25 million dollars to buy New Mexico and California (and the lands between), and to establish the Texas border at the Rio Bravo. The US would also assume $3.25 million in debt that Mexico owed to American citizens from the Mexican Revolution. The offer was made in secret, but soon became public knowledge. The Mexican people were incensed. Even though the Mexican government was too unstable to enter any negotiation, the people considered American asking for such concessions to be an insult. Slidell came back to America, convinced that war was the only solution.

Polk hedged his bet by also sending Jane McManus Storm to Mexico in a last-ditch effort to reach a diplomatic solution. Storm, as a New York newspaper and magazine writer had actively promoted Texas in her editorials and called for annexation of Texas as a first step toward achieving Manifest Destiny. It is probable that she coined that phrase, in an editorial in one of John L. O'Sullivan's magazines, the Democratic Review. O'Sullivan was credited with originating the phrase in an unsigned editorial, but computer analysis indicates Jane wrote the piece.

Storm was a good choice for this task. She had interviewed President Polk several times and he was impressed with her. Jane spent several years in Texas and was acquainted with most important politicians there. Mirabeau Lamar dedicated a book of poetry to her. She was the only woman ever allowed by the Mexican government to be deeded land as an empresario. She was thirty-eight years old, remarkably intelligent, and a born diplomat. Jane was incisive, intuitive, and attractive, but her efforts to achieve peace with Mexico were unsuccessful. She decided to stay on in Mexico as a war correspondent.

Polk gave up on diplomacy. He sent Zachary Taylor and 3500 US troops to Texas to start a war. Taylor and his troops spent some time in Corpus Christi, but the Mexican Army ignored them. Ulysses S. Grant, a young lieutenant, three years out of West Point, saw his first combat in this war. In his memoirs, he commented on Taylor's role in creating the conflict. "The presence of United States troops on the edge of the disputed territory farthest from Mexican settlements was not sufficient to provoke hostilities. We were sent to provoke a fight, but it was essential that Mexico should commence it..."

Finally, they crossed the Nueces into the no man's land that Mexico claimed as her own. Skirmishes with the Mexican army followed, and an all-out battle occurred when 1,600 Mexican soldiers discovered Captain Seth Thornton and 80 American troops on patrol on the north side of the Rio Grande. In the one-sided battle that ensued, 11 Americans were killed and 6 wounded. The rest were captured and imprisoned in Mexico. The wounded were returned on a wagon to Taylor's camp. The Mexican guide who drove the wagon said his commander had no way to care for the wounded.

Polk addressed congress on May 11, 1846, asking for a declaration of war. He said, "...But now, after reiterated menaces, Mexico has passed the boundary of the United States, has invaded our territory and has shed

American blood on the American soil. She has proclaimed that hostilities have commenced, and that the two nations are now at war."

After solid opposition and contentious debate, Congress passed the declaration of war two days later, on May 13, 1846. The Mexican army was not ready to fight a war, especially one against a well-trained, efficient army such as the one headed by Zachary Taylor. The Mexican privates were laborers and peons, pressed into service by officers who were more akin to war lords than competent soldiers. The enlisted ranks had no loyalty to the state and felt no patriotic duty to serve their country. Any sentimental loyalty they felt was for their villages. Many of them had been fighting each other and were confused when ordered to fight side by side against the Americans.

On the other hand, Taylor's troops were well-trained, mature, disciplined soldiers. The officers were competent and well educated, many from the military academy at West Point. U.S. Grant said, as he looked back in his memoirs, "The victories in Mexico were, in every instance, against vastly superior numbers. There were two reasons for this. Both General Scott and General Taylor had such armies as are not often got together. At the battle of Palo Alto and at Resaca-de-la-Palma, General Taylor had a small Army, but it was composed exclusively of regular troops, under the best of drill and discipline. Every officer, from the highest to the lowest, was educated in his profession, not at West Point necessarily, but in the camp, in garrison, and many of them in Indian Wars...."

When war was declared, American troops immediately moved in and captured Santa Fe and cut off any supply from the Santa Fe Trail. On the Pacific coast, the American army occupied the upper part of California and the navy blockaded everything in Baja California and the Mexican west coast. The navy also blockaded the Mexican east coast in the Gulf of Mexico.

Santa Anna, who was exiled in Cuba at the time, contacted the Mexican president, Valentin Gomez Farias, and offered his help to lead the Mexican Army against the American invaders. He said he had no desire to be president but only wanted to help his country by lending his military expertise in the time of need. The desperate Farias invited him back to head the army.

At the same time, Santa Anna was secretly meeting with representatives of the United States. He offered to arrange a peaceful end to the hostilities and sell the United States all the disputed lands in Texas, along with upper California and New Mexico, for a reasonable price, if the U S would help him get back into power in Mexico. Polk gave him a $2 million deposit, and ordered the blockade lifted for his safe return to Mexico.

When Santa Anna arrived in Mexico, and was given command of the military, he immediately went back on his word to everyone. He took over the presidency of Mexico and vigorously attacked the American forces. Mexico seemed incapable of self-government, much less conducting a war with the United States, but Santa Anna was determined to succeed. The people of Mexico over-looked his faults and saw only that Santa Anna had not deserted them in their time of need. They revered him as a great patriot and ignored his many shortcomings.         At the start of the war, several companies of Texas Rangers, under the leadership of Capt'n Jack Hays, were mustered into service as scouts and guides for the American Army. Zachary Taylor was dismayed by the Rangers for their non-military bearing, lack of discipline, and contempt for military courtesy, but said they were the best fighting men he had ever seen. The rangers served with distinction throughout the war and became universally feared by the Mexican people. They were called "Diablos Tejanos," (Texas Devils) and were dreaded as *Rinches* (Rangers.) The American press chronicled their exploits and made larger than life heroes of the Rangers.

J. Pinckney Henderson, the first governor of the state of Texas, after only two months in office, took a leave of absence to command a troop of Rangers. He led his troops competently in many battles and skirmishes as Taylor moved toward Mexico City. When the war was over, Henderson returned to Austin and resumed his duties as governor but chose not to run for re-election.

Richard King and his good friend Miffin Kenedy, river boat captains, prospered throughout the war, delivering supplies and ammunition for the army up and down the Rio Grande River. King, a natural entrepreneur, began to invest in real estate with his profits.

In far north Texas, on April 29, 1846, Col. Leonard Williams headed a trading party camped on the Canadian River. He noticed a blue-eyed girl that he took to be Cynthia Ann Parker. He offered a handsome amount of ransom, but the elders of the tribe refused to discuss the matter. Cynthia Ann would have been about twenty years old and had been with the Indians ten years.

General Taylor and his army marched south from the Rio Grande. Because supply lines were so long, rather than continually reinforce Taylor, Polk decided to send another army and invade Mexico at Vera Cruz. On March 9, 1847, General Winfield Scott, in the first amphibious landing in American history, landed 12,000 troops at Vera Cruz and marched toward Mexico City.

Samuel H. Walker left the Rangers to become a member of Zachary Taylor's Mounted Rifles in the US Army. He and his group served as scouts and guides for Taylor's army. He stayed with Taylor thru the early battles of the war and performed outstanding service. After the battle of Monterrey, Walker resigned from the US Army and reactivated his commission as captain of the Texas Rangers. He went to Washington on a mission for the Rangers and visited with President Polk.

During his time in Washington, Walker traveled to New York City to meet with Samuel Colt and work with him on the design of a new handgun for the army. Colt welcomed his input and named the weapon the Colt Walker. Because of Walker's recommendation, President Polk had the US Army order 1,000 of the handguns. Colt had 100 extra made for promotional purposes and public sale and presented one of the first to Cap'n Jack

Hayes. The Walker Colt was the most powerful black powder handgun ever made. A secondary result of the order was the salvation of Colt's company from bankruptcy. Colt had the guns made by Eli Whitney, Jr. at his factory in Connecticut.

The Walker Colt was a six-shot, single action revolver with a nine-inch, rifled barrel. It weighed 4 ½ pounds unloaded, and fired .44 caliber balls, with a 60-grain powder load. It was designed as a saddle gun, to be carried in a saddle holster. With a special accessory wooden stock, it converted to a small rifle. It was effective to a hundred yards and became the sidearm of choice for the Texas Rangers.

Samuel Walker returned to the war, joined his Texas riflemen and was attached to the First Pennsylvania Volunteers to help combat guerrilla warfare. His black bean finally turned up on October 9, 1847. He was killed in action at the little village of Huamantla. After his death, the Rangers went on a rampage and took vengeance on the innocent citizens of the village. That added to their reputation as "Diablos Tejanos."

Jane McManus Storm witnessed the amphibious assault and siege of Vera Cruz and sent back dispatches to New York newspapers and magazines. She travelled by horseback, stayed with the army, and covered the battles through the surrender of Mexico City and the capture of Chapultepec. She was the first ever female war correspondent, and the first war correspondent to be "embedded" with the troops. She spent most of the money she made with Texas real estate on legal fees back east. Among other legal battles, she sued Aaron Burr's talkative maid for slander.

At President Polk's request, Jane helped negotiate the Treaty of Guadalupe Hidalgo at the end of the war and was likely responsible for clauses which gave women equal status with men in certain property disputes. After the war, she married William Cazneau, a close friend of Mirabeau Lamar. She and Cazneau worked together to develop the city of Eagle Pass on the Rio Grande and later moved to a plantation in the Dominican Republic.

Capt'n Jack Hays, after the war, resigned from the Rangers and led a wagon train to California. He was elected Sheriff of San Francisco in 1850, and later, as a surveyor, laid out the city of Oakland. Although offered commissions on both sides, he chose to sit out the Civil War. He became wealthy, with investments in real estate and ranching. Jack Hays died of natural causes on April 21, 1883, San Jacinto Day. He is buried in Oakland.

A list of young American officers in the Mexican/American war reads like a who's who of generals in the Civil War. In addition to US Grant, generals from the north include George B. McClellan, William T. Sherman, George Meade, and he of the sideburns, Ambrose Burnside. Southern generals Robert E. Lee, Stonewall Jackson, James Longstreet, Joseph E. Johnston, Braxton Bragg, and Sterling Price participated in the war, as did the president of the Confederacy, Jefferson Davis.

As a result of the war, the Texas border was established at the Rio Grande. In addition, Mexico ceded all of California, Nevada, and Utah, most of Arizona and New Mexico, and parts of Colorado and Wyoming to the United States. The United States paid Mexico $15 million and assumed debts of $3.25 million that Mexico owed American citizens.

Polk was castigated by political opponents. Speakers on the floor of Congress hung their heads in shame because the United States acted as a bully and wrested territory from a much weaker nation. With all the objections and embarrassment, all the oration and posturing, at the end of the day, the Texas border was defined by the Rio Grande and America stretched from sea to shining sea. Manifest Destiny was no longer a phrase invented by a magazine writer. It was reality.

## CHAPTER TWELVE

# Civil War and Reconstruction

At the time Texas was annexed into the Union, senators were not elected in Texas, but appointed by the legislature. Sam Houston was appointed Senator, along with his long-time friend, Thomas Rusk. There was some question in the minds of Houston's friends (and enemies) as to whether he could stay away from booze long enough to be an effective voice for Texas, but to Houston's (and Margaret's) credit, Sam remained sober. To the amusement and amazement of some of his friends, Sam even became active in the Temperance League.

Early in Houston's time as a Senator, Henry Clay introduced the Compromise of 1850 which established the modern borders of Texas. Other provisions of the compromise included accepting California as a free state with its current boundaries, and admitting Utah and New Mexico as territories, with the slavery issue to be resolved by popular vote in each territory. Texas was paid $10 million and ceded one half of New Mexico, one third of Colorado, and parts of Wyoming, Kansas, and Oklahoma to the United States. The Compromise of 1850 resolved the slavery issue in the western territories, established the permanent borders of Texas and postponed the Civil War.

Richard King - Texas State Historical Society

In 1852, Richard King bought the Spanish Santa Gertrudis Land Grant of 15,500 acres for $300.00. He purchased the land from the heirs of the original owner and established the King Ranch. For the rest of his life, he continued to add land to the original ranch.

After King bought the land grant, as if on schedule, all of South Texas and Northern Mexico suffered from an extreme drought which forced small cattlemen to sell their herds. Captain King arranged to buy all the cattle in a small Mexican town, Cruillas. Driving the cattle on his way home to Texas , King realized that the villagers had sold him all the livestock they owned. They would make it through that year on the money he paid, but what about the years after that? They would have no cattle or horses to breed and sell. He turned around and went back to Cruillas.

King realized that he needed laborers and vaqueros and stockmen, and the Mexicans needed jobs. He offered a deal to all the villagers. He would provide homes, schools, hospitals and jobs to as many of them as would move across the border and work on his ranch. Most of the people accepted the deal, and about a hundred families loaded all they owned in wagons and followed Captain King to Texas.

These people became known as Kineros, or "King's Men." With materials furnished and wages paid by Captain King, they built their homes, their schools and their hospital. They worked the cattle, trained the horses, cleared the land, built the fences, and helped build the King Ranch.

Meanwhile, for the entire 13 years (February of 1846 until March of 1859) he spent as a senator, Sam Houston worked tirelessly to preserve the Union. He backed, spoke for and voted for bills unpopular in the South because they were, in Houston's mind, good for the nation. In 1848, he incurred the wrath of Southern Democrats by voting for the Oregon Bill, which prohibited slavery in that state. Houston, in his words, was a "Southern man for the Union" and supported the Missouri Compromise of 1820, which prohibited slavery north of Latitude 36-30', not coincidently, the northern border of the Texas panhandle. The Kansas-Nebraska Act of 1854 allowed slavery if residents voted for it. Houston opposed the Act because he thought it would divide the nation. His tenure in the senate was effectively over when the Texas legislature officially condemned his position on the Kansas-Nebraska Act. He finished his term, and the legislature replaced him in 1859 with John Hemphill.

On December 19, 1860, Charles Goodnight, working as a scout, led a group of Rangers to a Comanche camp on the Pease River near present-day Vernon. The war chief, Peta Nocona, and his two sons escaped the attack, but the Rangers captured several squaws, old men, and children. Goodnight noticed one of the squaws was a white woman with blue eyes and took her to Sul Ross. The captured squaw was Cynthia Ann Parker. Cynthia Ann had lived with the Indians, as a member of the tribe, for 24 years. She had married an important chief, Peta Nocona, and had three children. Nocona honored her by taking only one other wife. Cynthia Ann had no desire to be rescued.

When it became apparent that Houston would not be reappointed to the Senate, he ran for governor of Texas in 1857. He lost to Hardin R. Runnels, but during the race, Houston made a speech in Victoria, telling of the heroic deeds of Margaret Theresa Wright, a local woman Houston believed should be given the title of "Mother Of Texas." Houston was well acquainted with Jane Long, who also lived nearby, and knew how she coveted that title. He felt Margaret Wright earned it by her actions after the Goliad Massacre.

Margaret Robertson married her first husband, James Williams Hays, before she was twenty. He died in 1812, possibly fighting for Andrew Jackson in the Battle of New Orleans. Margaret, a widow with three children, moved in with Felix Trudeau, commander of the garrison at Natchitoches, Louisiana. After ten years and two more children, Trudeau died in 1822, and Margaret moved with her five children, to Texas. She applied, as a widow, for a league of land in the De Leon Colony, near Victoria. Before the title was transferred, she married John David Wright in 1828. She and Wright had two daughters, Amy Ann and Tennessee, but the marriage was not a happy one. Wright abandoned her in 1835 and moved to Mexico to escape prosecution for bad debts.

Wright returned in 1842. He had secretly obtained title to the ranch before he left for Mexico, and, as male head of the household, took over Margaret's property upon his return. Wright discovered that in his absence, Margaret had bought half a league of land and deeded six hundred forty acres to her son, Peter Hays. Wright was furious and filed suit to reclaim the land, even though he had never owned it.

Wright lost the suit, and the first appeal. While the second appeal was pending, Peter Hays was mysteriously killed in an ambush. Margaret filed for divorce on March 6, 1848, charging her husband with habitual cruelty, fraudulent land transfer, and the murder of her son. After a bitter court battle and three appeals, the Texas Supreme Court awarded her a divorce and half the joint property, over 5,500 acres and almost 600 head of cattle.

Margaret Theresa Robertson Hays Trudeau Wright deserves the title "Mother of Texas" that Houston bestowed on her. She saved the lives of the escaped Goliad survivors in 1836. She seems to have been the first female in Texas to reserve a cattle brand, the CT, which she registered with the Republic of Texas in 1838. She may have been granted the first divorce in the new State of Texas, in 1848. She was a courageous pioneer and patriot, an early rancher, and the mother of seven children. Her youngest daughter, Tennessee, was expelled from the Primitive Baptist Church they attended for "improper walking." The attractive teenager evidently wiggled her bottom more than was thought necessary by the elders of the church. Margaret died in Victoria at age 89, on October 21,1878. Sam Houston felt she earned the title "Mother of Texas," by heroic deeds during the revolution.

Houston challenged Runnels again, in 1859, and defeated him, making Houston, who had been governor of Tennessee from 1827 until 1829, the only person ever elected as governor of two different states in the Union. Houston, a staunch Unionist, was governor of Texas, and Texas was well on the way to secession. During the debates leading up to secession, Houston said, "Let me tell you what is coming. After the sacrifice of countless millions of treasure and hundreds of thousands of lives, you may win Southern independence, but I doubt it. The North is determined to preserve this Union."

The Texas legislature voted to secede from the Union on February 2, 1861 and voted to join the Confederate States of America on March 3, 1861. Houston refused to take an oath swearing allegiance to the Confederacy and was evicted from his office on March 16, 1861. Abraham Lincoln is said to have offered him 50,000 Union troops to maintain his office, but Houston declined the offer, choosing not to be the cause of bloodshed in his beloved state.

Bloodshed in Texas has been, since earliest times, the norm. The vote for secession failed in some counties and was very close in others. Deep in the hill country, the German residents did not believe in slavery, and had promised loyalty to the Union when they settled. Only a few years later, they were asked to forget that pledge and pledge allegiance to the Confederate States. Many of them did not speak English, and this adjustable morality was confusing. They stayed to themselves and tried to avoid confrontation over the slavery issue. Their non-German neighbors did not trust their motives, could not understand their language, misunderstood their clannishness, and, in some cases, coveted their well-tended farms.

Confederate soldiers under Captain James Duff were sent into the "German Belt," north and west of San Antonio, to protect the settlers from Unionists and perhaps draft some Germans into the Confederate Army. Duff and his troops patrolled the area as vigilantes, searching for Unionists behind every tree, and meting out "justice" as he saw fit. Duff's troops arrested and hung two German citizens at Fredericksburg, and threatened the German communities of Comfort, Sisterdale, Fisher, San Marcos and New Braunfels.

A group of German farmers banded together under Fritz Tegener and prepared to go to Mexico. Depending upon which story you believe, they planned to cross over the Mexican border, make their way to New Orleans, and join the Union army, or they planned to sit out the war in Mexico. Sixty-four men gathered at Turtle Creek, just south of present-day Kerrville, and struck out across country toward Mexico. Duff heard of this and dispatched ninety-six troops under Lt. Colin McRae to arrest the defectors and bring them back for trial.

McRae's troops caught the Germans on August 9, 1862. The Germans, unaware that they were being followed, camped on the banks of the Nueces River near present-day Carrizo Springs. Their freedom brought on a festive mood, and they stayed up late, drinking beer and singing songs of their homeland. McRae's troops, who obviously misunderstood that part about "arrest and bring back for trial," surrounded the camp and planned to attack at dawn.

Two of the Germans were posted as sentries, and they stumbled onto the Confederates about One AM. Even though their plans were disrupted, the moon provided enough light for McRae's men to attack. The Germans stood off two charges, but eventually gave up to the superior forces. At least one third of the defectors fled at the beginning of the battle, and five more, including Tegener, ran into the woods at the end of the fight. According to fragmentary evidence, nineteen Germans were killed in the initial battle, and nine wounded. The wounded were taken into the woods and shot. Nine others were killed by the Confederate cavalry which trailed them and caught up when they tried to cross the Rio Grande. McRae lost two men killed and eighteen wounded. About twenty-five of the Germans escaped. Some made their way to New Orleans and joined the Union army. Others went to California or hid out in Texas or Mexico for the duration of the war. The Confederates buried their dead but left the Germans where they fell.

After the war, four years to the day, on August 10, 1866, the German-language Treue der Union Monument was dedicated in Comfort, Texas. The bones of the men killed at the Nueces were gathered and buried in Comfort by relatives and local citizens. An 1865 American flag, with thirty-six stars, flies at perpetual half-mast near a limestone obelisk over the common grave. The names of the victims are carved in stone on the monument.

Historians, to this day, argue about what to call the incident. To one side, it was plainly the Battle of the Nueces. Another group, with equal fervor, claims it was the Nueces Massacre.

Texans enjoy a fight and are good at it. Over the course of the Civil War, Texas contributed 90 to 100 thousand men to the Confederate war effort. Wood's Texas Brigade enlisted 5353 men during the war, and only 617 remained to surrender at Appomattox. General Robert E. Lee preferred Texas soldiers because he could count on them. He knew that their fighting spirit had been born in the Texas Revolution, and honed in the Mexican-American War. When asked what to do in combat, Lee said, "See those Texans over there? Watch them and do what they do."

Sam Houston's oldest son, Sam Junior, went against his father's wishes, and joined the Confederate army. He was wounded and left for dead on the battlefield at Shiloh. A Yankee doctor discovered he was still alive. Sam carried a bible in his shirt pocket which identified him and stopped a bullet that would have killed him. The doctor had him moved to a field hospital and nursed him back to health. Upon recovery, Sam was imprisoned in Camp Douglas, a prisoner of war camp outside Chicago. He was traded in a prisoner swap and returned home to his grateful parents.

Gainesville, a small settlement near the Red River, some 80 miles north of the ferry crossing on the Trinity River that would become Dallas, was settled by a mixed group. Most were from the South, but only a few owned slaves. The slave-owning minority, because of their wealth, controlled the local government, including the court system. Many of the farmers chose not to own slaves for moral reasons and were unsympathetic to the southern cause. Animosity between the groups led to conflicts and the slave owners called in Confederate Troops. Martial law was declared.

Between one hundred and fifty and two hundred Union sympathizers were arrested. A civilian court was convened. It lacked legal status in the state of Texas, but that fact was ignored. The appointed judge and seven of the twelve jurists owned slaves. Without benefit of a proper defense, forty-one "Unionists" were found guilty and hanged, one or two at a time over a two-day period. The Texas governor, Francis R. Lubbock, applauded the action as just and fair treatment of dissidents.

Great Hanging At Gainesville

A park in downtown Gainesville contains historical markers telling of the Gainesville Hangings. Historians, as usual, disagree about what happened. Were the unionists hanged innocent of any crime, or did they actively plot against their confederate neighbors? Evidence indicates there was guilt on both sides of the question.

On January 1, 1863, at three o'clock in the morning, the first battle of the Civil War on Texas soil began. Confederate forces under General John B. McGruder attacked the Union forces occupying Galveston Island. Having no iron-clad ships available, two Confederate ships, armored with bales of cotton, sailed from Houston to take on six union vessels harbored at Galveston. The Rebels, sailing their cotton-clads, sunk the *USS Harriet Lane*, and ran the *USS Westfield* aground, forcing the Union Navy to blow it up to keep it out of Confederate hands. A young Englishman from Austin, Ben Thompson, was wounded fighting for the South in this battle. The Union soldiers ashore saw the Navy ships abandoned, and thought the Navy was surrendering. They immediately surrendered, and Galveston remained in Confederate hands until the end of the war.

In the summer of 1863, Sam Houston fell ill. With his removal from office as Governor, he had retired from politics and lived with Margaret and his family in the rented "Steamboat House" in Huntsville. He liked the area because it reminded him of his native Tennessee. On July 23, Sam developed pneumonia, and died on July 26, with Margaret and his family at his bedside. His last words were, "Texas, Texas,… Margaret."

Sam Houston, U.S. Senator, 1856

Margaret Lea Houston, through her unconditional love and unquestioning loyalty to Sam Houston, gave Texas and the United States a sober, intelligent and courageous voice of reason. She took a man well on his way to becoming a common drunk, reformed him, led him to religion, and salvaged his self-respect. She provided peace and tranquility at home that allowed him the freedom to pursue his political ambitions. Sam Houston fought for national unity as a United States Senator for 13 years. He was Governor of Texas. The Constitutional Union Party tried to draft him into the 1860 U. S. Presidential race. Without Margaret Lea Houston, Texas, the United States, and the world would have been deprived of Houston's wisdom and guidance, and Sam Houston might well have gone down in history as a drunk who got lucky at San Jacinto.

The second Civil War battle on Texas soil took place on September 8, 1863. The Union army sent 5000 troops and twenty-two ships to invade Texas. The plan was to sail up the Sabine River, land troops, capture the railroad, then ride into Houston and the interior of Texas. Lt. Dick Dowling and forty-four Confederate soldiers were dispatched to their duty station at Ft. Griffith to spike the cannons and disable the fort, which was deemed incapable of stopping such a formidable force. While stationed at the lonely outpost, to fight boredom, Dowling and his troops practiced with the old smooth-bore guns in the fort. They placed distance markers in the channel as aiming stakes and felt comfortable in their ability to hit any ship that came within range. Dowling decided not to withdraw without a fight.

Four iron-clad gunboats led the Union navy up the Sabine, firing at the fort as they advanced. When the Union gunboats came within range, the rebels returned fire with the four thirty-two pounders and two twenty-four pounders they had been sent to disable. Dowling's extra training paid off. His men were deadly accurate. One of their first shots exploded the boiler of the lead Union ship, and a second shot disabled the tiller on another ship, causing it to run aground. With two of its new ironclad gunboats disabled and blocking the channel, and deadly artillery ready to destroy any ship that came within 1200 yards, Union General William B. Franklin called off the invasion and returned to New Orleans.

At the end of the day, Dowling's forty-four men took possession of two Union gunboats with 13 heavy cannons. The northern forces suffered two dozen killed or badly wounded, 37 missing in action, and 315 captured.

Most of the missing were thought to be black Union soldiers who slipped back home to Louisiana. The Confederates suffered no casualties.

After Lee's surrender on April 9, 1865, Texas veterans made their way home. On May 13, 1865, former Texas Ranger Col. John S. (R.I.P.) Ford and a troop of Confederate soldiers soundly whipped a Yankee force under Col. Theodore H. Barrett at Palmito Ranch near Brownsville, Texas. Word of Lee's surrender had reached both armies in deep south Texas. At least a week before the battle, a traveller tossed a New Orleans newspaper with stories of Lee's Surrender and Lincoln's Assination to a group of soldiers on the dock. With that news, many Confederate troops left for home. Others chose to stay and continue fighting. The battle was the last conflict of the Civil War and one of only three that took place on Texas soil. It was a matter of pride in Texas that the Union Army never occupied the state.

Captain King and Miffin Kenedy operated a thriving river boat business during the Civil war. Yankee ships blockaded the port at Brownsville, but international law prevented interference with any ship flying the flags of neutral nations. King and Kenedy moved their headquarters across the river to Matamoros, hoisted Mexican flags, and used their riverboats to load Texas cotton bales onto foreign ships in the harbor. Both men ploughed their substantial profits into their ranching operations.

The assassination of Lincoln prolonged and complicated reconstruction, especially in Texas. Lincoln's approach was as a patient father, working to settle a dispute between two spoiled children. The opposition favored punishment of the wayward child. Some in congress insisted upon severe punishment, and Andrew Johnson lacked the personality or ability to enforce Lincoln's lenient policies. When he tried, congress impeached him and came within one vote of removing him from office.

Re-admission to the Union was not an automatic action, as most Southerners would have liked. Republicans gained a majority in Congress, overrode Johnson's vetoes, and established a set of criteria for a state to be readmitted to the Union. Debts from the war had to be dealt with. Ex-Confederates were to be disenfranchised. Slaves were to be freed and allowed to vote. Returning veterans and freed slaves needed food, shelter and jobs of some sort. In addition, there was an unspoken desire in the Northern-dominated congress to punish the South for the insurrection.

Texas, on the other hand, wanted to return to the lifestyle it had enjoyed before the war with as little disruption as possible. The Texas legislature set about to comply with the terms of Presidential Reconstruction, the most lenient option available, and set up a Reconstruction Convention. Presidential Reconstruction required that the convention draft a new state constitution, nullify the act of secession, abolish slavery, and repudiate the debts incurred by the Civil War. It soon became apparent that Texas would only comply with the minimum requirements of the law. The legislature refused to adopt the thirteenth and fourteenth amendments to the US Constitution which abolished slavery and gave adult male Negros the right to vote. Texas appointed two senators that had encouraged secession and elected representatives to Congress with deep Confederate ties. Texas voters selected James W. Throckmorton as governor, a conservative with strong objections to the Union Military presence.

The United States Congress refused to seat the representatives that Texas sent to Washington. They enacted the First Reconstruction Act on March 2, 1867 which divided the South into five military districts with the Union Army in charge of each district. The existing government in each state was considered "provisional." Texas, in the fifth district, fell under the jurisdiction of General Charles Griffin. Griffin ordered General Phillip Sheridan to remove Governor Throckmorton from office, naming him an "impediment to reconstruction." Sheridan also removed several judges for the same reason. Over the next two years, the military removed hundreds of city and county officials that were believed to be less than sympathetic toward the Union.

Congressional Reconstruction required additional effort by the Texas legislature. A new state constitution that allowed all adult males, regardless of race or previous servitude, the right to vote had to be written and adopted. The Fourteenth Amendment to the US Constitution had to be approved by Texas voters. When these conditions were met, congress would consider readmission.

Texas finally met all the conditions and ratified the appropriate amendments in February of 1870. Congress accepted the conditions, and U.S. Grant signed the bill readmitting Texas to the Union on March 30, 1870. At the same time, Edmund J. Davis, a former general in the Union Army, was elected Governor and took office.

Life for the average Texan changed little during the years of war and reconstruction. Most residents were rural and life on the farm was always hard. In 1870, the largest city in Texas was Galveston, with some 13,000 residents, followed by San Antonio, Houston and Jefferson. The population was growing in every part of the state. Families from the deep south had lost everything in the war—their homes and farms were destroyed, their crops burned, their livestock scattered. Cheap land was available in Texas and settlers came by the thousands.

Texas Plantation owners adapted to the loss of their slaves by establishing a tenant farmer system which divided huge plantations into small plots. Sharecroppers farmed the land and paid for the use of it with a share of the crop. The result was not a redistribution of wealth as envisioned by liberal thinkers, but a continuation of the status quo, with the same rich individuals controlling the economy, and the working poor having little chance for advancement. Cotton became the chief crop throughout the state and sharecroppers became not much more than legal slaves.

Cynthia Ann Parker continued to live with relatives in North Texas. The state legislature voted her a league of land and a $100 per year pension for five years. She did not want the land or money and, if not locked in her bedroom, would attempt to escape. Her daughter, Prairie Flower, died of influenza. Cynthia Ann, deprived of her Indian family and living with strangers, refused to eat. She died with a broken heart in 1870.

During the Civil War, the western frontier, the line between Anglo settlements and Indian territory, had been pushed back by more than a hundred miles. The Union Army established a line of forts along the frontier to protect settlers and control the Indians. President Grant also put Quakers in charge of the Indian reservations in the hope that their peaceful nature would have a calming effect on the tribes. Grant also knew the Quakers, famed for their honesty, would not steal supplies meant for the Indians.

Some of the Indians slipped off the reservations and raided in Texas. Rangers or soldiers were not allowed to follow them into Indian Territory, and when they returned, the Quaker agents protected what they considered their poor, misunderstood charges. As to the forts, no self-respecting Comanche ever attacked a fortified position. If the army sent two hundred men out on scout, they would see nothing. When the army sent ten men out to gather firewood, if they found them at all, they were tortured and mutilated.

General William T. Sherman, military commander of everything west of the Mississippi River, decided to personally inspect the situation in Texas. He thought the problem was exaggerated and was sure he could find a solution. Sherman left San Antonio on May 2, 1871, with his Inspector General, two aides, and seventeen troopers to inspect the forts along the frontier. They visited Fort Concho, Fort Griffin, and Fort Belknap without seeing any sign of Indians.

As Sherman's party approached Fort Richardson, near Jacksboro, on May 17, 1871, they were watched by two hundred Indians, hiding in the brush near Salt Creek. The soldiers had nothing of value to the Indians, and would most likely put up a fight, so they were allowed to pass, unmolested. The next day, the patience of the Indians was rewarded when Henry Warren's wagon train came along the same road. Warren had a contract to deliver supplies to the army and was on his way to Fort Richardson with twelve wagon loads of corn and other staples.

The Comanche killed and mutilated seven of the men, including Warren. They burned the wagons, stole the supplies and mules, and escaped back into Oklahoma. Three drovers escaped the massacre and told the story to General Sherman at Fort Richardson. Sherman immediately sent Col. Ranald Mackenzie, the base commander, and three companies of cavalry in pursuit of the Indians.

One of the wagoneers was found with his tongue cut out, stretched horizontally on a wagon tongue and roasted over an open fire. This made quite an impression on General Sherman, because he knew that easily could have been his troop. This incident changed Sherman's mindset, and the US Army's policy toward the Indians. Sherman no longer doubted the stories he had heard of Indian atrocities. The army ceased to remain in a defensive posture and follow the Quaker peace policy. Sherman ordered Mackenzie to aggressively attack any Indians found off the reservation. Mackenzie was to take troops into the Llano Estacado, the age-old dominion of the Comanche. The U.S. Army was on the offensive and Indians would go to the reservations and stay or face annihilation.

The cattle industry grew in Texas after the Civil War. Rangy, long-horned cattle roamed the brush and pear country of South Texas and were free for the taking. Richard King and Mifflin Kenedy, after the Mexican-American and Civil Wars, established ranches in South Texas and trailed large herds of longhorns to the railroads in Kansas. Huge profits were made. Free cattle in South Texas were worth $10 to $20 each at the railhead. Growing cities in the east wanted beef and were willing to pay for it.

Charles Goodnight and Oliver Loving

In the Spring of 1866, Charles Goodnight and Oliver Loving partnered to blaze the Goodnight-Loving trail from the San Angelo area west to the Horsehead Crossing of the Pecos River, then up river to the army post at Ft. Sumner, New Mexico. The army needed beef to feed the Navajo Indians held there. Goodnight altered an army surplus Studebaker wagon and invented the "Chuck Wagon" for this drive. He and Loving made the trip two more times in the next year. Loving was attacked by Indians on their third trip and died from his wounds. Goodnight finished the drive, kept meticulous records and paid Loving's share of the profits to his family. He delivered Loving's body back to Palo Pinto County, Texas. Larry McMurtry told the story in the book "Lonesome Dove."

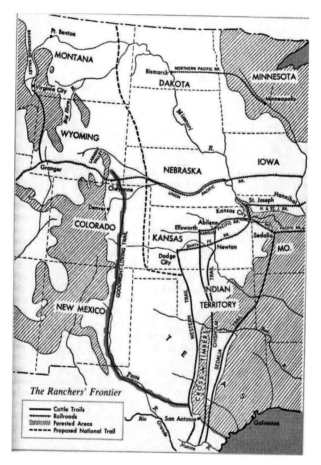

Goodnight Loving Trail - Texas State Historical Society

After the Civil War, there was little organized law enforcement in Texas, and bands of outlaws roamed the land, especially in the northeast counties. To help curtail the growing lawlessness, the legislature created the State Police and the Texas Militia. Many freed slaves took jobs in the State Police, and this complicated enforcement. White citizens were reluctant to take orders or direction from blacks, even if they were policemen. Some of the blacks used their new-found authority with a bit too much enthusiasm. Racial strife added to the tension as the police went about their duties. Governor Davis used the State Police as his personal army to put down any resistance to his edicts and enforce questionable legislation.

Davis pursued a one-man crusade to equalize and educate ex-slaves and punish whites for their former abuse. More than one third of the State Police were freedmen, and most had little training in law enforcement.

Jane McManus Storm Cazneau, and her husband William Cazneau, moved to their plantation in the Dominican Republic in 1855. She remained politically active, and worked secretly with her friend, President U.S. Grant, sharing a dream of making several states out of the Islands in the Caribbean. Jane's son, William Mont Storm became a successful inventor with over thirty patents to his name. William Cazneau died of yellow fever in 1876, and Jane died in 1878, while returning from a business trip to New York City. Her ship sank in a storm in the Bermuda Triangle.

The famous outlaw, John Wesley Hardin, killed his first man (an ex-slave) at age fifteen, in what may have been self-defense. When three State Police officers came to arrest him, Hardin killed them from ambush with a shotgun. That was not self-defense. By late fall of 1868, the fifteen-year-old had killed four men and would spend the rest of his life outside the law.

In November of 1873, Edmund Davis was defeated by Richard Coke, a former Confederate officer, by a two to one margin. Calling the election illegal, Davis barricaded himself in the governor's office, which was on the first floor of the capitol building. The new governor and members of the legislature were forced to climb a ladder to their offices on the second floor. Davis appealed to President Grant to keep him in office with help from the U.S. Army, but Grant ignored his plea and Davis vacated the office in January of 1874. He locked the door and took the key, forcing Coke to break in to occupy the governor's office.

Edmund Davis left the state in disarray. Texas legislators were working in Austin to retain the status quo for affluent whites. Poll taxes and other restrictions were being enacted to disenfranchise negros, Mexicans, and poor whites. Outlaws ran free in the state, with law officers unable to combat the lawlessness. Texas Rangers were organized, then disbanded for lack of funds to pay them. Comanche ruled the Llano Estacado, and no one near the frontier was safe.

The Constitution of 1876 was passed during Coke's term as governor. Under this constitution, Coke was a part of a three-member board that set up the Agricultural and Mechanical College of Texas, now Texas A&M University, and hired the faculty. Part of his speech advising entering students was considered so eloquent that all members of the Corps of Cadets are required to memorize it to this day. He said, "Let your watchword be duty, and know no other talisman of success than labor. Let honor be your guiding star with your superiors, your fellows, with all. Be as true to a trust reposed as the needle to the pole, stand by the right even to the sacrifice of life itself, and learn that death is preferable to dishonor."

Richard Coke was a Democrat. Edmund Davis was the last Republican Governor elected in Texas for a hundred and five years.

# CHAPTER THIRTEEN
# Gunfighters and Lawmen

During and right after the Edmund Davis administration and Reconstruction, outlaws flourished in Texas. The Rangers were underfunded, State Police were corrupt, and local law enforcement was inadequate to combat the problem. Several outlaws and a few lawmen reached legendary status, but most faded unknown into history. Some of these outlaws were gunfighters, and some of the gunfighters were lawmen. Many worked on both sides of the law.

On one of his trips taking cattle to Colorado on the Goodnight-Loving Trail, Charles Goodnight hired a young cowboy named Clay Allison from Cimarron, New Mexico. Clay worked hard, kept to himself, and followed Goodnight's rules about drinking and gambling. Over the next few years, Clay worked for Goodnight sporadically. They remained friends, but Goodnight wouldn't hire him after he gained a reputation as a gunfighter.

After serving under Confederate General Nathan Bedford Forrest in the Civil War, Allison returned to the family farm in Tennessee. He lacked self control and had an unruly temper. Clay killed a Yankee soldier who tried to repossess the farm and the whole family moved to New Mexico Territory. In the Cimarron area, he participated in several lynch mobs, and instigated some of them.

Clay Allison

His reputation as a gunfighter started in January of 1874, when Allison killed a gunfighter named Chuck Colson, who was said to have killed seven men in Texas, New Mexico, or Colorado. The two were having dinner together, and got into an argument. Colson reached for his gun and it got tangled up in the table leg. That gave Clay Allison enough time to pull his gun and shoot Colson in the head. Allison was arrested but immediately released when witnesses testified that he fired in self-defense. When asked why he would have dinner with a man who was likely to shoot him, Allison said he didn't want to send a man to Hell on an empty stomach.

Allison was proud of his ability with a handgun and practiced drawing and shooting when he could afford to buy ammunition. When asked what he did, he once replied that he was a "shootist," and may have coined that term.

Over the next few years, Clay Allison killed several men in self defense, and moved around the country, living for a time in Sedalia, Missouri, and later in Dodge City, Kansas. He knew Bat Masterson and Wyatt Earp in Kansas, and probably Ben and Billy Thompson. According to Charlie Siringo, Masterson and Earp knew and respected Allison's reputation and there was no trouble between them.

After living in Kansas for a short time, working as a cattle broker, Allison bought a ranch near Mobeetie in the Texas panhandle and planned to settle down. He married America Medora McCulloch, "Dora," a girl from Sedalia, Missouri, on February 15, 1881.

Allison sold his ranch in 1883, and moved back to New Mexico. Dora gave birth to a little girl, Patti Dora Allison, on August 9, 1885, in Cimarron, New Mexico. The little family bought a ranch on the river near Pecos, Texas.

On July 3, 1887, Clay Allison was hauling supplies to the ranch when a sack of grain started to fall from the wagon. Clay reached to stop the falling sack, lost his balance and fell off the wagon, which rolled over him, breaking his neck and killing him instantly. Seven months later, on February 10, 1888, Dora delivered Clay Pearl Allison, another little girl.

It is said that Clay Allison killed over a dozen men in his lifetime. He died at age 45. A marker on his grave says, "He never killed a man that didn't need killing."

Gunfighters of that day did not duel like Hollywood heroes in the middle of the street at high noon. Most gunfights were spontaneous affairs, in darkened barrooms between two half-drunk participants. The winner was usually the most nearly sober one who managed to hit his opponent with a well-aimed or outright lucky shot. If they met in the street, in the daylight, both started shooting half a block away and the one with the rifle usually won. Because of the cost of ammunition, there was little outright practice.

Consider the death of John Wesley Hardin in an El Paso barroom. One afternoon, John Selman and Hardin had words and Selman left the bar. Around midnight, Selman returned. He walked in, pulled his pistol and shot Hardin in the back of the head. End of story. In his trial for murder, a hung jury resulted in Selman's release, pending a retrial which never happened. Anyone could tell it was self defense—give John Wesley Hardin an even chance and he will kill you.

Ben Thompson

Billy Thompson

Ben and Billy Thompson were born in England and moved to Austin, Texas, in 1851, when Ben was eight and Billy was six. Ben, being the oldest, was very protective of Billy and their four-year-old sister. Ben worked at odd jobs during his adolescence, until he discovered a talent for gambling. Billy mostly didn't work at anything, but depended on Ben to provide for his needs.

Ben killed his first man in New Orleans in 1859, just before the Civil War. The man was abusing a woman and Ben came to her aid. Ben served with distinction in the Civil War and was wounded in the battle of Galveston. After the war, Ben fatally shot a teamster during an argument. He fled to Mexico and joined Maximilian's forces, but returned to Austin when he heard that his sister was being abused by her husband. He beat his brother-in-law so severely that he was convicted of attempted murder and served two years in Huntsville State Prison. He eventually received a full pardon and an early release.

Billy, in the meantime, shot a stable boy in Aransas Pass. The teenage boy slapped Billy's horse away from a feed trough and Billy called him on it. The boy invited Billy to put away his gun and fight it out with fists. Instead, Billy shot him, and ran away. Self defense was not involved. Billy just lost his temper and killed the youth.

The Thompsons moved to Kansas and Ben, with a partner, Phil Coe, opened a saloon in Abilene. "Wild Bill" Hickok was the town marshal, and the new saloon owners soon got crossways with him over their advertising methods. John Wesley Hardin was in town, hiding under the name Wesley Clemmons, and Ben tried to get the unstable Hardin to confront Hickok. Hardin demonstrated good judgment and told Ben that if Hickok needed killing, he should do it himself. Hickok killed Ben's partner, Phil Coe, in a gunfight while Ben was recuperating from an accident. Both he and Hickok left town without confronting each other.

Ben and Billy Thompson settled in Ellsworth, another Kansas railhead town with plenty of entertainment for cowboys fresh off cattle drives. Billy accidentally shot and killed his friend, Sheriff Chauncey Whitney, as he stood with Ben and Billy in a confrontation over a gambling dispute. The others involved, a local lawman and a gambler, pressed charges, but Billy was released when witnesses confirmed that the shooting was accidental.

In 1875, Ben left Kansas and moved to Mobeetie, in the Texas panhandle, adjacent to Fort Elliott. Army camps attracted gamblers, and Ben became friends with a fellow gambler, Bat Masterson. Masterson killed a soldier in a dispute over a woman. Ben Thompson stepped in and saved Masterson when other soldiers tried to lynch him. The two became fast friends and worked together to settle a dispute for the Santa Fe Railroad Company.

Bat Masterson

In later years Masterson became a writer in New York City. When asked to compare gunfighters he had known, he made the observation that three qualities make up a competent gunfighter. First, he must be fearless. A gunfighter must be able to function without fear of consequences. He must be able to control his emotions and act without regard for the outcome of any confrontation.

Second, he must be proficient with the tools of his trade, the firearms. In the daylight or the dark, he must be able to draw, cock, aim, and fire any weapon automatically, in any situation. He must be able to perform with several different firearms, with different ammunition, in different circumstances.

Third, and perhaps most important, he must be deliberate. He must take his time, pick his target, take careful aim, and kill his enemy. Masterson knew a number of truly brave men who were excellent shots and had been killed in gunfights because they were in too much of a hurry.

Masterson said the one man he knew with all these qualities, the man who would be ultimately successful against anyone he knew, was Ben Thompson.

Ben took the money he earned from the railroad and opened the Iron Front Saloon at Sixth and Congress Avenue in Austin. In June of 1880, Billy needed help again. He was in jail in Ogallala, Nebraska, because of a shooting. Ben enlisted his friend Masterson and they "rescued" Billy from jail and went back to Dodge City. The police in Aransas Pass continued to seek Billy over the stable boy incident, but their warrants evidently did not reach the authorities in Kansas.

Ben Thompson wore silk top hats and English clothing and spoke with a clipped British accent. When he was sober, he was personable and friendly. The townsfolk of Austin respected him and in 1881, the city of Austin hired Ben to be city marshal. The crime rate dropped dramatically. The next year, in a private dispute, Thompson shot and killed Jack Harris, the owner of Vaudeville Variety Theater in San Antonio. He was indicted and resigned his position with the city. After he was tried and acquitted, he did not resume his position as city marshal.

On March 11, 1884, Ben and King Fisher, an old friend visiting Austin, took the train to San Antonio. Fisher was on his way home to Uvalde and Ben, a bit drunk, decided to ride part way with him. Ben was loud and rowdy on the train. In San Antonio, they continued to drink. While having a drink at the White Elephant Saloon, they ran into Ben's brother, Billy.

That evening, around 10:30, Ben and Fisher went to the Vaudeville Variety Theater, perhaps to mend relations with the new owners, or perhaps looking for trouble. Word of their intended visit had reached the owners, and the gunfighters were expected. Details are fuzzy, but Ben Thompson and King Fisher, two of the deadliest gunfighters in Texas, were ambushed and killed. According to the front page story in the next day's San Antonio Light, both men were riddled with bullets and died instantly. Ben Thompson tried get his gun out but an off duty policeman, working as a bouncer at the club, grabbed his hand and held the gun down while others shot him. Ben tried to free himself and shot five times into the floor. When Ben fell to the floor, one of the assailants stepped up, put a gun to his head and shot him point blank. Fisher got one shot away. Ben may have wounded a man named Foster in the leg, or Foster may have shot himself as he hurriedly pulled his gun. Foster died later, after a botched amputation.

The San Antonio Paper reported that when the shooting started everyone in the club wanted outside. People jumped from the second floor windows, crowded the doorways, and rushed through the kitchen. Billy Thompson rushed over from the White Elephant Saloon and was detained and searched at the front door. The police feared he might seek revenge, but he was unarmed. He was released to claim his brother's body.

The assassinations were planned and deliberate and there were multiple shooters, but no one was ever charged in either killing. In spite of public outrage, the San Antonio District Attorney or the police department expressed little interest in the case.

King Fisher was thirty at the time and was buried on his ranch in Uvalde. Ben, age 40, was buried in Austin in a large funeral at the Oakwood Cemetery. Billy was eventually arrested and tried for the murder of the stable boy in Aransas Pass. He was acquitted because all the witnesses had died or moved on. Billy died of a stomach ailment in 1897, at 52, still known as Ben Thompson's unpredictable and troubled younger brother.

King Fisher

John King Fisher was born near Dallas in October of 1853. Fisher grew up outside Austin and lived in Goliad for a time. As a teen, he started using the name King and made money by buying wild horses, breaking and training them, then selling them at a profit. King Fisher was a good-looking boy with a wild streak, a favorite with the girls. He had a few brushes with the law and spent a few months in jail before he was out of his teens.

At a relatively early age, Fisher worked "security" for large ranches in South Texas. He became very good with a gun and began to dress flamboyantly, with elaborate vests, fancy sombreros, and silk scarves. Ranch "security" in those days, consisted of protecting the herds from rustlers by simply shooting any unauthorized people found on the ranch, especially

Mexicans. During this time, Fisher joined a gang that rustled cattle in Mexico and brought them into Texas to sell. Soon King Fisher became head of the gang, mostly by killing his competition.

To consolidate his activities, he bought a ranch near Eagle Pass on the Rio Grande and used it to stage his rustling exploits. To discourage visitors, he put up a sign at a fork in the road near his property. "This is King Fisher's road. Take the other one." Mexican cattle could be sold in Texas with no questions asked, and the same rules applied in Mexico with Texas cattle. Texas Rangers arrested Fisher several times, but could not convict him of any crime because no one would testify against him. Some of his neighbors were very loyal to Fisher as a friend. Others were simply afraid of him.

King Fisher married and settled down. He and his wife had four daughters and Fisher phased out his illegal activities, sold his ranch and moved to one near Uvalde. He continued to dress outlandishly and had a pair of chaps and a vest made from the skin of a Bengal Tiger. He carried nickel-plated, ivory-handled six guns and wore silver spurs.

For a time he was sheriff of Uvalde, a not unusual switch for a reformed gunfighter. He was an effective lawman and respected in the community. In 1883, he trailed two stagecoach robbers, Tom and Jim Hannehan, to their ranch near Leakey. They resisted arrest and he killed Tom Hannehan in the shootout. Jim surrendered, gave up the money they had stolen, and went to prison for a time.

King Fisher was buried in Uvalde. For years after, on the anniversary of Tom Hannehan's death, Tom's mother would build a bonfire on Fisher's grave and dance around it, chanting until the wee hours.

One of the most famous outlaws ever in Texas was Sam Bass, a kid from Indiana. Bass was an easy-going fellow, not a gunfighter, but a good shot and proficient with firearms. Sam was not prone to outbursts of temper or unreasonable anger. He was not a killer, he was a train robber.

Sam always wanted to be a cowboy, and moved to Denton, Texas, to fulfill that dream. He found work with the local sheriff, "Dad" Egan, cleaning stables, grooming horses, milking cows, doing odd jobs, and hauling supplies around the county. Sam worked hard, saved his money, and earned the respect of the Denton community. He also became an expert on all the back roads, thickets, and trails in the county.

Sam Bass

Sam bought a mare with his savings and began to race her. The "Denton Mare," as she was known, won most races. Sam quit his job and began to live off his winnings. He also began to hang out with a crowd of young toughs in barrooms, drinking and gambling. That was more fun than working, and Sam didn't hold a regular job after 1875, when he was 24 years old.

Sam and a new friend, Joel Collins, took a herd of cattle to Nebraska and sold them. They used the money to prospect for gold in South Dakota, and ended up broke. Sam and Joel joined a gang and started robbing stages, but that didn't provide enough money to be worth the risk. The gang decided to rob trains.

In Big Spring Station, Nebraska, on November 11, 1877, the six-man gang robbed its first train. The small safe had only $450, and the big safe, with the big money, was equipped with a time lock and could not be opened. The thieves discovered some wooden crates and broke one open. The crates contained $60,000.00 worth of newly minted, $20.00 gold pieces, heading from the San Francisco mint to an eastern bank. The gang split the money and separated. Most were caught within a week and Joel Collins was killed in a shootout with lawmen, but Sam and Jack Davis made it back to Texas with their share of the gold coins.

Sam explained his new wealth as good luck in the gold mines of Dakota, and shared his wealth with his friends. Sam spent his money freely and was generous to a fault. Even so, it is unlikely that he spent $10,000 in three months, and many people around Denton think Sam must have buried the money. Rumors surround a local cave as a hiding place for the Bass gold and treasure seekers continue to pester landowners in the area.

Whether because of necessity or for entertainment, by February of 1878, Sam and his gang were back to robbing trains. In the following three months Sam and his gang robbed four trains around Dallas, netting $1300.00 in the first robbery and very little in the others. The robberies were amateur affairs. Some of the witnesses thought the robbers were either very nervous or drunk. In two cases, they failed to find large sums of cash the express men had hurriedly hidden, and Seaborn Barnes got shot in the legs at a shootout in Hutchins, Texas.

The train robberies upset the voters and consequently, the politicians. The governor leaned on the Texas Rangers, and an all-out effort to stop Sam Bass and gang was mounted. Jim Murphy, in exchange for some charges being dropped and a share the reward money, agreed to re-join the Bass Gang and inform the Rangers of their plans. The Bass Gang, because of Sam's knowledge of the Denton countryside, led the Rangers on a merry chase. They appeared and disappeared at will, and generally made the Rangers look silly. Then Murphy sent information about the planned robbery of the bank in Round Rock.

Texas Ranger Major John B. Jones, surprised that Sam Bass was moving so far south, sent three Rangers ahead, then he and Deputy Sheriff Morris Moore of Travis County went to Round Rock to watch for the Bass Gang. Soon, word leaked out and lawmen from all over the area hurried to Round Rock to get in on the action and perhaps share in the reward money.

Friday morning, July 20, 1878, Sam and his four-man gang went into Round Rock for a final look at the bank. They planned the robbery for Saturday afternoon and wanted to case the job and get the "lay of the land."

Jim Murphy used an excuse to leave the group and go down the street to Old Town. He hoped to contact Major Jones and make him aware of the gang's plans. Sam, twenty year-old Frank Jackson, and Seaborn Barnes tied their horses in an alley and went up the street to Kopperal's General Store, on the corner of Mays and Georgetown Avenue. Ranger Dick Ware met the strangers on the street as he crossed to the barber shop, but paid them no mind.

Deputy Sheriff Grimes of Williamson County and Deputy Sheriff Morris Moore of Travis County watched the strangers as they entered Kopperal's store. Grimes noticed that one of the men carried two guns, which was one more than the law in Round Rock allowed. He decided to investigate, and Deputy Moore waited outside.

Inside the store, Sam was buying some tobacco. Still not aware that this was the Bass gang, Grimes, inflated with authority, flashed his badge and asked to see their guns. All three outlaws pulled their guns and shot Grimes. He was dead before he hit the floor with six bullets in him and his gun still in its holster. Deputy Moore rushed in, shooting. He hit Sam in the hand, and was then shot in the chest. The outlaws stepped over him and ran for their horses.

Across the street, Ranger Ware was getting a shave at the barber shop. Hearing the shooting, he pushed the barber aside, and jumped from the chair. Still wearing shaving lather, he drew his gun and ran out into the street to engage the outlaws. Major Jones rushed out of the telegraph office down the street. Jim Murphy stayed hunkered down in Old Town.

A one-armed man named Stubbs picked up Grimes' pistol and helped the Rangers from the front porch of the store. The outlaws had made it to their horses and were trying to get mounted while several Rangers, one wearing a barber's smock and shaving cream, shot at them. The one-armed man tried to reload Grimes' pistol. Ranger Harold, using his rifle, may have hit Sam Bass at this time. Seaborn Barnes was hit in the head and died instantly, probably shot by Ranger Ware. With help from Frank, Sam managed to get mounted and he and Frank rode away. Sam, shot through the lower body, fell off his horse at the edge of town. Frank ignored the flying bullets and helped Sam back on his horse. The two made their getaway heading out the Georgetown road.

The Rangers and the townspeople agreed to postpone the search for Sam Bass until the next morning. They didn't want to risk a night-time gun-fight with an unknown number of gang members.

Near midmorning the next day, they found Sam Bass, seated and propped up against a tree. He was badly wounded. Sam's code of ethics would not let him rat out his friends. He told Major Jones, "It is ag'in my profession to blow on my pals. If a man knows anything, he ought to die with it in him." Sam also said, when asked about killing Deputy Grimes, "if I killed him, he is the first man I ever killed." Sam Bass died of his wound on July 21, 1878, his 27th birthday. He is buried in the Round Rock Cemetery.

Jim Murphy lived the rest of his short life in misery and constant fear that some friend of Sam Bass would kill him. On June 7, 1879, he committed suicide by taking poison. Frank Jackson may have become a prosperous rancher in New Mexico, or he may have died in prison in Arizona. Both stories are claimed to be true.

The city of Round Rock installed bronze plaques in the sidewalk, street, and on the floor inside the store, marking the places where lawmen or outlaws died. One plaque, out in a vacant lot near the water tower, marks the place where Sam fell from his horse and Frank bravely helped him as they got away.

Pink Higgins

John Pinckney Calhoun Higgins was born March 28, 1851, in Macon, Georgia, but grew up near Lampasas, Texas. While still a teenager, he worked as a cowboy on cattle drives to the railheads in Kansas, and picked up the nickname, "Pink." He joined The Law and Order League to actively fight horse thieves, cattle rustlers and outlaws. Higgins participated in several hangings and fought skirmishes with Indians still active in the area. A Winchester rifle became his weapon of choice.

His reputation as a gunfighter started in the mid 1870's during what became known as the Horrell- Higgins Feud. A family feud ordinarily takes place between two families. In this one, Pink Higgins took on the four very dangerous Horrell brothers. It started when Higgins swore out a warrant, accusing all four Horrell brothers of rustling his cattle. With a home town jury, the brothers were acquitted.

In January of 1877, Pink ran into Merrit Horrell in the Matador Saloon in Lampasas. Merritt had rustled some Higgins cattle. Pink is supposed to have walked over to Horrell and said, "This is to settle some cow business," and pumped four rifle bullets into Horrell. He turned himself in to the Rangers and was acquitted because of self defense.

There were some skirmishes between the factions, then, in June of that year, the Horrells ambushed Higgins and some friends on the Town Square in Lampasas. Two Horrell hired hands and two of Higgins' friends were killed. In July, the Texas Rangers came to Lampasas, and Major John B. Jones negotiated a peace between the factions which effectively ended the feud. A few months later, the same Ranger, Major Jones, was instrumental in capturing Sam Bass and his gang in nearby Round Rock.

In 1882, Higgins divorced his wife, Delilah, who, true to her name, was unfaithful. The next year, he married a fifteen year old girl, Lena Sweet, to care for his three children, and moved to a ranch near Spur. He and Lena had seven children, six daughters and one son. The son and one daughter died as infants. His two older sons (by Delilah) both became prominent lawyers.

Also in 1882, Sam Horrell, the only one of the brothers left alive, moved his family to Oregon, permanently ending the feud. He died peacefully in California in 1932.

In West Texas, Pink worked security for the Spur Ranch and caught and hanged several rustlers. His last gunfight happened in 1904, with an ex-sheriff, Bill Sandifer. Both men had worked security for the Spur Ranch, but couldn't get along. The problem may have stemmed from the fact that Sandifer was distantly related to the Horrells. In any case, the Spur Ranch fired both men.

Sandifer rode out to Higgins' Ranch to settle their differences, once and for all. Higgins rode out to meet him. They exchanged words, dismounted, and then Bill Sandifer started firing. Pink's horse was shot in the flank, and Sandifer was jumping around, firing in every direction. Higgins kneeled down, took careful aim with his Winchester, and shot Sandifer dead. The only witnesses were Higgins' daughter and brother-in-law. He was never indicted or arrested. The sheriff of Spur hired him as a deputy a few weeks later.

Pink Higgins died of a heart attack in Spur on December 18, 1913. He is said to have killed 14 men in gunfights.

Henry Andrew "Heck" Thomas—Lawman

Henry Andrew Thomas, another Georgia boy, was born in Athens, Georgia, on January 3, 1850. He picked up the nickname "Heck" in his childhood and it stuck with him. During the Civil War, he served as a courier boy for his uncle, who was a Confederate General. He was just twelve years old.

After the war, Heck's father became police chief of Atlanta, and Heck started his law enforcement career as an Atlanta policeman at age seventeen.

Unlike many lawmen of the day, Heck never crossed the line to become an outlaw. He was always a lawman. In 1875, he moved his family to Galveston, Texas, and took a job as a railroad guard for the Texas Express Company. He guarded the express car on the Houston and Texas Central Railroad, a line that ran between Galveston and Denison and was often hit by train robbers.

In March of 1878, at Hutchins Station, near Dallas, Sam Bass and his gang attempted to rob Heck's train. Heck was wounded in the shootout that followed, but managed to shoot Seaborn Barnes in the legs. Bass's gang went away empty handed. Heck had hidden $25,000.00 cash in an unlit stove and put dummy packages in the safe. The train was well underway when Bass and his gang discovered their mistake. Heck was promoted to a Fort Worth detective for the company, and by 1879 was made Chief Agent.

In a close race, Heck failed an attempt to be elected Sheriff and joined the Fort Worth Detective Association, continuing in the law enforcement business. In 1885, he began pursuit of the notorious Lee gang, headed by two brothers, Jim and Pink Lee. These outlaws ambushed and killed four members of a posse searching for them and were stealing horses and cattle in North Texas and Oklahoma. The settlers were enraged, the Indians were enraged, and law enforcement was enraged. Rewards totaling $7000 were being offered.

Thomas performed one of his trademark dogged pursuits and four months later, he and Jim Taylor, a friend that Thomas recruited for his marksmanship, cornered the Lee brothers in a hay meadow near Dexter, Texas. As was his custom, Heck gave the outlaws a chance to surrender. They chose to fight, and both brothers were killed in the shootout that followed. The newspapers proclaimed the successful work of the lawmen, and they split the reward.

Heck used his friend, Jim Taylor, several times down through the years. Taylor was good company on the trail and known as one of the best shots in Oklahoma. They worked together well and Heck swore Taylor in as a deputy whenever he used him, so there was never a question about splitting the rewards.

Shortly after the Lee shootout, Thomas was appointed Deputy U. S. Marshall and assigned to work for the infamous "hanging judge," Isaac Parker, in Fort Smith, Arkansas. On his first trip into Indian Territory, Thomas caught eight murderers, a bootlegger, a horse thief, and several lesser criminals. This would become typical for Heck, and he would apprehend over three hundred criminals during the seven years he worked for Judge Parker.

When Thomas left Judge Parker, he continued as a U. S. Deputy Marshall, and concentrated on the most-wanted outlaws. The work was dangerous, but the rewards were higher. He received gunshot wounds that required hospitalization at least six times during his years as a lawman. Heck always gave the outlaws an opportunity to surrender, but sometimes he didn't give them much time to make up their minds.

He aligned himself with two other Deputies, Chris Madsen and Bill Tighman, and the three took on the nickname "The Guardsmen." Over the next few years, the Guardsmen chased the Dalton Gang, the Doolins, and several other well-known outlaws. They were sent to Perry, Oklahoma, a boom town that sprung up overnight in the Oklahoma land rush. Perry boasted 25,000 people and 110 saloons. The Guardsmen cleaned it up.

Heck and a posse of local citizens cornered Bill Doolin, of a gang called the "Wild Bunch," and offered him a chance to surrender. He chose to fight and was killed in the shootout. The Dalton Gang was wiped out a few weeks later in a raid on Coffeyville, Kansas. According to Emmett Dalton, the only survivor of the gang, they knew that Heck Thomas was on their trail and would not give up. Instead of continuing to run, they decided to rob two banks in Coffeyville, and use the money to escape to South America. Heck was close enough in pursuit to identify their bodies the next day. Heck knew the outlaws because in earlier days, two of the Daltons had worked with Heck as deputies.

In 1902, Heck Thomas moved to Lawton, Oklahoma, and became police chief. He led a relatively quiet life for the next seven years, and then retired after a heart attack. Heck died of natural causes in 1912.

John Wesley Hardin

Perhaps the Baddest of the Bad when it comes to Texas gunfighters, was John Wesley Hardin, the son of a Methodist preacher who started killing at age fifteen and, except for a seventeen year stint in Huntsville State Prison, continued until the day he died. Hardin was pathological about a lot of things—killing was one of them, lying was another. While in prison, Hardin studied law and wrote an autobiography. His autobiography claims he killed forty-four men, but official records indicate the total was more like twenty-seven. Many stories about his exploits are exaggerated in his book, and some simply never happened.

One popular story concerns his killing of a man for snoring. According to the tale, Hardin was trying to sleep in a hotel one night, and the man in the next room was snoring loudly. Hardin yelled, trying to wake the man up so the snoring would stop. Having no luck waking the man, and no luck sleeping with the snoring, Hardin got up, went down the hall, kicked open the door, shot the snoring man, then went back to a peaceful night's sleep.

According to Hardin, that never happened. The incident took place in Abilene, Kansas, at the American House Hotel. Hardin and two friends had been out drinking, and one of them was sleeping in the room next door. During the night, Hardin was awakened by the loud snoring of his friend. Hardin yelled and beat on the wall, but the snoring didn't cease. Finally, in desperation, Hardin shot through the wall four times to wake the guy and shut him up. The second shot hit the snorer in the head, killing him instantly.

Hardin, after the shooting, saw the Abilene sheriff, Wild Bill Hickok, hurrying across the street. He slipped out the window and spent the night in a convenient haystack, then left town early the next morning. Wild Bill was trying to add to his reputation as a gunfighter, and Hardin was convinced Hickok would arrange to shoot him if he ended up in his custody.

Hardin, complaining about the untrue stories written about him, said he was supposed to have killed four or five men for snoring. He said, "That's just not true. I only killed one man for snoring."

John Wesley Hardin went into prison at age twenty-three and came out at age forty. He lived a bit less than two years after he was released, and, so far as is known, only killed one man in that time. Otherwise, he had a busy year. He was released from Huntsville on February 17, 1894. He passed the examination and was admitted to the bar on July, 21, 1894. He married a fifteen year old girl on January 9, 1895. She left him a short time later but the marriage was never legally dissolved.

According to a 1900 newspaper article, just after he was released from prison, Hardin and a friend were visiting on the street in Gonzales. A Mexican was "sunning himself" on a wooden box down the street. Hardin bet $5.00 he could knock the Mexican off the box with the "first shot." Hardin won the bet, but was charged with "negligent homicide." The terrified Mexican was only wounded by the gunshot, but broke his neck when he fell off the box.

Hardin moved to El Paso to practice law after his teen bride left him. On August 19, 1895, John Selman shot him in the back of the head, then put three more bullets in him as he lay dead on the floor. Selman testified that he saw, in the barroom mirror, Hardin reaching for his pistol and he had no choice but to shoot him. The trial ended with a hung jury, and Selman was shot dead in a barroom before the appeal came to trial.

I read that there were 160 gunfights in Texas between 1865 and 1900, more than any other state. I don't doubt that Texas had more gunfights, but I wonder about that number. Who keeps score and how? If they just read all the newspapers, how can they be sure everything was reported?

Revolvers became widely available after the Civil War, and all the soldiers knew how to use them. Indians were still a problem in Texas and there was some need, especially for frontier dwellers, to carry guns for self-protection. Human beings, especially adolescent males, are fascinated with anything dangerous. Give a young man a gun and his imagination will run wild. The gunfighters were not forty-year old farmers or shopkeepers. Those guys were home eating supper. If they had a gun at all, it was for hunting, shooting snakes or varmints, and displaying over the mantle.

The men who fought gunfights at the local saloons didn't have a wife and family to go home to. They went to a bar for company. They could talk and laugh, maybe gamble a bit, brag and tease the whores, tell jokes and have a drink or two. Good clean fun. Sometimes one of them would have a little too much to drink, or a stranger would make a smart-assed comment, and things might get out of hand. Someone might get shot and they might die, but that was not often. Maybe four or five times a year in the whole state of Texas. Of course, that would add up in thirty-five years.

# CHAPTER FOURTEEN
# Ranald Slidell Mackenzie
# and the Red River Wars

While the lawmen were dealing with outlaws and gunmen, the army had its hands full with the Indians. General William Tecumseh Sherman did not have to send Col. Mackenzie's troops out to arrest those responsible for the Salt Creek Massacre. In late May, 1871, a day or so after he and Mackenzie arrived at reservation headquarters in Fort Sill, White Bear (Satanta) bragged about the raid to anyone who would listen. Lawrie Tatum, the Quaker in charge of the reservation, attempted to defuse the situation, but the war chief was proud of the raid, and wanted to be sure that no one else got credit for it. He named Big Tree (Ado-ete) and Sitting Bear (Satank) as two other participants and bragged that they brought forty-one mules into their village, along with barrels of corn, coffee, flour, and sugar.

General Sherman ordered the immediate arrest of all three chiefs. Sherman was on the front steps of the Fort Sill headquarters, with a few dozen armed soldiers standing around, and Indians scattered about the yard. There was a tense moment as the soldiers raised their weapons and the Indians reached for theirs. Tatum, or perhaps Satanta, quieted the braves and the soldiers were allowed to arrest the three chiefs.

Sherman expected his orders to be obeyed. His rank was such that the only person he called "Sir" was the President of the United States. It never occurred to him that a bunch of reservation Indians might not obey a general in the army. He may have realized later that was the second time in a week that he escaped death by a narrow margin.

Sherman decided to have the chiefs tried in state court in Texas, breaking with tradition, which would have required a military court martial. In the military view, killing an opponent in an act of war is one thing. In civilian terms, murdering an innocent drover while stealing merchandise is something completely different. Sherman wanted the death penalty, which he knew a military court could not deliver, so he decided to prosecute the case in civil court. The trial was set for Jacksboro, Texas, in the jurisdiction where the crimes occurred.

As the chiefs were prepared for transfer to Jacksboro, Satank told his family he would not suffer the white man's justice and would never stand trial. He asked that they look for his body along the road to Texas. As the prisoners were being loaded, Satank refused to get into the wagon. His hands and feet were tied with leather thongs, but he fought the guards, and was knocked to the ground. The guards picked him up and threw him into the wagon. Satank wrestled a blanket over his head.

The guards assumed that Satank covered himself from shame and embarrassment, but he hid under the blanket so he could chew the bindings off his wrists. As the wagon creaked along, Satank chanted his death song. Suddenly, he leapt from under the blanket and stabbed a guard with a knife he had hidden in his clothing. As he wrestled the guard's rifle away, other guards shot him, and he fell dead in the middle of the road. The army left him there and his family was afraid to claim the body. After a few days, Mackenzie sent soldiers out to gather the body and had Satank buried at Fort Sill.

The trial of Satanta and Ado-ete (Big Tree) took four days in early July of 1871, and they were found guilty and sentenced to hang. The Reconstruction Governor Edmund Davis felt pressure from several sources—The Quakers with their peace policy, Comanche threats that the hanging would cause an all-out war, the liberal press, the Bureau of Indian Affairs, and misguided Eastern Congressmen who favored peace with the Indians at any cost. Finally, in answer to a request from President Grant, Davis gave in and commuted the sentences to life imprisonment. Both chiefs were paroled within two years. Satanta went back to raiding, was caught and sent back to Huntsville Prison where he eventually committed suicide. Big Tree became a Baptist preacher and lived to be eighty years old. He died in 1929.

Ranald Slidell Mackenzie was born in Westchester County, New York, on July 27, 1840. His father was born Alexander Slidell, but had his name changed to Mackenzie to claim the inheritance of an uncle. (Mackenzie was his mother's maiden name). Alexander Slidell Mackenzie was a captain in the navy and author of several books, but he made an unfortunate career choice when he hanged the son of the Secretary of War for mutiny. He was exonerated of all blame, but the incident dogged him for the rest of his naval career.

Ranald Slidell Mackenzie began his education at Williams College and finished at the Military Academy at West Point, where he graduated first in his class in June of 1862. After graduation, Mackenzie went directly into the Army of the Potomac as a second lieutenant.

Mackenzie had a distinguished career in the Civil War. He fought in the second Battle of Bull Run, Antietam, Gettysburg, and Petersburg. During these campaigns, he was wounded several times. During the siege of Petersburg, at Jerusalem Plank Road, his right hand was mangled, and he lost two fingers. The Comanche later gave him the name "Bad Hand."

By June of 1864, Mackenzie had received several battlefield promotions and, because of bravery in action, was brevetted to Lt. Colonel in the regular army. He was not popular with the troops that served under him—Mackenzie was considered harsh and demanding by the rank and file—but was well respected by his peers and superiors. U.S. Grant called him "the most promising young officer in the army."

After the Civil War, Mackenzie was promoted to colonel of the Forty-first Infantry, a black regiment headquartered at Ft. Brown in Texas. The unit moved to Fort Clark and later to Fort McKavett. On February 25, 1871, he assumed command of the Fourth United States Cavalry at Fort Concho, and in March moved it to Fort Richardson.

Immediately after the Salt Creek Massacre, Mackenzie and General Sherman discussed the idea of seeking out the Comanche in their camps on the Llano Estacado. Mackenzie's job would be simple--find the Comanche and force them back to the reservation or annihilate them. He began to explore the uncharted High Plains in his first efforts to find the Indians. With the help of an ex-Comanchero guide, Polonio Ortiz, he discovered Indian trails crisscrossing the plains. The Comanchero showed him reliable water sources less than thirty miles apart, which, in turn, gave access to virtual highways across the formerly mysterious wasteland. These expeditions gave Mackenzie and his black troopers solid knowledge of the Llano Estacado geography.

On October 3, Mackenzie received the official order from General Sherman to go forth and kill Comanche. This was the end of anything like tolerance. No more would the army engage in defensive measures only. No longer would the Quaker peace policy be observed. General Sherman was out of patience. After all, he could have been killed at Salt Creek or Fort Sill.

Early in October of 1871, Mackenzie had his first battle with Quanah, a young war chief of the Quahadi, the most warlike and dangerous band of Comanche. Mackenzie's forces included eight companies of his Fourth Cavalry, two companies of the Eleventh Infantry, and twenty Tonkawa scouts. After moving west for more than four days, they set up a base camp at Duck Creek, near present-day Spur. The next day, Mackenzie chose to leave his infantry secure at the base camp to await supplies from Fort Richardson. Meanwhile, Mackenzie and the cavalry could move faster to try and find the hidden Quahadi village and attempt to surprise the Comanche in their heartland.

On October 9, Mackenzie and his cavalry set up camp in Blanco Canyon, perhaps the first white soldiers ever to see that canyon. The camp was southeast of present-day Crosbyton. That night, just after midnight, Quanah attacked. The Indians charged through the camp at full gallop, shouting, shooting and stampeding the soldier's horses. They killed one trooper, managed to steal about seventy horses, including Mackenzie's favorite mount, and disrupted the camp. The soldiers chased the Comanche up the canyon walls to the caprock, but the Indians faded into the night.

With the onset of daylight, Mackenzie and his cavalry, led by the Tonkawa scouts, followed the Comanche trail. The Indians were slowed by their family members, who packed the village and joined the retreat. After four days, Mackenzie's troops got near enough to mount an attack, but a sudden blinding snowstorm allowed the Quahadi to escape. The blue norther obscured the tracks of the Comanche and the cavalry, dressed in summer uniforms, had to stop and build fires to keep from freezing. Mackenzie abandoned the chase near present-day Plainview, and the Quahadi vanished into the Llano Estacado.

On the way back to the base camp at Duck Creek, the Tonkawa discovered two Comanche scouts, following and keeping tabs on the troop. In the skirmish that ensued, the Indian spies were killed, and Mackenzie took an arrow in the leg, the seventh wound of his military career. After two more weeks, Mackenzie was forced, by the weather, his wound and dwindling rations, to give up the chase. He returned to Fort Richardson on November 17, 1871.

Mackenzie considered the expedition a failure, but he learned valuable lessons. He penetrated to the heart of Comancheria and drove a Quahadi band from its homeland. He explored and mapped an area that, so far as anyone knew, had never been seen by a white man. He found that troops could survive on the Llano Estacado and learned to protect his horses and plan for drastic weather changes.

There is evidence that Blanco Canyon had been seen by white men before Mackenzie and his soldiers got there. Over three hundred years before, in 1541, Francisco Coronado and his conquistadors camped in Blanco Canyon near present day Floydada. The location is known because pottery shards, Spanish horseshoe nails, and crossbow points were found there in 1993. While camped in the canyon, Coronado's daily log tells of a "tempest," a violent hail and rainstorm that shredded their tents, broke up their cooking pottery, and wounded some horses. The Spaniards had never seen such violent weather, but it is not uncommon in the Texas Panhandle.

During the summer of 1871, while Mackenzie learned the secrets of the Llano Estacado, and chased hostile Comanche, Charles Goodnight was busy extending the Goodnight-Loving Trail from New Mexico north to Colorado, and eventually to Wyoming.

By this time, Jack Hays had been in California for over twenty years. He had already been sheriff of San Francisco, laid out the city of Oakland as a surveyor and amassed a fortune in real estate. He became active in politics and was gaining influence in the local Democratic Party.

In Chicago, a city of 325,000 people, the great Chicago Fire started as Mackenzie's troops moved into Blanco Canyon on October 8th. The fire burned out of control until rain aided the fire fighters on October 10th. Mrs. O'Leary's cow was judged not responsible, but over three hundred people were killed, and 100,000 people lost their homes. John Warne Gates was sixteen that year, and both his brothers had died, leaving him an only child. He learned to play poker, watching professional gamblers in long-running games at the railroad station.

The point to all this is that most of the country was blithely marching along, growing and prospering. Most Americans were living good, safe, productive lives, while the settlers in Texas were sleeping with shotguns near at hand and nervously lying awake during nights of the full moon. The dreaded Comanche Moon.

In early July of 1872, Mackenzie left Fort Concho with almost 300 troops, a dozen officers and 20 Tonkawa guides. They returned to Duck Creek and established a base camp. After several scouting trips from the base camp, the troop headed west, using trails shown them by the Comanchero guide Polonio Ortiz. They searched for signs of Comanche and/or stolen cattle. These were no longer the green, inexperienced soldiers that had been embarrassed at Blanco Canyon. Mackenzie drilled them daily. They were competent and well-trained in everything from polishing brass to marksmanship and hand-to-hand combat.

The soldiers probably tramped through Ransom Canyon, where the Comanche brought white captives to be ransomed. From there they would have circled present day Lubbock in Yellow House Canyon and exited past the lakes area that has been a gathering place for Indians for over 12,000 years. They headed west toward present Clovis, New Mexico.

Mackenzie was a hard taskmaster, but especially hard on himself. His leg wound from the Blanco Canyon arrow had healed, but he was still bothered by Civil war wounds that had not properly healed. Riding all day was wickedly painful for him, and as a result his personality suffered. He was moody, difficult to please, and rarely found humor in anything. He found very little to praise.

On August 7, after resupply at Fort Sumner, New Mexico, the troop moved on to Fort Bascom. Ortiz led them back east across the Llano Estacado, skirted Palo Duro Canyon, and followed Blanco Canyon back to the base camp at Duck Creek. After a few day's rest, on September 21, 1872, the troop struck out due north, determined to find the base camp of the elusive Comanche. The Tonkawa scouts reported that it was on the North Fork of the Red River.

Mackenzie did not know it at the time, but his route through the canyons near present-day Matador, Turkey, and Clarendon was a favorite pathway of the Comanche. In the sheltered canyons here, beneath the caprock, their villages had protection from the weather, yet easy access to the hunting grounds of the vast Llano Estacado.

September 28, scouts reported a large village of Comanche on the North Fork of the Red River, some ten miles southeast of present-day Pampa. The troopers advanced to within a half mile of the village before being discovered, then charged when the alarm was sounded. The battle lasted less than thirty minutes.

Mackenzie's Raiders, as they were starting to be known in the press, charged into the village with their guns blazing. The villagers were completely surprised. Many were killed and 130 women, children and old people were taken prisoner. Makenzie lost three killed and three wounded.

Mackenzie reported twenty-three Comanche killed, but there were almost certainly more. Many of the Comanche dead were submerged in a pit to keep them away from the Tonkawa Scouts. The Tonks mutilated the bodies of their enemies, and they hated the Comanche.

Everything in the camp was burned. The tents, the lodge poles, buffalo robes, moccasins, winter food supplies, everything of value was burned. The captured horses were placed in a corral for the night and put under double guard. Before dawn, the Comanche stole them back, including the horses of the Tonkawa scouts. After this experience, Mackenzie decided it was not possible to keep Comanche horses. From this point on, he had them shot.

The prisoners were marched to the base camp at Duck Creek, and on to Fort Concho. Mackenzie planned to trade them back to their families if the families promised to live on the reservations. This ploy worked, and several chiefs moved back to Fort Sill. Some of them stayed.

Mackenzie did not get the opportunity to continue battling the Comanche. A band of Kickapoo Indians who lived in Mexico were raiding in Texas. Since the end of the Civil War, they had been stealing cattle and horses. The Mexican government was either unable or unwilling to stop them. The Kickapoo rode into Texas, rustled cattle and horses, killed and scalped a few settlers, then crossed back into Mexico where they were protected by the government. In January of 1873, President U.S. Grant, under increasing pressure from Texas politicians and citizens, ordered General Sheridan to send Mackenzie's Fourth Cavalry to Fort Clark on the Rio Grande to stop the raids. Grant chose that unit because it was in Texas at the time, and army inspectors listed it as the best cavalry unit in the U.S. Army.

General Phil Sheridan and Secretary of War William Belknap visited Mackenzie in April to discuss the Kickapoo situation and issue face to face verbal instructions. Their orders were not in writing because the raid could cause an international incident and it was important that they disavow any responsibility. Mackenzie was on his own.

Sheridan respected Mackenzie from their relationship during the Civil War. This raid would raise the general's opinion of the young officer and cement their friendship.

After a month of careful planning and close surveillance by civilian scouts, Mackenzie crossed the Rio Grande just after dark on May 17, 1873, with six companies of his Fourth Cavalry, a total of 360 men and 17 officers. Mackenzie pushed his men through the night on a circuitous route to avoid settlements. After a sixty-three-mile forced march through the desert, they attacked the Kickapoo village near Remolino just before dawn.

The attack completely surprised the Indians, who offered little resistance, and the battle was over in a few minutes. Mackenzie's men burned the villages, three in all, with a total of 180 dwellings. Most of the Indians fled into the hills, but Mackenzie reported nineteen killed and forty women and children captured. The army lost one killed and two wounded. Mackenzie pushed his troops through the night and safely crossed back into Texas at dawn on May 19th. The captives were taken to San Antonio and eventually transferred to Fort Sill, in Indian Territory.

The response to the raid was universally favorable, except, of course, in Mexico. The Texas legislature voted to officially thank Mackenzie for the raid. General Sheridan praised him for his initiative, and, from this time forward, called on him for his most difficult assignments. The Kickapoo ceased all raids into Texas for fear of another devastating attack. Many moved deep into the mountains. The Mexican Government, nervous because of its involvement, chose not to make the episode into an international incident. The captives were sent to Fort Sill, and by the end of 1874 more than half the Kickapoo resettled on the reservation, which vindicated Mackenzie's captive policy.

The Comanche realized that white men were killing buffalo to remove the Indian's source of food. Hundreds of buffalo hunters flooded the plains, ignoring the Medicine Bow Treaty, killing and skinning buffalo and leaving the bodies to rot. The Indians, to stop the carnage, and to survive, had to stop the hunters and skinners.

In far north Texas, at an abandoned fort near the Canadian River called Adobe Walls, Kit Carson and 300 men had fought a thousand Indians in 1864, and were lucky to get out with their scalps. Ten years later buffalo hunters, merchants, gamblers and card sharks gathered there. Two merchants, a trading post, and a saloon moved in to serve the hunters and hide men working the area.

A new Comanche medicine man, Isa-tai, claimed to have strong medicine, which made him immune to the bullets of the white man. He joined with Quanah Parker, the fiery half-breed son of Peta Nocona and Cynthia Ann Parker, to lead an attack against the buffalo hunters at Adobe Walls. Their plan to attack just before dawn and kill the sleeping hunters in their beds made good sense, especially if they painted themselves yellow, which Iso-tai claimed made them immune from white man's bullets.

Just before dawn on June 27, 1874, at least 250, and according to some sources, as many as 1000 Indians, mostly Comanche and Cheyenne, attacked the sleeping hunters. Iso-tai joined the group completely naked and painted yellow. Even so, his medicine was not strong, and things went wrong from the first. Many of the Indian ponies stumbled in prairie dog holes, throwing their riders before they reached the encampment. To complicate matters, the hunters were not asleep, but wide awake, drinking. The hunters "forted up" inside the sod saloon and picked off Indians with short guns through makeshift shooting holes in the walls. The sod would not burn, so the Indians could not burn the building and were left to scurry around outside while the hunters took potshots at them.

After about four hours, the Indians withdrew to a nearby mesa to hold a war council. The Indians felt they were safe, more than a half mile from the fort, until one was shot off his horse. As Isa-tai contemplated the failure of his medicine, his yellow horse was shot from beneath him. The buffalo hunters had broken out the single shot Sharps "Big Fifties". These "Buffalo Guns" shot a one-half-inch diameter slug, propelled by 125 grains of black powder and were powerful enough to knock over a horse at 1,000 yards.

The buffalo hunters in camp were not amateurs, or teenage adventurers, but grizzled professionals. Some were young, but all were competent, experienced hunters, who killed for a living. They were an especially tough crew, even for the panhandle at that time. Bat Masterson, future sheriff of Dodge City, Billy Dixon, who would go on to win the Medal-of-Honor (one of the few ever given to a civilian), and several future well-known outlaws were among the twenty-eight men there. One woman, the wife of cook William Olds, fought alongside her husband.

Satanta had distinguished himself in the first battle of Adobe Walls, against Kit Carson. Now, fresh out of Huntsville prison on parole, and sworn to live peacefully, he helped plan the raid. At his trial, he protested that he didn't take part in the fighting, but his presence there broke the terms of his parole. When he returned to the reservation after the battle, he was arrested and returned to prison in Huntsville. In October of 1878, he committed suicide there by diving from a high window into a brick courtyard.

The Indians lost their taste for battle after the first day. Isa-tai's medicine was useless, even for those who went naked and painted themselves yellow—he claimed it failed because the Cheyenne killed a skunk the day before the battle. Quanah Parker was wounded, not seriously, but Indians considered the wounding of a chief to be bad medicine. The Indians did not attack the fort after the first day. On the third day, a group of fifteen Indians looked over the battlefield from atop a mesa almost a mile away. Billy Dixon borrowed a Sharps "Big Fifty" from the storekeeper, took careful aim, and fired. One of the Indians fell dead. Dixon always claimed it was a lucky shot, but for the Comanche, it was the last straw. They loaded their gear and went home.

Four hunters lost their lives in the battle, three during the initial attack, and one unlucky fellow who accidentally shot himself in the head as he climbed a ladder dragging a loaded rifle. No one knows precisely, but most authorities agree that about twenty-five Indians died. Sometime after the battle a group measured the length of Billy Dixon's shot. They set the distance at 1538 yards, almost nine tenths of a mile.

The Indians, sorely disappointed in Isa-tai's lack of good medicine and their failure to take out the hunters, vented their frustrations by raiding all over the plains. Raids as far north as Kansas, west to New Mexico, east into Oklahoma, and deep into south Texas are blamed on the failure of this battle. Quanah took his followers on the warpath in Texas.

The carnage following Adobe Walls pushed the white man's patience past the limits. In July of 1874, Grant gave Sherman permission to have the army take over the reservations. The five-year experiment with the Quaker peace policy had failed miserably and was discontinued. Grant ordered the army to use any means possible to seek out and deal with any Indians who refused to remain on the reservation. No restrictions were imposed on the army's movements. They were ordered to cross into Indian Territory at will and chase renegades wherever they tried to hide. Even the liberal press agreed with these provisions.

General William T. Sherman and General Phil Sheridan had worked together for months on a plan for the "Red River Wars." It was to be the final solution to the Indian problem and was to be the largest full-scale offensive ever unleashed by the U.S. Army against Native Americans. Grant gave the go-ahead, and these two Civil War soldiers put three thousand troops in the field against about eight hundred Indian braves, who carried their women and children on the war path with them.

The plan for the Red River War involved moving five columns of troops into the Texas Panhandle from five different directions. One troop worked due south from Fort Dodge, Kansas. One came east from New

Mexico, and one moved west from Fort Sill. Still another column started northwest from central Texas and Mackenzie worked due north from Fort Concho. All planned to use Mackenzie's knowledge of the terrain and dog the Indians with relentless pursuit until they were trapped and driven out of the Llano Estacado.

Each of the separate units had its own supply chain and enough supplies to stay out indefinitely. They would squeeze the Indians between columns of bluecoats until the savages begged for a chance to go back to the reservation. The panhandle of Texas is a big place, with lots of canyons and mesas, gullies and dry washes and hiding places. The soldiers were going to squeeze the Indians relentlessly—just as soon as they found them.

The Indians knew they would lose any pitched battle. They were outnumbered by better armed and equipped soldiers, so they watched and when it became necessary, they moved. They ran off horses in the night and disappeared in the daytime. They attacked small patrols and evaded the columns of cavalry.

Mackenzie set up his base camp at the now-familiar Duck Creek campground near Spur, and for a month or so, sent scout patrols in all directions. They fought a few skirmishes with roving bands of Comanche but could not discover any large Indian camps. In early September, the rains started. The average yearly rainfall in that country is around 20 inches, but some years that all comes in one month. Thick mud covered the plains, slowing the horses and sticking the wagons.

After leaving his infantry and one company of cavalry to guard the supplies, Mackenzie abandoned the wagons and loaded the mules with twelve days' rations and struck out across country to Tule Canyon. Comanche attacked in force one night, trying to steal the horses, but Mackenzie had double-hobbled them and increased the guard. When the Indians first charge failed, they circled the camp for a couple of hours, then faded into the night. Bad Hand had learned his lessons.

The Tonkawa scouts followed a trail to the edge of Palo Duro Canyon. When they looked down into the canyon, 900 feet below, they saw five Indian villages and a large herd of horses. They hurried back and reported this to Mackenzie. It was the news he'd been waiting for. Mackenzie pushed his men through the night, across Tule Canyon, up over the Caprock and along the edge of the Llano Estacado. Just before dawn on September 28, seven companies of American Cavalry looked down from the canyon's edge on the sleeping Indian villages.

The scouts found a goat trail down into the canyon and within an hour all seven companies descended and stood on the canyon floor. The Indians, knowing they were safe in their home camp, had posted no guards. As soon as the Indians discovered soldiers, they attacked from every quarter, trying to give their squaws and families time to escape. Mackenzie's troops charged and the Indians retreated up the side of Blanca Cita Canyon which intersected Palo Duro just upriver from the villages.

The battle did not last long. When the squaws and children were safe, the braves retreated up out of the canyon and disappeared into the Llano Estacado. Only a few Indians were killed and Mackenzie had one trooper wounded. Mackenzie did not follow the Indians—he had what he wanted. Five empty villages with every buffalo robe, every piece of jerky, every winter blanket, every tent, every lodge pole, and every sack of government-issue flour, coffee, sugar, tobacco, and cornmeal. In short, everything the village needed to survive the winter. Without these supplies, the Indians would suffer long, slow, and sure starvation. Mackenzie ordered everything burned.

It was three o'clock in the afternoon before the last of the supplies and tents were burned. The entire village was ash. To paraphrase General Grant's instructions to General Sheridan, "A crow would have to carry provisions to cross the canyon."

Mackenzie and his troops herded the 1500 or so Comanche horses out of Palo Duro and across the plains to Tule Canyon. The next morning, about three hundred of the best horses were cut out for use of the troops, and the rest were systematically shot. All day long, horses were roped, dragged into the canyon and shot. The bodies rotted, until nothing but bones remained. For many years, visitors to Tulia were taken out to "see the horse bones." Finally, in the 1920's the bones were ground up and sold as fertilizer.

With the Battle of Palo Duro Canyon, the Red River Wars were essentially over. Some small skirmishes followed, and Mackenzie's Calvary defeated a small band of Comanche near present day Tahoka on the south plains. That was his last fight with the Comanche. Mackenzie searched in vain for Quanah's band of Quahadis, and most of the plains Indians, starving, turned themselves in to the reservation. The first bands to come in were treated harshly, their horses taken, and the leaders imprisoned, but it soon became apparent that these people were so thoroughly beaten that further punishment was unnecessary.

Sheridan ordered Mackenzie to cease his searching and report to Fort Sill as commander of the Comanche and Cheyenne Reservations. Mackenzie took command of Fort Sill on March 16, 1875, and immediately sent out a peace party in search of the last remaining band of Comanche, Quanah's Quahadis. After some negotiations, on June 2, 1875, Quanah Parker led four hundred Quahadis and fifteen hundred horses in surrender to Fort Sill authorities. The Red River Wars were truly over.

Quanah Parker settled into life on the reservation and soon became, in the eyes of the white men, the chief of all the Comanche. The Comanche were not accustomed to a supreme chief, but they were also not accustomed to living in one place, tilling the soil, and being dependent upon white men for food and shelter. Quanah worked out leases with ranchers, that allowed them to graze their cattle on Indian land for a fee. During this time he developed a strong, lasting friendships with Texas ranchers Burk Burnett and Charles Goodnight.

Parker became well-known and friends with influential people, including some local and national politicians. He built a large frame home called Star House on the reservation and lived there with his six wives. Theodore Roosevelt and other famous people visited Quanah at Star House, and he appeared in county fairs, rodeos, and other festivities in Texas and Oklahoma. He maintained his friendships with Texas ranchers, and grew to be close friends with his old enemy, Ranald Mackenzie.

Quanah Parker died at Star House in 1911, and is buried at Fort Sill, next to his mother. Cynthia Ann Parker and his sister Prairie Flower.

Mackenzie was too valuable as an Indian fighter to leave on the desk job at Fort Sill. After Custer became famous by getting killed at Little Big Horn, in the summer of 1876, Sheridan sent Mackenzie to Wyoming to "influence" the Sioux to move back to the reservation. He did this job in his usual quiet and efficient manner. During the next several years Mackenzie successfully faced Indians in Colorado, New Mexico, and Arizona. He dealt with Utes, Apache and Navajo, and was easily the most effective Indian fighter in American history. In 1882, he became the youngest brigadier in the Regular Army, and, a year later, was brought back to San Antonio to head up the Department of Texas. Unfortunately, by this time, he was showing signs of mental illness.

Mackenzie had fallen in love with a San Antonio widow, a nurse, and they planned to wed. Mackenzie bought a small ranch in Boerne, and planned to retire there, in the hill country that he had grown to love. As the date for the wedding drew near, his behavior became erratic. One morning, after a drunken spree, he was found badly beaten and tied to a wagon wheel in a seedy neighborhood in San Antonio. On the day before his wedding, he broke up a chair in a merchant's shop and attacked the merchant with one of the chair legs. In spite of protests from the bride, the wedding was delayed. An army doctor ruled that the general suffered from "General Paresis of the Insane."

General Paresis of the Insane comes as a consequence of Third Stage Syphilis and occurs ten to thirty years after exposure. Mackenzie's symptoms included erratic behavior, headaches, lack of social inhibitions, insomnia, asocial behavior, and deterioration of judgment. The army doctor in San Antonio said he was unfit for military service and recommended he be confined to an asylum.

To make the transition possible, Mackenzie's friend, General Phil Sheridan, issued sham orders transferring Mackenzie to Washington, D.C., to reorganize the army. Mackenzie's sister came from New York to accompany her incoherent brother back to his homeland. He was admitted to Bloomingdale Asylum in New York City, where he was again judged "totally unfit for Military service." The army discharged him on March 24, 1884 and granted him a full pension. He spent the last five years of his life in and out of mental institutions and died at his sister's home on January 18, 1889. He is buried at West Point.

About a year after Mackenzie chased the Indians out of Palo Duro Canyon, Charles Goodnight moved 1600 cattle into the canyon and set up what he called the Old Home Ranch, 250 miles from the nearest railroad and over a hundred miles from the nearest neighbor.

Goodnight liked to make deals. He tracked down a local outlaw named Dutch Henry and made a deal with him. If the outlaw would stay on his side of a certain creek, and leave Goodnight's cattle alone, then Goodnight wouldn't have to send all his well-armed cowboys after him. They could be neighbors and friends. Dutch agreed and they sealed it with a drink from a bottle of brandy that Goodnight kept in his saddle bags. Neither ever broke the agreement.

Goodnight also made a deal with Quanah Parker. In 1879, Parker was allowed off the reservation, to lead his band in a Buffalo hunt. Goodnight met Quanah on the plains and noticed that the Indians were starving. He volunteered to furnish two beeves every other day, if the Indians would leave his herd alone. Quanah agreed and the Indians kept off Goodnight's ranch. Goodnight delivered two beeves every other day. When asked if the Indians kept their end of the bargain, Goodnight said, "I never knew one that didn't."

CHAPTER FIFTEEN

# Panhandle Ranches

Unfortunately, while Col. Mackenzie was chasing the Indians out of the Panhandle, and Charles Goodnight was setting up a ranch in Palo Duro Canyon, the legislature was meeting in Austin. The Constitutional Convention of 1875 drafted a new constitution and the voters approved it. The Texas Constitution of 1876, the seventh constitution in Texas history, took effect in February of that year. It is a long, wordy document, so unwieldy it has been amended more than 800 times. Texans still live with it today.

On a positive note in 1875, a patent was issued for a product that would have more influence on the development of the Texas ranching industry than any other--barbed wire. Early 1876, two salesmen from Illinois came to Texas to sell this wonderful product to the farmers and ranchers who needed it most. The Texans didn't know they needed it, so Pete McManus, a seasoned pro, and John Warne Gates, a 21 year old trainee came upon an idea to demonstrate the need.

They got the necessary permits and had a barbed wire enclosure built in Military Plaza in downtown San Antonio, across from the Alamo. After the salesmen gathered a crowd, several rangy longhorn steers were herded into the pen and the gate was closed. Cowboys tried to spook the longhorns into crashing through the fence. The fence held, and in less than an hour, the confused cattle huddled together in the center of the pen, unwilling to go near the wire. McManus and Gates set up tables in the lobby of the Menger Hotel and took deposits and orders for enough barbed wire to swamp the Washburn-Moen factory.

When Gates returned to Illinois, he asked for part ownership of the business. The owners refused and Gates started his own company. He soon bought out the Washburn-Moen Company and hired Pete McManus and gave him Texas as a sales territory. McManus became the most successful barbed wire salesman of all time.

During the early years, a competitive product called "Bob War" was marketed in Texas. The product never caught on, perhaps because Texans felt they were being ridiculed by the Yankees who made it. Texans are funny that way.

One of the things that concerned the lawmakers of the great State of Texas was a sense of fair play. It was not fair for a cotton farmer in Washington County to have to pay property taxes, when a farmer in the panhandle paid none. The whole panhandle was a trackless waste. Some people lived out there, raising cattle and farming, but there were no counties, no county sheriffs, no county judges, no county tax assessors, and no county tax money coming in. Now that the Indians were gone, that just would not do. The legislature sent out surveyors and started laying out counties in the panhandle.

On July 27, 1877, a six-man surveying party came up out of Blanco Canyon onto the plains. The men all walked. Two horses pulled their heavy wagon. More animals would require more water, and it was not available in this arid land. The wagon carried all their equipment and provisions and enough water to last until more could be found. They located the northeast corner of Lubbock County and marked it the only way they could out there, with a mound of dirt. They worked west along the northern boundary of the county until they came to the North Fork of the Yellow House Canyon, which helped locate the west boundary. They turned south along that line. The group had two surveyors, two helpers, and two land speculators. Speculators tagged along for the opportunity to locate railroad land and sell it to eastern investors.

Texas had kept its public land when it was annexed by the Union, and made its own deals with the various railroads, and other companies, using land as a liquid asset instead of cash. Texas would soon trade land for its capitol building, and it would trade millions of acres for its railroads. Speculators located the land covered by railroad company script, purchased it for fifty cents to a dollar an acre, and hoped to sell it at a profit.

The constitution of 1876 called for counties to be no smaller than 700 square miles and no larger than 900 square miles. The counties should be as close to square as possible, with the county seat near the geographic center. Adjustments were available for special cases.

Obviously, Brewster County was a special case. It was organized in 1878, after all these rules were made, but it contains 6,169 square miles—three times bigger than the state of Delaware and 500 square miles bigger than Connecticut. The county seat, Alpine, is in the northwest corner, at least fifty miles from the center of the county. The county was named after Henry P. Brewster, a Secretary of War in Ed Burnet's temporary cabinet. Brewster was Sam Houston's personal secretary at San Jacinto and accompanied him to New Orleans to have his wounds treated after the battle.

The counties of the panhandle were created so quickly, picking names became a problem. The legislators had laid out fifty-four perfectly good counties up there but had only about twenty or so heroes to name them after. The wily legislators used the list of signers of the Texas Declaration of Independence along with any politically active unknowns they found listed in former Texas Governments.

William S. Fisher, another little-known secretary of war in Ed Burnet's temporary cabinet, got a county named after him. Armstrong County was named after a prominent pioneer ranching family, but no one is sure which prominent Armstrong family. With all that, it is unfortunate that one of the counties got named after Robert Potter, the first Secretary of the Texas Navy. The word that comes to mind at the mention of his name is "sleazeball."

The legislators made up for Potter by naming one county for Deaf Smith, perhaps the greatest unsung hero of the revolution. "Deef" Smith took part in almost every battle of the revolution. He provided Travis, Bowie and Houston with invaluable scouting information, and never missed when asked to take out a Mexican officer with his long rifle.

Smith had decided to sit out the war—being married to a Mexican woman, he was already under Mexican control. When a Mexican officer refused to allow Smith into San Antonio to visit his wife, Smith instantly became a revolutionary by shooting him. He had been away for several weeks, and the officer just didn't understand. Smith really needed to see his wife.

Lubbock County was created in 1876, along with the rest of the panhandle counties, but it wasn't officially open for business until 1891. To be activated as an official county in the state of Texas, certain conditions had to be met. A petition signed by one hundred-fifty qualified voters who lived in the county was required. A County Judge and other officials had to be appointed. Census records of Lubbock County show that in 1880, and 1890, most residents of Lubbock County were single young men, transients under twenty-five years old, who were either sheep herders or cowboys. Lubbock, by the way, was named after Thomas S. Lubbock, a bona fide Civil War hero and the brother of Texas Civil War governor Francis R. Lubbock.

Paris Cox, at age 29, operated a sawmill in Boxley, Indiana. He was a Quaker, married with two children, both boys. In 1875, a Texas railroad agent offered to trade certificates for fifty thousand acres of unlocated Texas land for Cox's sawmill. Cox took the deal, even though he had never been near Texas.

Cox came to Texas in 1878, made his way to the panhandle, and camped in southeastern Hale County. He was impressed by the soil and vegetation of the high plains and determined to settle above the Caprock. He was especially impressed with some land in Crosby County and went to Austin to arrange to have it surveyed and recorded. He moved his family, and three other Quaker families onto his property in the fall of 1879. Because of a mistake in the survey, his little village was actually just inside the Lubbock County line.

Cox had a well dug and he and his boys built a half-dugout to live in. The other families chose to live in wood-framed and reinforced tents and suffered mightily during the long cold winter of 1879-1880. As the weather started to warm in March, a violent sandstorm leveled their tents and scattered their belongings over the panhandle. All three families gathered up what they could find of their things and went back to Indiana.

Paris Cox and his family stayed, and in June of 1880 his wife gave birth to a little girl, Bertha, who was the first white child born in Lubbock County. There is no indication that Mary, Cox's wife, lobbied to be known as the "Mother of Lubbock."

Cox had a lot of land to sell and dreamed of establishing a Quaker Colony on the high plains. By 1882, ten families joined the Coxes and formed the village of Maryetta on the Crosby-Lubbock County line. In 1886, the name was changed to Estacado, and it became the county seat of Crosby County.

Sometime in 1877, a sheep herder named Zachary Taylor Williams became the first permanent resident of Lubbock County. The census of 1880 listed Paris Cox and family as residents of Crosby County, and Williams had settled on three sections of prime grazing land in the canyon along the North Fork of the Prairie Dog Fork of the Brazos, which included Buffalo Springs. Taylor had three employees living with him. The 1880 census listed 25 residents of Lubbock County, mostly young men passing through as sheep herders or cowboys. Sometime in 1882, George Singer built an adobe house and opened a store in Yellow House Draw on the west side of Lubbock County.

A pioneer of Lubbock County, Rollie Burns, described Singer's store. "I rounded a bend in the canyon and saw Singer's store, diminutive and forlorn, nestling on the southwest side of a lake which formed the headwaters of the Yellow House. The lake covered several acres and was fed by springs. When I rode up, a dozen or more horses were tied to the hitching rack out in front.

In and around the store was a motley crowd of cowboys, a few Mexicans, and a half dozen Apache Indians. I mailed my letter, bought a drink of whiskey and some candy, stood around a while, and started back."

J. Evetts Haley combined the stories of several old men into this description of Singer's store. "When the roundups drew to a close and jingling spurs struck music from the floor of his store, Old Man Singer was in his glory. Pack horses were hobbled out, bed rolls thrown upon the floor, and when night came, the old man left the cowboys in charge and went home. Until far in the morning the good old game of poker held forth in earnest. When the money was gone, a cowboy reached up and pulled down a box of stick candy or a plug of tobacco from a shelf, "sweetened the pot," and the game went on. Another went broke, and another, and down came a pair of California pants to be bet against a couple of shirts. Singer appeared in the morning after the struggle was over. Never did a padlock fasten his door, and never was his confidence betrayed to the loss of a cent by these men who gambled in zest but would have shot at a word."

In 1886, a demented Mexican burned Singer's store. The mild-mannered Singer caught and killed the Mexican, then rebuilt his store about a half mile down the canyon.

In contrast to the primitive conditions in the panhandle of Texas, John Warne Gates prospered in the Chicago area. As he accumulated more barbed wire factories, he started a steel mill to supply them, using the "open hearth" process, which was less costly and more efficient than the Bessemer method generally in use at the time. When he controlled several steel mills, he worked out a merger with J.P. Morgan to form U.S.Steel. Morgan, working behind the scenes through the board of directors, had Gates excluded from the management of U.S. Steel, and the two became lifelong enemies.

Gates took his act to New York City and became active in construction, finance, and real estate. He financed and built the Plaza Hotel and lived there with his family in a sixteen-room suite for the rest of his life. Because of his flamboyant business ventures and extravagant lifestyle, he earned the nickname, "Bet a Million Gates."

In 1879, surveyors came back to Lubbock County and headed west and north. The State Legislators had earmarked 3,000,000 acres in the panhandle to be sold, and the proceeds used to build a new State Capitol Building. The proposed ranch sprawled over parts of ten panhandle counties and was laid out along the New Mexico border from Yellow House Draw west of Lubbock, north to the Oklahoma border. The counties involved were Dallam, Hartley, Oldham, Deaf Smith, Parmer, Castro, Bailey, Lamb, Cochran, and Hockley. The ranch varied from twenty to thirty miles wide and meandered for 200 miles along the New Mexico border. Winter came two weeks earlier in the northern pastures than it did in the south.

Chicago investors John V. Farwell and his brother, Charles B. Farwell organized a syndicate, with mostly English investors, to build the Capitol Building. Mathias Schnell was successful bidder on the building and laid the cornerstone, but in May of 1882 he assigned all interests to Taylor, Babcock, and Company, a partnership of Abner Taylor, A.C. Babcock, Charles B. Farwell and John V. Farwell. Babcock inspected the ranch land before agreeing to the job, starting in Old Tascosa in late March and working his way south to Yellow House Draw before the end of April.

The meticulous Babcock noted the 1880 J.T. Munson survey of the property defined the Northwest corner of the state at the point established by the 1859 survey of John H. Clark. The Clark Survey was accepted and approved by congress in 1891. Only one little problem. Clark was off by a half mile, and the western boundary of the state, and the ranch was not on the 103rd meridian but a half mile west of the meridian.

Finally, in 1911, the issue was laid to rest. U.S. President Taft and John V. Farwell worked together to get congress to pass a joint resolution approving the Clark line. The resolution was passed on February 16, 1911 and saved a half-mile wide strip of land, 310 miles long, for Texas.

On the other side of the Panhandle, surveyors mislocated the Northeast corner nine times, starting in 1850. The Supreme Court finally commissioned a survey to settle the question in 1929. Local ranchers complained that they went to sleep in Oklahoma, and woke up in Texas.

Other disputes involving Texas borders did not turn out so well. The Red River forks about fifty miles before it reaches the 100th meridian, which forms the eastern border of the Texas Panhandle. Naturally, Texans assumed the border followed the north fork, and the United States held that the border followed the south fork. In 1860, Texas claimed the triangle shaped area, named it Greer County and established a county seat. In 1896, the Supreme Court ruled the county was a part of Indian Territory and belonged to the United States, not Texas. Texas was forced to give up Greer County. The court has ruled several times that the Texas/Oklahoma border is the south bank of the Red River, not the center or the north bank. Therefore, all the oil under the river belongs to Oklahoma. Same with Lake Texoma. The whole lake, and all the oil under it, is in Oklahoma.

The cornerstone of the state capitol building was laid on Texas Independence Day, March 2, 1882. Over a thousand workers, many of them convicts, worked on the building, which was dedicated on San Jacinto Day, April 21, 1888. The architect, Elijah E. Myers, also designed the Colorado and Michigan capitol buildings. The Texas Capitol is one of the largest and most elaborate capitol buildings in the United States and is seven feet taller than the national Capitol. It cost $3,744,630.60, labor and material, of which $3,224,593.45 was paid for by the Farwell Syndicate, in exchange for 3,050,000 acres of panhandle ranch land.

The Italian Renaissance Revival Style building was designed to be constructed of Texas limestone, mined at nearby Oak Hill. The limestone, with a high iron content, discolored when exposed to the elements. The stone was structurally sound, but Texas could not have a splotchy, rusty-colored state capitol.

The owners of a granite mountain in Marble Falls, some fifty miles to the north, volunteered to provide all the Texas granite needed at no cost to the state. A three-mile spur was added to the railroad line and Texas Sunset Red Granite from Marble Falls sheathed the entire capitol building. Eighty-six granite cutters from Scotland were imported and added to the workforce.

In 1936, the W.S. Bellows Construction Company of Houston proudly started work on the San Jacinto Monument to commemorate the Centennial Year of Texas Independence. When the star was lifted to the top of the monument, to the chagrin of many Easterners and the delight of Texans, it turned out to be almost 13 feet taller than the Washington Monument. Oh, well. Like the Capitol building, it is too late to change.

The Farwell Brothers sold debenture bonds in England to raise operating funds for the XIT Ranch. They installed four-wire barbed wire perimeter fences, then cross fenced ninety-two pastures with more than 1500 miles of fence. Three hundred thirty-five windmills were installed, averaging thirty-five feet high, pumping water from 125 feet down. Several of the taller windmills blew over in violent West Texas windstorms. Beginning in 1887, 125,000 to 150,000 cattle were carried on the range, mostly longhorn. Purebred Hereford and Angus cattle were imported to improve the bloodlines. By 1900, the XIT was the largest ranch in the world.

The XIT brand had nothing to do with "Ten Counties in Texas" despite the cowboy legend. The brand was designed by Ab Blocker, a trail driver, who drew it in the sand with the heel of his boot. It was simple, easy to do with a five-inch straight iron, and hard for rustlers to alter.

Speaking of untrue cowboy legends, the Chisholm Trail does not exist in Texas. Jesse Chisholm, a merchant with a trading post in Kansas, opened a new post on the Red River at a crossing near Montague, Texas. He blazed a trail across Kansas and Oklahoma between the two trading posts, to allow him to service and supply both locations. O. W. Wheeler first used the Chisholm trail to drive 2400 head of cattle to market in 1867. Trail drivers made their way across Texas as best they could, then picked up the Chisholm Trail at the Red River crossing and followed it across Oklahoma to the railroads in Kansas.

In the late 1870's and early 1880's, the panhandle began to boom. T. S. Bugbee established a ranch on the Canadian River, about eighty miles north of Goodnight. The XIT, with 150,000 cattle, sprawled along the western boundary of the state and the lawless village of Tascosa grew up nearby. The town of Mobeetie prospered near the Oklahoma border, adjacent to Fort Elliott, and Clarendon sprang up between them. Charles Goodnight called Mobeetie the roughest town he'd ever seen, except for Cheyenne, Wyoming. In contrast, Clarendon was established by a preacher and named for his wife. The deeds for local real estate contained a prohibition clause and the town was called "Saint's Roost" by local cowboys. According to a local legend, a drunken cowhand who caused trouble in Tascosa was once sentenced to ten days in Clarendon.

George Littlefield eventually bought over 312,000 acres of XIT land out west of Lubbock County. Small farmers began to move in from the north and east. Charles Goodnight added more and more land to his holdings and, always a visionary, recognized the need for fences. He began to fence his home ranch with newly patented (1874) barbed wire.

Goodnight, seeking an investor to help him expand his holdings, hosted a Buffalo hunt in Colorado for John Adair, an Irish financier, and his adventurous American wife, Cornelia. Adair, shooting from horseback, took a bead on an elk and rotated in the saddle as the elk moved. He squeezed off a shot and might have hit the elk had he not shot his own horse in the back of the head. The horse collapsed, dead before it hit the ground. Adair was slightly injured in the fall and Goodnight, after a lot of thought, went ahead with the partnership negotiations.

In June of 1877, Charles Goodnight and John Adair became partners for a five-year term and formed the JA Ranch. Goodnight didn't especially like John Adair, a difficult individual in addition to being a bit klutzy, but he wanted to enlarge his ranch operations and could not do it without taking on a financial partner. With larger herds of cattle, Goodnight had an opportunity to improve his financial standing, but, more important to him, more cowhands meant more protection from the hazards of living on the plains.

With stray bands of Indians and outlaws still running loose over the high plains, an ample number of young, gun-toting cowhands came in handy.

In 1884, in Davenport, Iowa, a group of investors, eager to cash in on the fortunes being made in the cattle business, formed the Western Land and Livestock Company, with capital stock of $800,000.00. The company set up offices in Fort Worth and hired David Boaz as general manager. Boaz was instructed to buy or lease land, fence and water it, stock it with cattle, and begin ranching operations as soon as practical.

Boaz felt the Yellow House Canyon in Lubbock County was the best location still available and immediately bought three sections near a spring at the entrance to what is now the Buffalo Lakes reservation. He bought the land from a sheep rancher, Zachary Taylor Williams, and established the headquarters of his ranch near that spring. In the 1950's, the site was the headquarters of the V-8 Ranch.

Boaz purchased 74,200 acres of land at prices ranging from 25 to 40 cents per acre. He then leased all the school lands in the southern half of Lubbock County, and any privately-owned tracts he found available. With this accomplished, he had a continuous pasture 14 miles wide and 28 miles long, comprising the south half of Lubbock County. He fenced the perimeter and cross fenced the property into three large pastures.

Boaz bought 200 saddle horses for $8,000, drilled ten water wells and erected windmills to serve them. He hired cowboys to do the work, but his biggest expense was cattle. Because he was in a hurry, he bought twenty thousand stock cattle for $25.00 each, a total of half a million dollars. He bought the cattle at the very top of the market. Two years later, a stocker cow could be bought for $5.00.

The Iowa investors, patriotic to their state, chose IOA as the name for their ranch. It was pronounced "I-O-WAY." Unlike the XIT brand, IOA offered several easy choices for alteration and rustling was a problem from the outset.

The IOA Ranch started operation at the same time the disastrous drought of 1886-1887 set in. From June of 1885 until the fall of 1887, there was almost no rain. When the rains returned in 1887, cattle prices had plunged and the meager calf crop did not offset losses from the hard winter and the continued drought.

J.K. Millwee, the competent ranch manager, resigned in the face of all these setbacks, embarrassed that he could not make a profit. Rollie Burns was hired to take his place. The cattle operation of the ranch never yielded a profit, but the stockholders might have saved their capital investment if their creditors had been patient. As it worked out, a creditor filed for foreclosure and the sheriff of Lubbock County sold the lands in question on the steps of the courthouse on the first Monday in November, 1901. J. W. Kokernot of Brewster County bought the properties, and later sold for a nice profit.

Charles Goodnight turned over the JA Ranch to John Adair's widow, Cornelia Richie Adair, in 1887 and moved to the Quitaque area to continue ranching on his own. During their ten year association, Goodnight increased the size of the JA to over 1,350,000 acres and produced healthy profits for the partnership, even after Adair was repaid for his capital investments, including a ten percent fee. The JA Ranch is still operated by Cornelia Richie Adair's heirs.

The XIT Ranch made little profit on its cattle operations and sold its last cattle in 1912. The cattle business was initially set up only to provide a use for the land until it could be colonized and sold off to small farmers and ranchers. After 1901, part of the ranch was subdivided and sold to retire the bonds that had been issued to obtain operating capital. In 1915, a Real Estate Trust was established to administer the disposition of the property. The trust ceased to operate on the last day of December, 1950.

In 1902 and 1903, Elana Zamora O'Shea taught school at the Santa Gertrudis Division of the King Ranch. Two older Kineros often came to visit with her after class. She read to them from Mexican newspapers and told them of the Texas history her students were studying. One evening, she mentioned the Goliad Massacre and they became very excited and asked about the "Angel of Goliad."

One of the Kineros was Matias Alverez, who said he was the son of Telesforo and Panchita Alavez. He took the teacher to meet his mother, Dona Panchita Alavez, the Angel of Goliad. The lady was in her nineties and bed-ridden at the time. According to O'Shea, "she died on the King Ranch and is buried there in an unmarked grave....Old Captain King and Mrs. King knew her story and respected her identity."

It is not known whether Panchita and Telesforo got married or simply continued their affair. Later in life, Panchita may have married a man named Alverez, which might have caused some confusion in the names.

In any case, Panchita's son, Matias Alverez is the great-grandfather of three Cavasos brothers. Bobby Cavasos, a running back who was the first All-American at Texas Tech, went on to become foreman of the Laureles Division of the King Ranch. Bobby's brother, Richard, was the first Hispanic to become a four star general in the U.S. Army. Their older brother, Dr. Lauro Cavasos was the first Hispanic to serve in the U.S. Cabinet. Dr. Cavasos was president of Texas Tech University and Secretary of Education under Presidents Reagan and George H.W. Bush.

Growing up in any part of Texas is a blessing. Texans are proud of their state and its history. In deep East Texas, at Jefferson, the attitudes and accents are slanted in an Antebellum South direction. The people are Texans, but they are cautious, slow to warm up to strangers and reluctant to accept new ideas. They creep around back in the shadows of the forests and look out at the bright sunshine on the prairies. They choose to stay back in the shade, lest everyone know their "business." They work hard in the muggy heat, and some of them amass fortunes by accumulating timberland.

In Southeast Texas, in Port Arthur, Texans tend to fade into the bayous and swamps. Their accents are Cajun, indistinguishable from their Louisiana neighbors. They eat crawfish, dance to Zydeco music, and gamble on any and everything. Most of them never accumulate a fortune but work hard during the week and spend all they make playing hard and gambling on the weekends.

In 1899, John Warne Gates was asked by a friend in Texas to bail out an oil field operator, Patillo Higgins. Higgins, a wildcatter, had drilled 575 feet down on top of a salt dome near Port Arthur and had no money to finish the well. Gates formed the Texas Company to finance and finish the venture. When the papers were all signed, "Bet a Million" Gates owned 46% of the venture, John Lucas owned 12%, and Higgins worked for wages with no ownership interest.

On January 10, 1900, the well known as Spindletop blew in and spewed 100,000 barrels per day into the atmosphere. At the time, that was more oil than was being produced by all the existing wells in the United States, combined.

By the time Spindletop became productive, Gates had gained control of the Port Arthur docks, the railroad, and a refinery. Drilling for oil, transporting it, or refining it required dealing with one of Gates' companies. His Texas Company became Texaco, and he built a home in Port Arthur, even though his primary residence remained at the Plaza in New York. He built a hospital to serve the area and named it after his mother, Mary.

People in Central Texas, at Waco, lean again toward the Old South. They are also Texans, and are deeply religious to all outward appearances, but a bit hypocritical under the surface. A few "old families" rule the society pages, the churches, and the business life of the town. Fortunes are made in "the heart of Texas" in the cotton fields or the insurance business.

Along the Red River in North Texas, Wichita Falls accents pick up the old west, with a cowboy twang. Texans who settle there must be able to weather miserably hot summers and brutally cold winters. Wealth is not always accumulated there—it is often won by a wildcatter in the oil fields, then lost three months later in a poker game.

Out in the West Texas town of El Paso, the accents are Spanish and the fortunes come from questionable sources. One of the stipulations of the Compromise of 1850 made El Paso a part of Texas. Texas gave up half of New Mexico, one third of Colorado and parts of Kansas, Oklahoma, and Wyoming, but retained the Big Bend area and El Paso, and gained a rich Hispanic heritage and cultural ties to Mexico.

El Paso, in addition to heritage and culture, boasted a prosperous red-light district. In the early 1880's, two local madams feuded over the services of a popular "Soiled Dove"and came to blows on the front steps of a brothel. Miss Etta Clark shot Miss Alice Abbott in the groin area with a forty-four pistol. According to the doctor, the bullet passed through her body in the vicinity of the pubic arch, but missed any vital organs. The El Paso newspaper mistakenly reported that she was shot in the Public Arch, and history was made. For years after, Miss Abbott was asked about the condition of her public arch. Miss Clark was found not guilty by reason of self defense. She might not have been guilty, but she was certainly not innocent.

Coastal Texas, Galveston, Aransas Pass and Corpus Christi for example, is seafood country. In Corpus, the Texan accents are tinted with a Mexican influence, more so than other parts of the state. Because of the port, fortunes are made in shipping, especially petroleum products. Soon, Liquid Natural Gas will be exported in tankers from a gigantic facility under construction. Southwest of Corpus, past the cotton fields, the King Ranch dominates the landscape. Cotton is also king out there. The high school football team in Robstown is called the "Cottonpickers."

We've covered the Panhandle/South Plains area in depth. The accents on the plains are slow cowboy drawls, sprinkled with wonderful descriptive phrases. No one comments that a lady wears a nice perfume. They say, "That Ole Gal smells like the top dresser drawer." An outlaw doesn't draw a gun. He "reaches in his pocket and pulls out a thirty some odd."

The High Plains promises little and delivers much. Consider the High School building in Lubbock. Absolutely unique architecture, ornately detailed, flawless construction. It is the kind of building one might expect to see in Southern California, or perhaps in the Andalucian area of Spain. Yet right there on 19th street, in a city that considers proper architectural embellishment an accent color painted on the front door, stands the Tom S. Lubbock High School, with a Moorish bell tower (no bell), buff colored brick, red clay tile roof, and ceramic tile accents.

Lubbock High School

The contractor ran out of money before he finished the building, but rather than cheapen the construction, he sold some property and finished the job according to the original specifications with his own money. Since the early thirties, generations of high school kids have prepared for their lives in this building, many unaware of its significance.

Fortunes on the high plains are made the old-fashioned way. Farmers work for years acquiring land, suffering through hail storms and droughts, living at the mercy of the weather, the markets and the banks. When they go, they leave the whole package to their heirs. Some of their heirs preserve and expand the package, and others lose it all. The chief excuse for losing everything has always been, "Them stupid, ignorant bankers loaned me more money than I could pay back."

Texas cities, Dallas, Houston, San Antonio, and Austin are vibrant and unique in their own way. Dallas, the newest of these, did not exist when Texas was born. It is urban, refined and cosmopolitan. Houston is brash, confident and proud of itself. San Antonio is old, (perhaps the oldest city in North America), Spanish, and remarkably diverse and interesting. Austin is weird and works hard to stay that way.

Texans in every part of the state know that they live in the best possible place on earth. Every young man, in every section of the state, dreams of acquiring some land. The amount of land he needs to fulfill his dreams is only limited by his ambition. Some farmers would be happy with 160 acres, while some ranchers want 160 sections. All of them know it will take hard work and luck to make their dreams come true, but this is Texas. God sweetened the pot when he made this land. With any luck at all, anywhere in this wonderful state, you just might strike oil.

There are men who were not born in Texas, but should have been. Sam Houston is one, as is John Warne Gates. Also on this list, so far as I'm concerned, is Conrad Hilton. Although he was born in San Antonio, a little village in New Mexico, he started his hotel business in Cisco, Texas. He understood Texas. Hilton said, "There is a vastness here, and I believe that people who are born here breathe that vastness into their soul. They dream big dreams and think big thoughts, because there is nothing to hem them in."